CAMBRIDGE LATIN TEXTS

Editorial Board:
Chairman, E.J. Kenney; Executive Editor, D.J. Morton

LIBELLUS: SELECTIONS FROM
HORACE, MARTIAL, OVID AND CATULLUS
HANDBOOK

FOREWORD

This selection of poetry by Horace, Martial, Ovid and Catullus differs from preceding *Cambridge Latin Texts* in including four authors rather than one. It attempts (i) to provide students with a select range of Roman poetry from the last years of the Republic and the first century of the Empire; (ii) to provoke inquiry and research into Roman life by focusing on the sort of poetry which springs directly from the people and concerns of contemporary society. The poems are divided into ten sections, each presenting material broadly relevant to a particular feature of Roman life: I Town; II Wealth and patronage; III Work; IV Entertainment; V Autobiography; VI Death; VII Love and sex; VIII Character studies; IX Travel; X Belief. These sections are not mutually exclusive. Equally, they are not intended to provide a balanced treatment of their theme. And they are certainly not intended to imply that the poems which compose them are to be viewed in the first instance as historical documents. They do, however, give the collection a sort of logic; they do sometimes set together interestingly different treatments of the same topic; and they do serve to assemble information about particular aspects of Roman society in a way that might persuade readers to look further afield for a systematic account. However, the primary aim in assembling this collection has not been to offer the reader a hotchpotch of source material, but to present him with poetry of intrinsic interest and importance.

In selecting pieces for inclusion, I have tried to balance the known and loved against a quota of less famous but no less interesting poetry. I have provided a mixture of long and short, serious and light-hearted, difficult and easy passages. Wherever possible, complete poems have been preferred to extracts. My selection from Catullus has been made from the poems not already anthologised in the previous *Cambridge Latin Text*: R.O.A.M. Lyne (ed.) *Selections from Catullus* (Cambridge, 1973). The result has been a mixture of 9% Catullus, 35% Horace, 33% Ovid and 23% Martial. I have inevitably included texts for which there is no accessible modern commentary and, even where such commentaries do exist, I have felt it unrealistic to assume, as most of my predecessors in the series have been able to do, that teachers will have the commentaries to hand. This has meant a rather fuller exposition of points of difficulty in this Handbook, supplemented by facing-page notes and vocabulary in the accompanying pupils' text.

The texts used are the *Oxford Classical Texts*, in all cases except Ovid *Fasti*. In these three passages (II.4; X.3; X.4) I have used the Teubner (1932) edition, but with one or two punctuation changes in line with the Teubner (1904) edition and/or the editions of Bömer (1958) and Le Bonniec (1965 and 1969). I have also standardised overall some variant spellings (e.g., 'exstructos' for 'extructos'; 'lagoenis' for 'lagonis') and have rewritten as '-es' the third-declension Form B (accusative) plural '-is'.

After a brief general Introduction, this Handbook contains a Commentary on all the poems in the selection. A conspectus of each section is followed by detailed treatment of individual poems and excerpts. This begins, where appropriate, with a note on the literary context. Next there is a section devoted to difficulties in the language and content, including the metrical scheme of poems not in hexameters or elegiacs: some specific suggestions are made about teaching methods, complementary to those in the Introduction (pp. 7–11). Each poem or passage is then discussed and analysed. These discussions cannot be, and are not intended to be, in any sense final or even authoritative. They are meant to provoke disagreement as well as assent. A list of questions follows each discussion. Topics of particular interest are illustrated by references to both specialist books and slides and general works likely to be in school libraries: these lists of references are not, of course, intended to be comprehensive, but it is hoped that they may provide useful material for exploration by both teacher and pupil. For recommendations on how the Commentary should be used, see below, pp. 8–11.

Many students using these books will be familiar with the *Cambridge Latin Course*. There is nothing, however, to deter those who are not. In particular, the references to grammatical cases are always given in both *CLC* and traditional terms – e.g. Form C (dative).

I am well aware of the inadequacies of this Handbook, and can only hope that it may have sufficient virtues to prove a helpful companion to the anthology. I am very grateful to Professor E.J. Kenney for his many perceptive comments and corrections; to the Cambridge School Classics Project staff, particularly David Morton, Patricia Smith, Pat Story and Margaret Widdess; to Hermia Lambie; to Robert Tibbott, Richard Smith and other colleagues at King Edward's School, Birmingham; to the Cambridge University Literary and Linguistic Computing Centre; to the Cambridge University Press; to Birmingham University Library for its hospitality; and above all to my wife, Fiona, for her patience and understanding during the past two years. In addition, I owe a great debt to the writers mentioned in the Bibliography. I hope I have not travestied their ideas too frequently, and I cannot do better than recommend teachers to these originals whenever time and libraries allow.

ABBREVIATIONS

CIL	*Corpus Inscriptionum Latinarum* (Berlin 1862–)
CLC	*Cambridge Latin Course* (Cambridge 1970–8)
L&S	Lewis and Short *A Latin Dictionary* (Oxford 1879)
LSJ	Liddell and Scott, revised Stuart Jones and McKenzie *A Greek-English Lexicon* (Oxford 1940)
OCD	*The Oxford Classical Dictionary* (Oxford 1970)
OLD	*Oxford Latin Dictionary* (Oxford 1968–)

CITATIONS

References to Roman authors are given as follows:
IV.2   = Section IV of this anthology, second poem
*1–28 = the original lines 1–28, not included in the excerpt of a
          poem in this anthology
Ovid, *Tristia* IV.2
Catullus, *Poems* 4

Modern authors are referred to as follows:
          Fordyce — where a single publication is cited in the Bibliography
          Casson, 1971 — where more than one publication is cited in the
          Bibliography
          Brunt, 1971 (2) — where more than one publication from a
          given year is cited in the Bibliography

Full references to the works concerned are in the Bibliography.

THE PUPILS' TEXT

Students will find on the pages facing the text three main types of assistance.

(1) Translations are offered of words and phrases which have not appeared frequently in the *CLC*. Where two or more translations are given, the basic or more regular senses of the word are normally put first. In most cases, the last word listed provides the most serviceable translation for the word in context; if this is markedly different from the standard meaning, it is prefixed by '*here* ='. Where the translation of a phrase does not reflect closely the form of the Latin, it is followed by a literal translation prefixed by '*lit.*'.

(2) Explanatory comments are added, where necessary, to give help with unfamiliar names and concepts. This help is usually in brackets following the translation.

(3) Italics are used to give assistance with the structure of sentences and phrases, either by omitting all but the key words or by introducing in brackets suppressed words and phrases or by altering the word order of the original.

Long vowels (but not all 'long' or heavy syllables) are regularly indicated, except in the italicised structure notes, where only those vowels are marked which seem particularly useful aids to comprehension.

More details of the grammatical forms of words are to be found in the Vocabulary, which contains all the words occurring in the text.

INTRODUCTION

1 Chronological framework

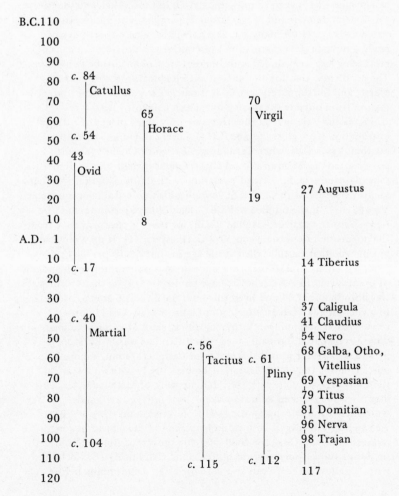

2 The authors

a *Biographies*

It is easy to overestimate the importance of biographical detail as an aid to appreciation of poetry; and this is particularly so in the case of classical verse, where the writer's subject matter and treatment can be so heavily determined by the conventions of the literary genre within which he is working. That said, there are a number of pieces in this collection which seem not to be first and foremost genre poetry but to offer genuine information about the poet's life and experience. Such poems need to be set in a biographical frame, because their audience would be expected to have at least a broad knowledge of the poet's career such that it could supply the details left unspoken and identify the understatement and exaggeration. Biography is also interesting for its own sake, and for many pupils who will have no opportunity of reading outside the examination prescriptions, it provides a means of presenting a more rounded and coherent view of an author's character. The problem is that for all our four authors biographical details are sparse, and for some very sparse. It is particularly difficult to find information from outside the poetry to act as a control.

For Gaius Valerius Catullus there are only three pieces of external information (for references see R.G.C. Levens in Quinn, 1972: 9). Suetonius says that, when Catullus apologised to Caesar for some poems attacking Mamurra (see VIII.1), Caesar invited him to dinner the same day and resumed friendly relations with Catullus' father. Apuleius identifies Lesbia with Clodia. St Jerome adds that Catullus was born at Verona in 87 B.C. and died in 58 B.C. aged thirty. Jerome cannot be right about the date of Catullus' death, for there is clear evidence from the poems that he was alive in 55 B.C. (Fordyce, ix). It may nonetheless be true that Catullus died at the age of thirty (this perhaps being recorded on his tombstone), and since there is no mention in the poems of events after 55 B.C., scholars have tended to assume that Catullus was born in about 84 and lived till about 54 B.C. The poems also refer to a villa on Lake Garda; the death of a brother in Asia Minor; and service under Memmius in Bithynia, which, since Memmius' tour of duty can be dated, probably means that Catullus was in Bithynia in 57–56 B.C. Other so-called facts about Catullus are much more tenuous, including the identification of Lesbia (VII.1) with an historical Clodia — in particular, with the infamous wife of Metellus Celer. This identification is taken as 'not unlikely' by Fordyce (xvii) and 'extremely probable' by Quinn (1973: xv–xix), and, if we accept it, we can begin to forge a connexion between Catullus' birth in a high-ranking family in Cisalpine Gaul, Metellus' governorship of this area (by no means fully Romanised) in 62 B.C., and Catullus' later association with Metellus' wife. We can also date the affair as beginning before

Metellus' death in 59 B.C., since Catullus refers to Lesbia's husband as alive. It is also possible to deduce from the poems that Catullus lived in Rome, while maintaining at least some contact with the North; and that he was one of a group of writers classified by Cicero as *poetae novi*, who were in reaction against contemporary styles of poetry (see III.1). His surviving poems number 116 and range widely in both length and poetic intent. There is no scholarly unanimity as to whether they were intended to be published in the order we have them, or even whether the collection we possess was actually put together for publication by Catullus.

Horace's poetry is full of autobiographical information, but the only significant external data are to be found in an anonymous *Life of Horace* based on writings of Suetonius, who had access under Hadrian to the correspondence of Augustus and was generally well placed to secure reliable information (Fraenkel 17). Quintus Horatius Flaccus was born in 65 B.C. at Venusia in Apulia, and he retained a lasting affection for the area of his birth (see III.3). His father (V.1) was a freedman of relatively slender means who nonetheless managed to send his son to Rome for a proper education in Greek as well as Roman culture. When he was about twenty, Horace went to Athens for more advanced studies, particularly in philosophy; and it was at Athens that he was recruited by Brutus to join the fight against dictatorship. In November 42 B.C. he was a military tribune in the army which was soundly defeated at Philippi. Horace's hopes of advancement were severely curtailed, and it is likely that his problems were increased by the confiscation of his father's property for the settling of veteran soldiers. The *Life of Horace* tells us that he then managed to procure for himself the job of *scriba quaestorius*, an official of some rank overseeing public finance and records. This may have been after the general amnesty of 39 B.C.; in any case it marks a considerable change for the better. Horace's early satiric poetry was fast gaining him a reputation, and during the 30s B.C. Horace published the two books of *Satires*, dedicated to the influential Maecenas. With support from Virgil, he was adopted by Maecenas as a client (V.1) and presented with a substantial estate in the Sabine Hills. The official relationship with Maecenas seems to have blossomed into friendship, and it brought Horace within the ambit of Augustus himself. 'Suetonius' has preserved the text of a letter from Augustus to Maecenas asking for Horace's services as a secretary (text in Fraenkel 17). Horace refused the offer, claiming that his health was not good enough, but Augustus remained friendly. When this exchange took place it is not possible to say, but in *c.* 23 B.C. Horace confirmed his literary standing with the publication as a unit of the collection of lyric poetry known as *Odes* I—III. The reception was not universally favourable, and it was to be some years before Horace returned to this type of writing. Other sorts of poem followed, including the *Carmen Saeculare*, commissioned by Augustus in 17 B.C. as part of the elaborate celebrations of the new Augustan era. Finally, and possibly as late as 8 B.C., Horace published a fourth book of *Odes*, and in this same year he died at the age of fifty-seven. He was buried by the side of Maecenas on the Esquiline Hill.

Our knowledge of the life of Publius Ovidius Naso depends almost entirely on his own writings, and particularly on *Tristia* IV.10 (excerpted in V.2; see note on Context). He was born in 43 B.C. His father belonged to an established equestrian family, originally of Paelignian stock, possibly clients of the great Roman family of the Messallae (Wheeler 3—7). Despite Ovid's complaints about lack of money, the family was wealthy enough to count for admission to the Senate (V.2.15); and this entailed at this time owning property worth 400,000 *sestertii* or more — though Syme (358—9) has argued that this was a relatively low hurdle. He had a sound traditional education in rhetoric at Rome (note on V.2.3). Ovid was a promising pupil; after further study in Athens and travels to Sicily and Asia Minor, he seemed bound for a distinguished political career. For a time he was content to progress along this route, becoming a minor magistrate (note on V.2.20) and perhaps also a member of the centumviral court (notes on VIII.5.5—6), over which he may at some time have presided as *decemvir stlitibus iudicandis*. It was at this point that Ovid decided to reject membership of the Senate and public office, in favour of devoting himself to poetry (notes on V.2.21, 26). He found a patron in Marcus Valerius Messalla Corvinus, a famous general and public figure who was cultivating a literary circle which numbered Tibullus (VI.3) among its members. That this group stood apart from that of Maecenas — containing *inter alios* Virgil, Horace and Propertius — 'may have some bearing on the problems of his exile' (E.J. Kenney in *OCD*, s.v. 'Ovid'). In 25—15 B.C. (see note on Context of IV.2) Ovid had published the *Amores*; he tells us in *Tristia* IV.10.57—8 that he had only just started to shave when he first gave public recitations of his 'carmina iuvenalia'. His work was popular, and other poetry followed, including *Ars Amatoria* and *Remedia Amoris* (*c.* A.D. 1 — see note on Context of IV.3). From about A.D. 2 Ovid applied himself to two mighty works — his complex and original epic poem *Metamorphoses*, never fully revised, and his poetic study of the Roman year, *Fasti* (see note on Context of II.4), of which only the first six months survive. Then in A.D. 8 Ovid was banished by Augustus to Tomis (modern Constanta) on the Black Sea; V.3 gives a moving account of his departure. The reasons for this *relegatio* are referred to obliquely by Ovid as 'carmen' and 'error'. The 'carmen' is the notorious *Ars Amatoria*, out of tune with Augustus' attempts at moral regeneration, but the 'error' has not yet been convincingly identified. Tomis was a most uncongenial place for a man of Ovid's temperament, and his frustration and sense of loss show all too clearly in *Tristia* (see note on Context of III.4) and

Epistulae ex Ponto (see note on Context of I.2). The date of Ovid's death is given by St Jerome as A.D. 17; there is no good reason to dispute this. His third wife had remained loyal to him in Rome protecting his property in the hopes of a reprieve (note on V.3.13). (*Relegatio* being a little less severe than *exilium*, the victim was entitled to retain his property and civilian rights.) We hear of one daughter (note on V.3.15).

Martial, like Ovid, acquired a reputation for loose living in character with the bawdiness of some of his verses. Like Ovid (e.g., in *Tristia* II.354), he defends himself vigorously against this charge: 'lasciva est nobis pagina, vita proba' (*Epigrams* I.4.8). Of this life only a few details survive — gleaned almost entirely from his own poetry. Marcus Valerius Martialis was born *c.* A.D. 40 at Bilbilis (about 3 km east of modern Calatayud, in central Spain). His parents were called Fronto and Flaccilla (VI.5), and their son laid claim to 'obstinate Spanish locks' and 'hairy legs and cheeks' (*Epigrams* X.65). Martial spent his schooldays in Spain, then followed the usual route (in *c.* A.D. 64) to complete his education in Rome; unlike Tuccius (II.5), he was not deterred by news of the patron—client system. In fact it appears that Martial depended on patronage for his existence in Rome. Certainly he makes frequent reference to his status as client (e.g. II.6; II.7), and it is likely that in his early years he counted the younger Seneca, a Spaniard, among his patrons. Peter Howell (in Michie 12) points out that Martial could almost certainly have obtained independence, had he wanted, by teaching rhetoric or practising as a lawyer. That he preferred to remain a client perhaps indicates some exaggeration in the picture Martial paints of himself as a poor, exploited client-poet, driven to extremes of flattery (I.4; VIII.5; X.6). There is evidence for friendships with Frontinus, author of the monograph on Rome's water-supply, the satirist Juvenal and Pliny the Younger. Martial's first surviving poems were published in a collection known as *Liber Spectaculorum* in order to mark the opening of the Colosseum in A.D. 80. The couplets of *Epigrams* XIII and XIV (see note on Context of IV.6) are also early works. Then, between A.D. 86 and 98 he published a heterogeneous collection of twelve books of *Epigrams*. Clearly his growing reputation brought relative prosperity. He was given equestrian rank perhaps by Titus, and the privileges of a father of three children (*ius trium liberorum* — V.5) by Titus and Domitian. Whereas *Epigrams* I.117 finds Martial living in a third-floor flat, he was in *Epigrams* VI.43 commending the delights of his estate at Nomentum and from A.D. 94 at least (*Epigrams* IX.18) he had his own small house in Rome. He also owned a mule-drawn carriage (in *Epigrams* VIII.61) and slaves (*Epigrams* I.101, and see VI.5 on Erotion). On the other hand, when Martial decided to leave Rome (*c.* A.D. 98) and retire to Bilbilis, the fact that Pliny the Younger presented him with his travelling-expenses may suggest that he is viewed by Pliny as none too wealthy (*Letters* III.21.2, excerpted in

CLC Unit IV 'domi' section IV) — though the letter perhaps implies
that this is more of a grand gesture than a helping hand. At Bilbilis
Martial accepted the patronage of a local lady called Marcella, who gave
him a country estate (*Epigrams* XII.31). There is some evidence from
his poems to suggest that provincial life, though initially a pleasant
change, began to pall before long. By about A.D. 104 Martial was dead.
Despite V.5 (see Discussion), there is no evidence for his having a wife
and family. Pliny (*Letters* III.21.6) doubted whether the *Epigrams*
would achieve the immortality Martial sought for them.

b Style

It is not easy to write concisely on style, since each of the four authors
not only leaves a personal mark on his material, but also is heavily
influenced by the genre within which he writes, if not also by his individual experience of life. Obviously much of the material from Horace's
Satires has more in common with Martial's work than with Horace's
own *Odes*. Furthermore, it could be argued that similarities of style are
even more noticeable than differences. Our poets, with their contemporaries, adopt a sort of stylistic *lingua franca*. This is conditioned by
their joint inheritance of a significant cultural legacy. They are heavily
influenced by Greek literature — borrowing established forms and
themes, such as the dedication poem and the attack on the abuse of
wealth; introducing Greek proper names and constructions into their
verse; and taking over many of the assumptions of the Callimachean
school of poetry, specifically its preference for the small-scale, precise
and unpretentious ('tenuis'), as against the grandiose and bombastic,
and for neatness of structure and cleverness of expression. (See further
on Catullus, Lyne 1—3; on Horace, Wilkinson, 1951: 116—22, and
Commager 35—41; on Ovid, Luck, 1963: 34—8; on Martial, Peter
Howell in Michie 14—15.) Equally, they are deeply affected by the
Roman experience and literary precedent. In particular, the epigrams
of Catullus and Martial, the *Satires* of Horace and Ovid's *Fasti* and
'autobiographical' verses draw on a living community and a tangible
environment. The structuring too of the elements of each sentence
within the metrical line does not differ much from one author to
another; for example, combinations of adjective and noun, usually
separated, are regularly preferred to adverbs, which do not carry so
much weight. Also, each poet reinforces the tradition within which he
works by cross-reference to, and remoulding of, the works of past and
contemporary writers. Many such references inevitably escape us, but
it is possible to find examples (in this selection) of Catullus using
Calvus; Horace reflecting Catullus and Lucilius; Ovid assuming familiarity with Tibullus, Horace and Propertius; and Martial building on the
language of Roman prayer. In addition, technical effects of varying

degrees of subtlety are attempted, in line with previous writers or else in reaction: sounds are recreated in verse, the range of poetic vocabulary is expanded to include the colloquial, old metres are stretched and new adopted, words are patterned for effect, puns are made and images developed. Such a polished style demands, and is demanded by, a well-educated readership who could understand recondite technicalities and appreciate learned cross-references.

No poet wrote exclusively for a learned clique, particularly not Martial, but all directed their work primarily at the chosen few and expected it to stand their scrutiny — even though most of their verse *could* be taken at a simpler level. Humour, for example, is generated often by means of sophisticated techniques such as parody and irony and the sort of defeat of expectation that is aroused in II.4 by Ovid's topsyturvy treatment of the Golden Age; but there is also plain exaggeration (cf. Suffenus the poet *manqué* of III.1) and the slapstick of the collapse of the drapery after Nasidienus' disquisition on gastronomy (IV.1). The common style did not preclude appreciation by the man in the street.

Few teachers will wish to explore with their classes the stylistic differences between individual authors. Nor are they likely to wish to examine in any detail the characteristics of the different poetic genres. Other reasons apart, there is the practical point that most users of this text will be reading only about a quarter of its content, in cross-section over several types of verse writing. Their very limited experience of, e.g., Roman satire will not warrant a specific introduction.

Note 1   Martial frequently lightens syllables which one might expect to be quantitatively heavy. Examples are: I.3.3 'rogŏ'; IV.4.1—2 'cerdŏ', 'fullŏ', 'caupŏ'; VII.5.1 'quaerŏ'.
            Horace similarly has 'nesciŏ' in VIII.2.2, 10; Ovid has 'putŏ' in VII.4.9.

Note 2   James Michie, *The Epigrams of Martial* (Hart-Davis/MacGibbon, 1973), has verse translations, often effective, of ten of the Martial poems in this selection: I.4; I.5; I.6; II.7; V.4; VI.5; VII.5; VIII.4; VIII.6; X.5. Translations can readily be found for most of the other poems and excerpts.

3 Treatment

There is no single correct way of teaching Latin poetry. The suggestions which follow rely on the presuppositions of the *Cambridge Latin Course*, and in particular on *CLC* Unit IV *Teacher's Handbook* 16—34. Useful ideas can also be found in the Introduction to M.G. Balme *Intellegenda* (Oxford U.P., 1970) and to the following two books intended for post O-level work: A.C.F. Verity *Latin as literature* (Macmillan, 1971) and C. Stace and P.V. Jones *Stilus artifex* (Cambridge U.P., 1972). The former includes (39—89) a systematic analysis of the critical process.

Perhaps the most persistent problem dogging the teacher of Roman literature is the difficulty of sustaining pace. An anthology has the inherent advantage of ever-changing subject matter, well adapted to the discontinuous study of Latin during the school week. The teacher can build on this by adopting the flexibility of approach repeatedly urged in *CLC* Unit IV *Teachers' Handbook*. One approach might be as follows. (Examples are largely from I.4.)

a Introduction

This should be brief. Pupils will be anxious to master the text and will not be receptive to detailed preliminary exposition. Remarks should be factual, stringently avoiding commendation. In the case of the longer extracts, the Context notes in the Commentary should be helpful at this point, and it might sometimes be worth reading a lively translation of the whole piece within its poetic context. I.4 needs little or no preamble, apart from some revision of the Roman method of keeping time.

b Presentation

Typically the teacher will (i) read a self-contained passage of about six lines of verse to the whole class, heavily stressing the phrase structure; (ii) set pairs of pupils to work exploring the surface meaning with the aid of the various types of assistance in the pupils' text; (iii) test pupils' grasp of the meaning by using simple, oral comprehension questions and/or translation; (iv) repeat this process until the extract is finished; (v) allow time for revision of the whole piece; (vi) reread the piece, or divide it up for reading by pupils. On I.4.1–6 comprehension questions could be asked as follows: what class of people is affected by the first two hours? What adjective is applied to the lawyers in line 2 and what is its point? What does 'varios' describe in line 3? Give examples. Which hour seems to be omitted? Whom is the peace and quiet for in the sixth hour (4)? What does 'septima' (4) describe? Is the tense of 'erit' (4) the same as or different from the tense of earlier verbs? What, in your own words, does line 5 mean? Translate line 6.

c Difficulties

It is important that the initial presentation should proceed without substantial interruption. With this completed, the teacher may well wish to revert to any points of difficulty. Some difficulties will have been anticipated and partially solved by comprehension questions. Others will emerge unexpectedly from pupils. Metre may well provoke anxiety, and it is probably best to err on the side of under-emphasis and to deal with it overtly only when pupils have been thoroughly immersed in the sound of the Latin.

(i) Syntactic structure and morphology

The notes on the facing pages of the pupils' text should deal with most oddities and awkward constructions. These are supplemented by notes in the Commentary, occasionally offering detailed examples of possible teaching technique. I have attempted to limit grammatical references to E.C. Woodcock *A New Latin Syntax* (Methuen, 1959). Four fundamental methods of dealing with incomprehension are (1) to reread the Latin with appropriate emphasis; (2) to revert to a simpler example of a troublesome phrase; (3) to use questions more or less loaded towards the required answer; (4) to resort to formal analysis. See further, *CLC* Unit IV *Teacher's Handbook* 19—21.

(ii) Metre

This should not be underemphasised to the point of oblivion. Metrical variety plays an important part in Latin poetry, and pupils should be made aware of this and should cultivate an ear for verse-rhythms. Some will be familiar with the hexameter, and possibly also the pentameter and hendecasyllabic, from *CLC* Units IV and V. Nevertheless, some revision will be necessary, and it may be worth making time early on for recapitulation of the basic principles of quantitative metre (Raven, Ch. 2). Once the text of a poem has been presented and read aloud, the teacher should (1) establish the typical units of unfamiliar metres, e.g. the double choriamb of III.3; (2) demonstrate the sound of a line or stanza; and (3) encourage readings by pupils. Close metrical analysis of a whole piece is not necessary: any close analysis should be an occasional exercise, and should be limited to specific verses in which metre is used pointedly (I.4.2). See further, advocating occasional learning by heart, *CLC* Unit IV *Teacher's Handbook* 30—1.

Readings of three of the pieces in this selection are available on disc as follows:

O. Skutsch *et al.*, *Latin Readings, Volume 1*, Discourses Ltd (for J.A.C.T.). DCL 1201:

> VIII.1 Catullus 43 (Band 12), read by K.F. Quinn
> VIII.2 Horace, *Satires* I.9 (Band 20), read by L.A. Moritz

A. Doughty *et al.*, *Vox Romana: Short Readings of Verse and Prose*, Discourses Ltd. DCL 502:

> VI.2 Horace, *Odes* IV.7 (Band 5), read by A. Doughty.

d Exploration

Once the class has fully grasped the surface meaning of the piece, it is time for discussion and analysis. It cannot be overstressed that the Discussions in the Commentary are not intended to be delivered undigested

to pupils. They are meant to assist the teacher with his own interpretation of the poem — an interpretation which may well differ in detail
or in substance from the Commentary. Only when the teacher has collected his own thoughts about a piece is he in a position to guide discussion in the classroom. *CLC* Unit IV *Teacher's Handbook* 23—31
should be referred to for detailed advice on method. The teacher should
have to hand a list of questions progressing from the factual towards the
interpretative. This list of questions should be viewed as flexible, and
should even be abandoned (where necessary) in favour of promising
leads thrown out by pupils. *CLC* Unit IV *Teacher's Handbook* suggests
questions about (i) how the piece should be read; (ii) how the poem
should be subdivided, with the aim of establishing changes of tone, etc.;
(iii) what precisely the writer intended by specific suggestive or ambiguous phrases; (iv) how the poem relates to pupils' experience, to be
handled with due sensitivity; (v) why the poet uses specific rhetorical
and literary devices in specific contexts. The Commentary contains lists
of questions following each Discussion. These only rarely encourage the
cross-comparison of poems within a section. This is something which
many teachers will wish to do for themselves, but which cannot properly
be done by a Handbook for an anthology which will very rarely be
studied *in toto*. The Handbook therefore concentrates on individual
poems, with the exception of the brief introductions to each section. It
is hoped that teachers will treat the questions with some discretion —
selecting, rephrasing or omitting as seems appropriate for the time available and the level of interest and ability of their class or groups. For
example, VI.3 question 7 (on Ovid's use of a Tibullan original) will not
be suitable for all pupils. No teacher should be unaware of the information on this topic provided in the Discussion, but it may be better
for some classes to tackle the poem with no more than a very general
awareness of Ovid's technique. Where a teacher does decide to raise such
problems, it is strongly recommended that this should only be attempted
after pupils have a sound grasp of the surface meaning; that detailed
comment and discussion should be limited to one or two important
areas of a piece as long as VI.3; and that the Tibullus lines (with translation) should be written in the blackboard or overhead projector for
close scrutiny by the class. Although this type of critical activity has not
been customary before the senior school, it *is* possible to engage in it
fruitfully before this stage, so long as the objectives are clearly defined
and limited. It could be argued that only by touching on such comparative analysis from time to time are pupils to be given a fair view of
Roman literature and a proper preparation (where this applies) for
sixth-form studies.

e Consolidation

Following class discussion, various types of activity are appropriate: (i) rereading of the original by teacher, or by pupils either within groups or to the whole class, live or taped; (ii) written analysis and assessment of the piece, preferably along broad lines of procedure mapped out by the teacher; (iii) activities, e.g. creative writing, artwork, research into social history, suggested by later questions in the Commentary, e.g. I.4 question 7; III.6 question 3; (iv) appropriate slides, prerecorded tapes and videotapes; (v) comparative material from English literature, if the pupils are responsive; (vi) group work on precise translation, as in *CLC* Unit IV *Teacher's Handbook* 29; (vii) systematic exploration of the theme of a whole section, e.g. IV Entertainment. It is recognised, of course, that the demands of the syllabus may well make the more time-consuming of these activities a very rare pleasure.

4 List of passages

I Town

number of lines

1 Horace, *Satires* II.6.78−117	si quis nam laudat Arelli	40
2 Ovid, *Epistulae ex Ponto* I.8. 29−40, 61−2	nec tu credideris urbanae commoda vitae	14
3 Martial, *Epigrams* III.52	empta domus fuerat tibi, Tongiliane, ducentis	4
4 Martial, *Epigrams* IV.8	prima salutantes atque altera conterit hora	12
5 Martial, *Epigrams* VII.61	abstulerat totam temerarius institor urbem	10
6 Martial, *Epigrams* XI.96	Marcia, non Rhenus, salit hic, Germane	4

II Wealth and Patronage

1 Catullus, *Poems* 26	Furi, villula vestra non ad Austri	5
2 Horace, *Satires* II.3.142−57	pauper Opimius	16
3 Horace, *Satires* II.5.93−104	obsequio grassare	12
4 Ovid, *Fasti* I.193−218	vix ego Saturno quemquam regnante videbam	26
5 Martial, *Epigrams* III.14	Romam petebat esuritor Tuccius	4
6 Martial, *Epigrams* III.46	exigis a nobis operam sine fine togatam	12
7 Martial, *Epigrams* IX.6(7)	dicere de Libycis reduci tibi gentibus, Afer	4

III Work

		number of lines
1 Catullus, *Poems* 22	Suffenus iste, Vare, quem probe nosti	21
2 Horace, *Satires* I.10.72—7	saepe stilum vertas	6
3 Horace, *Odes* III.30	exegi monumentum aere perennius	16
4 Ovid, *Tristia* IV.1.3—14	exul eram, requiesque mihi, non fama petita est	12
5 Martial, *Epigrams* I.79	semper agis causas et res agis, Attale, semper	4
6 Martial, *Epigrams* VI.35	septem clepsydras magna tibi voce petenti	6
7 Martial, *Epigrams* VII.83	Eutrapelus tonsor dum circuit ora Luperci	2
8 Martial, *Epigrams* X.62	ludi magister, parce simplici turbae	12

IV Entertainment

1 Horace, *Satires* II.8.54—85, 90—5	interea suspensa graves aulaea ruinas	38
2 Ovid, *Amores* III.2.65—84	maxima iam vacuo praetor spectacula Circo	20
3 Ovid, *Remedia Amoris* 201—12	nunc leporem pronum catulo sectare sagaci	12
4 Martial, *Epigrams* III.59	sutor cerdo dedit tibi, culta Bononia, munus	2
5 Martial, *Epigrams* XII.82	effugere in thermis et circa balnea non est	14
6 Martial, *Epigrams* XIV.16	quae scit compositos manus improba mittere talos	2

V Autobiography

1 Horace, *Satires* I.6.54—64	nulla etenim mihi te fors obtulit	11
2 Ovid, *Tristia* IV.10.15—40	protinus excolimur teneri	26
3 Ovid, *Tristia* I.3.5—26	iam prope lux aderat	22
4 Martial, *Epigrams* XI.39	cunarum fueras motor, Charideme, mearum	16
5 Martial, *Epigrams* II.92	natorum mihi ius trium roganti	4

VI Death

number of lines

1 Catullus, *Poems* 96	si quicquam mutis gratum acceptumve sepulcris	6
2 Horace, *Odes* IV.7	diffugere nives	28
3 Ovid, *Amores* III.9.29—60	durat opus vatum	32
4 Martial, *Epigrams* IV.18	qua vicina pluit Vipsanis porta columnis	8
5 Martial, *Epigrams* V.34	hanc tibi, Fronto pater, genetrix Flaccilla, puellam	10

VII Love and sex

1 Catullus, *Poems* 92	Lesbia mi dicit semper male	4
2 Horace, *Odes* III.9	donec gratus eram tibi	24
3 Ovid, *Amores* I.11	colligere incertos et in ordine ponere crines	28
4 Ovid, *Amores* I.12.1—10, 21—30	flete meos casus: tristes rediere tabellae	20
5 Martial, *Epigrams* IV.71	quaero diu totam, Safroni Rufe, per urbem	6

VIII Character studies

1 Catullus, *Poems* 43	salve, nec minimo puella naso	8
2 Horace, *Satires* I.9.1—21	ibam forte via Sacra	21
3 Ovid, *Amores* I.8.1—18	est quaedam (quicumque volet cognoscere lenam, audiat)	18
4 Martial, *Epigrams* III.43	mentiris iuvenem tinctis, Laetine, capillis	4
5 Martial, *Epigrams* VI.38	aspicis ut parvus nec adhuc trieteride plena	10
6 Martial, *Epigrams* VIII.79	omnes aut vetulas habes amicas	5

IX Travel

1 Catullus, *Poems* 4	phaselus ille, quem videtis, hospites	27
2 Horace, *Satires* I.5.1—33	egressum magna me accepit Aricia Roma	33
3 Martial, *Epigrams* X.12	Aemiliae gentes et Apollineas Vercellas	12
4 Martial, *Epigrams* XI.79	ad primum decima lapidem quod venimus hora	4

X Belief

number of lines

1 Horace, *Odes* I.34	parcus deorum cultor et infrequens	16
2 Horace, *Odes* III.18	Faune, Nympharum fugientum amator	16
3 Ovid, *Fasti* II.641–58	Termine, sive lapis sive es defossus in agro	18
4 Ovid, *Fasti* III.523–40	Idibus est Annae festum geniale Perennae	18
5 Martial, *Epigrams* IV.21	nullos esse deos, inane caelum	3
6 Martial, *Epigrams* IX.42	campis dives Apollo sic Myrinis	11

COMMENTARY

Section I

The six pieces in this section introduce the theme of town life. Their
view of town, essentially Rome, ranges from the critical (I.1, Horace's
Country Mouse) to the nostalgic (I.2, Ovid in exile pining for Rome).
Martial shows distaste for the fires (I.3) and 'varios labores' (I.4) of
Rome, but seems to take pride in its aqueducts (I.6) and the order of
its streets (I.5). Only one of the pieces, however, is primarily directed
at town life, and that is the one which makes the least specific reference
to Rome (I.1). Horace uses the technique of the fable and the smallness
of scale given by the two mice to exaggerate the extremes of luxury and
dangerous living which he connects with the big city; at the same time
he refines his telling of the tale to give it the more sophisticated appeal
expected by his (urban) audience. For Ovid (I.2), the city as such is
incidental to his hoped-for return from exile. Nonetheless, despite his
rhetorical denial in lines 1—2, the city is important to him as source of
the civilisation which Tomis fails to provide. The list of places in Rome
may be in part conventional, but the contrast with his imprisoned state
is made so strongly that the reader is given a powerful impression of
what Rome meant to the citizen in exile. Martial's four epigrams, more
than the lines of Horace or Ovid, use Rome largely as a backcloth. The
frequency of fires (I.3), the social whirl of the town (I.4), the change in
character of its streets (I.5) and the availability of water from the Aqua
Marcia (I.6) are all necessary constituents, but the prime subject matter
of the epigrams is always something different — *viz.*, the attack on
Tongilianus (I.3), the appeal for Domitian's literary patronage (I.4),
the flattery of Domitian (I.5), the assertion of Roman pre-eminence (I.6).

I.1 Horace, Satires II.6.78—117

Context

Horace is singing the praises of life on his small farm as compared with
the distractions and turmoil of being something of a celebrity in Rome.
The other-worldly fable of the two mice contrasts very strongly with

the realism of Horace's description of urban pressures, captured in snatches of conversation and gossip. The story is told by Cervius, a country neighbour of Horace, as a 'cautionary tale' (Brink 7) to discourage uncritical greed for wealth; at the same time, Horace is using Cervius' story-telling both to illustrate the non-triviality of conversation in the country, and more broadly to provide a further statement of the poem's central concern for country over town. The fable would be familiar from Aesop's version (see question 11).

Language and content

1 **Arelli:** no real-life Arellius can be supplied. On Horace's choice of names in the *Satires*, see Rudd, 1966, Ch. 5.

2 **sic incipit:** the subject is Cervius, the story-teller (see note on Context).

5 **ut:** for the sense suggested in pupils' text, see L&S II.C.4.e and Handford section 58.

6–7 **neque ille . . . invidit:** 'he was not the sort of mouse to grudge . . . '

7 **invidit:** here, unusually, followed by Form D (genitive) of thing begrudged.

8 **ferens:** present participles in Latin are occasionally used (as more frequently in English) with a past sense — 'after bringing'.

8–9 **aridum . . . dedit:** perhaps demonstrate on the blackboard how 'ore ferens' and 'dedit' refer to both 'aridum acinum' and 'semesa lardi frusta'.

12 **dapis meliora:** may be a colloquialism.

13 **ad hunc:** for 'huic', may be a colloquialism.

15 **vis tu . . . ?:** a formula (probably colloquial) for initiating a strong request.

18 **quo . . . circa:** no other examples remain of 'quocirca' in tmesis. Horace may have been imitating the extravagant tmeses of Lucilius.

20 **aevi brevis:** best taken together as a descriptive Form D (genitive).

24 **nox:** Night was supposed to drive her chariot across the sky.
ponit: for inverse 'cum' clauses, see Woodcock section 237; and cf. 'cum . . . excussit' (34–5).

26–7 **canderet, superessent:** the subjunctives may be generic, 'the sort of house where . . . ' (Woodcock sections 155–8), but 'subj. came to be used more and more in cases where its original modal force was either considerably weakened, or had even disappeared entirely, so that it was merely a stylistic substitute for an indic. . . . ' (Handford 139).

30 **succinctus:** cf. IV.1.17.

33–4 **bonis . . . rebus:** the teacher's reading should show that this is not governed by 'gaudet'. The rather bald Form E (ablative) is best taken as of attendant circumstances, but pupils should not normally be burdened with the terminology.

34 **agit:** there may be dramatic imagery here, suggesting that the Country Mouse is not yet fully converted — he is still aware of living out a rôle.

35 **valvarum:** even internal doors were regularly two-leaved.

36–7 **currere . . . trepidare:** historic infinitives.

Discussion

The forcefully placed 'olim' (2), like 'once upon a time', promises a story. Then in lines 3 and 4 we are introduced to the two mice. But these two lines are as rhetorically complex as the mice they describe are

ordinary. The quantitative heaviness of 'urbanum murem mus' sets up
the phrase as mock-portentous, and this impression is strengthened by
the highly worked chiastic patterns (ABBA and BAAB) of 'rusticus
urbanum murem mus' and 'veterem vetus hospes amicum'. Furthermore,
in each case Horace juxtaposes the same word in different forms with a
fourth-foot caesura between; and assonance and alliteration lend an
additional air of artistic contrivance. A deliberate tension has been created, as so often in this piece, between the simplicity of the story and
the sophistication of the technique.

The introduction ends with a characterisation of the Country Mouse:
he is 'asper', 'attentus quaesitis' and has an 'artum animum' (5–6). If
we know the story, as Roman readers no doubt did, we are expecting a
thoroughly sympathetic treatment of the Country Mouse. Horace surprises us with a catalogue of qualities which individually are typical
peasant virtues, but taken as a whole prove unappealing to an urban
audience. The mouse is a rough diamond ('asper'); frugal with what he
has acquired; and has a parsimonious or thrifty ('artum') mentality. All
these qualities are two-edged, and it is not easy to find English equivalents which walk the tight-rope between parsimony and thrift. Nonetheless, the accumulation of so many penny-pinching epithets in one
line gathers a certain pejorative force which is borne out by the stingi-
ness of what the Country Mouse offers. If the black-and-white contrast
of the fable is indeed a little grey at the edges, this would fit with Brink's
interpretation of the whole poem: 'Horace had a sense of the different
values inherent in town and country, and felt the pull of each' (Brink,
9). Of course, 'ut tamen artum / solveret hospitiis animum' does offer a
qualification, but we may well begin to wonder whether there is a touch
of irony here. It would be wrong to press this too far; but Horace does
seem to suggest that the Country Mouse is less generous than he imagines.
The proof of this pudding lies largely in the eating which follows.

The meals of lines 6–12 and 27–34 are evidently intended to be
contrasted by the reader — and not only for the manner of their ending.
A full appreciation of the points of contrast is not possible the first
time through. Words acquire more or less importance, and may even
modify their meanings, in the light of how the poem develops. Perhaps
the best way to provoke comparison is to tabulate the parallels:

	COUNTRY	TOWN
1	paupere cavo (3–4)	in locuplete domo (25)
2	sepositi ciceris; longae avenae; aridum acinum; semesa lardi frusta (7–9)	multa fercula de magna cena, quae inerant exstructis canistris (27–8)
3	ore ferens dedit (8–9)	veluti hospes cursitat, continuatque dapes, nec non verniliter ipsis fungitur officiis, praelambens omne quod adfert (30–2)

COUNTRY	TOWN
4a (agrestis) palea porrectus in horna esset ador loliumque (11–12)	(urbanus) purpurea porrectum in veste locavit agrestem (29–30)
4b fastidia (urbani) tangentis male singula dente superbo (9–10)	(agrestis) cubans gaudet; agit laetum convivam (33–4)

(1) The contrasts begin with the location: 'paupere . . . cavo' (3–4) being opposed to 'locuplete domo' (25). We are reminded that Cervius' story (see Context note) is directed against urban extravagance, not town life in general.

(2) The Country Mouse is as generous as his character allows, but his notion of hospitality is distinctly meagre. The extent to which it falls short of what was expected is emphasised by a process of anthropomorphism which begins as early as line 4. The use of terms like 'hospes' and 'amicus' (4), 'pater domus' (11) and the careful character-drawing in lines 5–6 set us thinking of persons; and there are few reminders of mousy status. The witty thing about the choice of country diet in lines 7–9 (West in Woodman and West, Ch. 5) is that, while individual items are eminently appropriate to mice, the four-course menu as a whole recalls the simplest fare of an agricultural labourer. The urban reader, who may not know a good mouse meal from a bad one, is thus made to see the food as unappetising and the hospitality as less than generous. The epithets clearly support this interpretation: the chick-pea has been put in reserve for a special occasion ('sepositi') and is likely to be rather old; the 'long' oat must surely be the wild variety with its long panicles; the unspecified berry is juiceless (and see *OLD* 7 for the miserly overtones of 'aridus'); and there are only half-eaten bits of bacon. Furthermore, Horace reduces to the singular all the titbits bar the bacon: the mouse brings forth one chick-pea, one oat and one berry. Of course, at first reading one interprets 'ciceris', 'avenae' and 'acinum' as poetic singulars, and (West in Woodman and West) it is only when one marks the contrast in 'multa fercula . . . exstructis canistris' (27–8) with its stress on plurality, excess ('superessent') and size ('multa', 'magna', 'exstructis' and perhaps, under the circumstances, 'canistris') that one becomes sure of the force of the Country Mouse's singulars. In fact, singularity is at least half guaranteed by 'singula' in line 10, and in line 8 by the strikingly concrete image of 'ore ferens acinum' — which incidentally reminds us that our mouse-host needs his 'hands' for walking. 'dapis meliora relinquens' in line 12 is wittily ironical, though I doubt (see *OLD* 2.b) whether 'dapis' necessarily conjures up the archaic splendour with which West invests it. Unlike the other items on the menu, 'ador' and 'lolium' (the Country Mouse's fare) were not consumed by humans. In sharp contrast, the meal in town is made to sound palatial. Line 27, which introduces the Town Mouse's food, is

a Golden Line (abCAB), of which Wilkinson says: 'Horace reserved its
monumental quality for special purposes . . . Two in succession
enhance the grandiosity of the town mouse's scene of operations'
(Wilkinson, 1963: 216). Line 26 (Wilkinson's second, and structured
aBCAb) is in fact not quite Golden, but is buttressed by an equally sub-
Golden line 28 (AbCaB).

(3) 'ore ferens . . . dedit' (8—9) captures succinctly the bluff style of
waiting adopted by the Country Mouse. Only two lines later he is to be
seen 'palea porrectus in horna' chewing away at his 'ador loliumque'.
With this unenterprising service compare the extravagant display affected
by the Town Mouse, who sees his guest settled, dresses for the part,
bustles around with consummate efficiency, and even plays the rôle of
the slave who, in the most fashionable households, tasted the food
before serving (cf. *CIL* VI.9005; *CLC* Unit III *Stage 27* 'cena'). 'prae-
lambens omne quod adfert' (32) picks up 'ore ferens' (8), and what
seemed an insignificant detail in line 8 is now set in strong contrast with
the finesse of the Town Mouse in line 32. The hustle and bustle is perhaps highlighted by alliteration of 'c' and 't', particularly noticeable in
lines 26, 28 and 30. There must also be some criticism on the part of
Horace and the reader, if not yet on the part of the Country Mouse, in
the clear suggestion that the Town Mouse's luxury entailed activity
proper to a slave (31—2).

(4) It is the Country Mouse who is described as taking his ease at
both meals, whether reclining 'palea . . . in horna' (11) or 'purpurea . . .
in veste' (29). We are given no picture of the Town Mouse's posture in
the country, though evidence for a starchiness incompatible with such
relaxed behaviour is provided by his 'fastidia' (9) and the expressive
characterisation of 'tangentis male singula dente superbo' (10) — where
the humour lies partly in the transferred epithet, 'superbo', and partly
in the disdainful skimming of each item with but one tooth. By contrast,
the Country Mouse is 'porrectus' (11 and 29), a word which implies an
abandoned posture — often used of people sprawled in sleep. The
general word for reclining, 'cubans', is found only in line 33 when the
Country Mouse is acting the 'laetum convivam'. I don't see why one
needs to evade (with West in Woodman and West) the conclusion that
the Country Mouse is 'rusticus' in the extended sense: he is shown us as
a peasant mouse who doesn't know the towny way of behaving at
dinner. We get no clue to the Town Mouse's posture even at the meal in
town. He is too busy rushing around to take any food himself.

After line 12, the story demands that the Country Mouse should be
persuaded to visit town. Aesop and the other fabulists give us distinctly
unsubtle speeches of persuasion, while Horace changes the whole tone
of the passage by injecting a dose of philosophy. If 'ad hunc' (13) is
indeed a colloquialism, then the contrast is even more pointed. The
philosophy here is a parody of half-digested Epicureanism. Horace him-

self was much in sympathy with the assumptions of Epicureanism, but
was sufficiently detached to smile at himself as a 'pinguem et nitidum
. . . Epicuri de grege porcum', in the *Epistle* to Tibullus (*Epistles* I.4.
15–16). (See also X.1.2, for the poet's apparent disenchantment.)
Similar sentiments to those of the Town Mouse are to be found in many
of Horace's later poems. Two points distinguish the Town Mouse's
homily as a piece of fun: (i) the crude concatenation of so much street
philosophy in so few lines; (ii) the inherent absurdity of a mouse utter-
ing philosophical technicalities. The Town Mouse's sentiments, which
taken as a whole are evidently philistine, nonetheless come over as
individually credible, and this gives a witty delicacy to the passage.
There is an obvious humour in the simple fact of such a pompous ser-
mon being delivered by a mouse. But Horace's humour goes further.
(i) Line 15 is a very reasonable exhortation for a pseudo-Epicurean to
make to his proselyte: it is an extraordinary thing for one wild beast to
say to another. (ii) Philosophers would presumably not intend creatures
like mice to count in the allotment of souls, for which they seem to
qualify if 'terrestria' (16) is taken literally. (iii) The commonplace
'magno aut parvo' (18) generally refers to 'the rich man in his castle,
the poor man at his gate', while here it is transposed into 'all creatures
great and small'. (iv) The philosopher who talks of the shortness of life
is not really bargaining for a mousy lifespan. (v) The underlying absurdity of Horace's philosopher-mouse is brought out by high-flown writing:
there is an unparalleled tmesis of 'quocirca' (see note above) and two
clear examples of bucolic diaeresis (18 and 20), which West sees as 'an
audible warning of approaching pomposity' (in Woodman and West 75).

The Virgilian phrase 'haec ubi dicta' (20) imparts an epic flavour.
But this grandeur, already undercut by the bucolic diaeresis of line 20,
is conclusively trivialised by the onomatopoea of 'leviṣ exṣilit; *i*nde' (21).
Not only do we hear the mice squeaking, but we are perhaps amused at
the implicit contrast between a burly Homeric hero who leaps lightly
because of his strength, and a mouse who leaps lightly because he is
tiny. The move to the town house is achieved with great economy; and
it thus balances the extended speechifying of lines 13–20. Lines 21–4
contain exit, journey, arrival at the town, passing of the walls, establish-
ment of the time and arrival at the house – all in a series of swift jump-
cuts. The heroic purposiveness of line 22 ('propositum', 'per-', 'aventes')
is well brought down to size in line 23, where the mice appropriately
crawl under the walls in the dark (note also the furtive sense of 'sub-').
The epic ambience is restored from line 24 by means of (i) the high-
flown diction of line 24; (ii) the virtual personification of 'nox' (24);
(iii) the pretentious 'ponit . . . vestigia' (24–5), undercut by the mental
picture conjured up by the last word of the clause, paw-tracks; (iv) the
strong colour-contrast of 'rubro . . . cocco' (25) with 'canderet . . .
eburnos' in 26 (see West in Costa 37ff.); (v) the Golden and quasi-

Golden Lines in 26—8. The effect of this mock-epic description is
exactly comparable with the inflated language of the philosopher-mouse
in the previous section: the mixture of the sublime with the ridiculous
is intentionally amusing.

The finale is introduced in line 34 by another inverted 'cum'-clause
(cf. line 24), just as the Country Mouse is settling into his rôle and
appears to be achieving the good life promised in line 19 (cf. 'in rebus
iucundis' in 19 with 'bonis . . . rebus' in 33—4). Note the leisurely pace
of the metre, with seven consecutive heavy syllables in both lines 33
and 34. By contrast, the elision in the fifth foot of line 34 speeds us
forward, with 'ingens' sounding distinctly ominous in the mousy micro-
cosm, but soon identifiable to the reader as no more than a noisy door.
In this way the mice are well brought down to size, and it takes no
more than the noise to shake them off their couches (where 'excussit
utrumque' in line 35 is an amusing verbal echo of 'cum ponit uterque'
in the very different circumstances of line 24). The whole effect is filled
out with some striking alliteration of 's', 't' and 'c'/'q' (the latter continuing in line 36). From this point, all the lines until the end are
enjambed, and the strongly dactylic metre races along with the
'utrumque', 'magisque', 'cavusque' jingle. 'currere' is brought forward
to begin line 36, with its urgency doubled by the historic infinitive; and
the feeling of terror is laid on thickly with 'pavidi', 'exanimes' and
'trepidare', while 'totum' and 'magis' act in support. So far, the only
stimulus of all this adrenalin has been the sound of the room door opening. The reader is at liberty to imagine reasons for this, such as the
slaves entering to clear up last night's dinner; but the mice naturally
react before they interpret, and this scene is presented very much
through their eyes and ears. The final straw is another, yet more threatening, sound. The house is no longer 'wealthy' as in line 25, but 'alta' (to
the mice); and to their ears it sounds through and through ('personuit',
38) with the baying of hounds — whom the pessimistic mice assume to
be first-rate hunters ('Molossis'), cats not being common before the first
century A.D. (Balsdon, 1969: 151).

The Country Mouse's final speech is brisk and his language simple,
unlike the wordy philosophising of the Town Mouse in lines 13—20.
For the Country Mouse, the 'silvae' are not 'ferae' (15) but coupled
with the mouse-hole as being 'tutus ab insidiis' (40). Against 'rebus
iucundis' (19) he sets 'tenui . . . ervo', and against 'living it up' ('vive',
20) he sets 'solacium', spiritual comfort. With 'cavus' (39), we are
reminded of the beginnings of the story.

A comparison with Pope's *Imitation*, lines 153ff., or the final chap-
ter of Orwell's *Animal Farm* might be instructive. For a more orthodox
view of the character of the Country Mouse, see John Berger's observations on styles of eating (*The Guardian*, 3 January 1976), from which
the following short excerpt is reproduced:

'The feast for the peasant . . . begins with food and drink. It does so because food and drink have been reserved or put aside, on account of their rarity or special quality, for just such an occasion. Any feast, even if it is impromptu, has been partly prepared for years. A feast is the consuming of the surplus saved and produced over and above daily needs. Expressing and using up some of this surplus, the feast is a double celebration — of the occasion which gives rise to it, and of the surplus itself. Hence its slow tempo, its generosity, and the active high spirits which accompany it.'

Questions

1 What does Horace tell us explicitly about the characters of the Country Mouse and the Town Mouse, and what can we deduce from their various activities in the fable? Are the mice intended to appear attractive personalities?

2 How do the two meals differ? Consider, e.g., the location, the types and quantities of food on offer, the behaviour of the host, the attitude of the guest, the conclusion of the meal.

3 What arguments does the Town Mouse use in lines 13—20? How persuasive are they?

4 What frightens the mice in lines 34—8? Which features of the situation does Horace emphasise, and why?

5 What is the moral of this fable? Is it what the Country Mouse says (38—40)? Does the story of the mice fulfil the purpose outlined for it (1—2)?

6 Imagine that you are making an animated cartoon of this passage. How would you cut your filming into sequences? Would you use 'voice over' at any point? Are there moments at which you would pan round a scene or zoom into close-up or adopt a particular angle? Is there sufficient visual detail in Horace's poetry, or would you have to invent more? Would you omit anything? Would you finish in the same abrupt way as Horace?

7 Make a comic strip of all or part of this fable. Try to bring out differences in scale and character.

8 If lines 2—4 had perished, what (if any) details would inform us that this was a story about mice rather than men? Distinguish hard evidence from general indications. Your list will not be long: why might this be so? Contrast Aesop's version of the same fable (see question 11).

9 How does Horace try to interest and entertain the reader? Consider his use of contrasting types of subject matter and language; humour; sound-effects.

10 Why have animal fables proved so attractive (cf. Aesop, La

Fontaine, *Peter Rabbit*, *Animal Farm*, *Watership Down*)? Is it
largely because the reader is made to feel in a comfortable
position of moral superiority? Why should Horace choose to
express this particular series of ideas in a fable?

11 How does the passage stand comparison with Aesop's telling of
the same fable?

'A field-mouse invited a friend who lived in a town house to
dine with him in the country. The other accepted with alacrity;
but when he found that the fare consisted only of barley and
other corn, he said to his host: "Let me tell you, my friend,
you live like an ant. But I have abundance of good things to
eat, and if you will come home with me you shall share them
all." So the two of them went off at once; and when his friend
showed him peas and beans, bread, dates, cheese, honey, and
fruit, the astonished field-mouse congratulated him heartily
and cursed his own lot. They were about to begin their meal
when the door suddenly opened, and the timid creatures were
so scared by the sound that they scuttled into chinks. When
they had returned and were just going to take some dried figs,
they saw someone else come into the room to fetch something,
and once more they jumped to take cover in their holes. At
this the field-mouse decided that he did not care if he had to
go hungry. "Good-bye, my friend," he said with a groan. "You
may eat your fill and enjoy yourself. But your good cheer
costs you dear in danger and fear. I would rather gnaw my
poor meals of barley and corn without being afraid or having
to watch anyone out of the corner of my eye."

A simple life with peace and quiet is better than faring
luxuriously and being tortured by fear.'
Trans. S.A. Handford (Penguin, 1954)

I.2 Ovid, Epistulae ex Ponto *I.8.29–40, 61–2*

Context

Ovid was banished in A.D. 8, and his *Epistulae ex Ponto* I–III were published in *c.* A.D. 13. He writes from exile to various addressees: 'although
my theme remains always the same, I have not addressed it to the same
readers, and the single cry that I utter seeks help through many people'
(Ovid, *Epistulae ex Ponto* III.9.41–2). Ovid's cry, of course, was for
release from confinement at Tomis. The verse-letters of Books I–III
were assembled arbitrarily (Ovid, *Epistulae ex Ponto* III.9.53): it is possible, but cannot be assumed, that individual letters were shown around
in Rome prior to publication. Our excerpt is from a letter addressed to
Severus, probably Cornelius Severus the author of an epic poem on the
war between Sextus Pompey and Octavian, rated highly by Quintilian.

Ovid tells Severus that Tomis is under siege by local tribesmen: he alone is both exile and soldier ('sum miles in exule solus': *7) and he pleads for, at the very least, transfer to a more peaceful locality (*73—4). His wish was not to be granted.

The immediate context is a complaint by Ovid that he has to put up with warfare in addition to his other troubles (*26) and a reminder that he has now been 'on the banks of the Styx' for almost four years (*27—8).

Language and content

1 **urbanae:** suggests Rome (as the following lines confirm) and carries overtones of civilisation as well as city life.

4 **cum cara coniuge nata:** cf. V.3.13—16. On Ovid's deep love for his third wife, see Wilkinson, 1955: 342—5.

5 **a . . . domo:** Ovid's house in Rome, preserved by the presence of his wife.

7 **fora:** in addition to the Forum Romanum (see plan of Rome in pupils' text 3), Augustus completed the Forum Iulium, left unfinished by Julius Caesar, and the Forum Augusti (*Res Gestae* 19—21, with notes by Brunt and Moore; Dudley 14—15 and 120—9). The Forum Augusti was begun in 37 B.C. and the Temple of Mars Ultor, which dominated it, was dedicated in 2 B.C. Ovid writes the praises of this temple in *Fasti* V.551—3, 563—6.

aedes: for a list of temples built by Augustus, see *Res Gestae* 19—21; Dudley 15. In addition to the many new temples erected, Augustus claims to have restored no fewer than eighty-two temples within Rome.

marmore: Augustus boasted that he had found Rome a city of brick, but left it a city of marble (Suetonius, *Augustus* 28.3).

theatra: Augustus tells us (*Res Gestae* 19—21; Dudley 14f.) that he repaired the Theatre of Pompey and built the Theatre of Marcellus. We know from Suetonius (*Augustus* 29.5) that the small but luxurious Theatre of Balbus (Pliny the Elder, *Natural History* XXXVI.12.60, mentions its onyx columns) was also built at Augustus' prompting (site undiscovered, *pace* map in pupils' text). For more details, see Dudley 178—84; Paoli 259 and 265, n. 26. The three theatres were all in the same neighbourhood, not far from the east bank of the Tiber. Suetonius (*Augustus* 43.5) tells an amusing story about the dedication of the Theatre of Marcellus.

8 **aequata . . . humo:** some *porticūs* (see below) covered a considerable area of ground. The levelling of the site, without bulldozers, would have been a massive undertaking (cf. *CLC* Unit II *Teacher's Handbook* 56 on the Fishbourne garden), and current building operations would no doubt have caught Ovid's eye before he left Rome.

porticus: Augustus built a Porticus of Octavia in 27 B.C. and a Porticus of Livia (Suetonius, *Augustus* 29.4), and possibly others that are not recorded. The Porticus of Octavia was part of a building complex which included Greek and Latin libraries and a lecture-hall, and housed 'one of the finest collections of paintings and sculpture in Rome, . . . mostly collected or commissioned by Augustus' (Dudley 178). We hear of an Aphrodite by Phidias, the Cupid by Praxiteles, a great equestrian group by Lysippus, and works attributed to Scopas. Colonnades were regularly placed behind the stage of theatres (Vitruvius, *De Architectura* V.9) so that the crowd had somewhere to go when it rained, and to provide

space for preparing stage sets. There was a well-known colonnade, the
Porticus of Pompey, behind Pompey's theatre. Propertius (*Elegies* II.32.
11—16) refers to its shady trees and columns and extravagant fountains,
and we know from Pliny that here too there were splendid works of art.

9   **Campi**: this open space to the north-west of Rome, where the energetic
went for athletic training and others simply to walk in the fresh air, was
gradually invaded by imperial building programmes. 'Agrippa, in particular, must rank among the greatest of the builders of Rome for his
development of the Campus Martius' (Dudley 17). Strabo writes enthu-
siastically of its surface covered with grass all through the year and says
that the total effect of the Campus is comparable with looking at a
theatrical backdrop (*Geographica* V.3.8).

9—10   **hortos, stagnaque**: Ovid probably has in mind the Horti Agrippae, near
the Thermae Agrippae in the Campus Martius. The Stagnum Agrippae
was in the Horti Agrippae; it was a large pool, later to be used by Nero
for mock naval battles (Tacitus, *Annals* XV.37).

10   **euripi . . . liquor**: probably a specific reference to the canal in the Horti
Agrippae. It was supplied by the Aqua Virgo (Frontinus, *De aquis* II.84)
and ran down to the Tiber. Seneca tells us (*Epistles*, 83.5) that he used
to take an annual dip on 1 January in the Euripus. The restricted
topography of lines 9—10 and the proximity of 'euripi' and 'Virgineus'
support the view that 'euripi' is singular and therefore Form D (genitive)
characterising 'liquor'. Alternatively, 'euripi' may be taken as Form A
(nominative) plural — either with singular meaning (in conjunction with
'stagna') or with non-specific reference to the canals and water-channels
of Rome.

Virgineus . . . liquor: the Aqua Virgo was the main artery for the north-
west water-supply, and in particular the Thermae Agrippae, the first
thermae in Rome. According to Frontinus 'it was called Virgo because a
little girl showed some streams to soldiers who were looking for water.
They followed these . . . and discovered a huge supply'; the intake was
at the eighth milestone along the Via Collatina, and its channel went
underground almost all the way into Rome, where it was carried on
arches from the Mons Pincius (*De aquis* I.10 and 22). In *Tristia* III.12.
21—2, Ovid refers to 'young men drenched in slippery oil' bathing their
tired limbs in water from the Aqua Virgo: it was clearly conveniently
near the main exercise area in the Campus Martius.

11   **puto**: strongly ironical.
     misero: Form C (dative) of disadvantage or deprivation.

13   **hostem**: see Context note, and *Tristia* IV.1.71—6 for elderly Ovid putting on armour.

14   **murus**: of Tomis.
     facit: the double grammatical subject can take a singular verb because
Ovid has virtually a single idea in mind — the wall with its locked gate.

Discussion

Ovid begins our excerpt with a startlingly uncharacteristic denial, couched
largely in emphatic spondees (1). His writings from exile are drenched
with nostalgia for Rome and the civilised life, yet here he is apparently
disclaiming any desire to return. The reader's attention is taken in a particularly bold fashion. But reality returns in line 2. Ovid has been exploiting an ambiguity in the repeated 'quaerere' — between long-term and
short-term goals. He does (of course) want to return to Rome, but this

is not the purpose of his present letter. He is prepared to settle for second-best — exile away from the front line of the Empire.

With 'quaerit et illa tamen' (2), Ovid is more direct; and, in the lines which follow, he gives us an exile's view of home. What appears to be a sentimental outburst (note the move from third to first person) is in fact carefully controlled. The first couplet (3—4) deals with friends and loved ones; the second (5—6) is a generalised introduction for the close detail of the third (7—8, central Rome) and fourth (9—10, the Campus Martius). The whole reverie is suggested by 'urbanae' (1), picked up by 'urbis' in line 5 as the focus narrows on to the urban topography, and concluded by 'urbis' in line 11. The duplication of 'subit' (4 and 8) is unimaginative, and the epithets of lines 3—5 ('dulces', 'cara', 'pulchrae'), though all abutting the caesura and leaving Ovid's attitude in no doubt at all, seem a little flat. 'domo' in line 5 leads one very smoothly from Ovid's family to the architecture of Rome, now characterised as 'pulchrae' (5) in what is probably the first of several implicit eulogies of Augustus' building achievement. Without line 6, the recital of buildings might be felt to follow too pat, and the line also serves to remind Ovid's readers that for him Rome is accessible *only* through the imagination. The mental process involved is nonetheless precise ('cuncta', '*per*videt', 'oculis . . . suis' — just as clear as actually seeing). The public life of Rome is then captured in four compressed lines. Business and the law ('fora', 7), worship of the state gods ('aedes', 7), entertainment, relaxation and the arts ('theatra', 7; 'porticus', 8), the beautiful open spaces of Rome ('Campi', 'hortos', 9), and its great aqueducts and water-channels — all in clear tribute to the man who had built or redeveloped so much of the city.

Ovid has now established the extent of his deprivation. The more attractive the picture Ovid paints of Rome, the less fair does it seem for him to be deprived both of Rome and of peace. 'at' (11), sharply adversative, brings him and his readers back to Tomis. 'I suppose my banishment from Rome does at least mean that I can enjoy the pleasures of the country', argues Ovid. The agreeable views of Rome which we have just experienced predispose us to react sympathetically towards such a plea.

Ovid defers his punch-line for twenty lines (omitted), in which he remembers the gardening he used to do in Italy; he does not aspire to that, but wishes he could at least have a plot of land to look after in the Tomis countryside. This seems a small thing to ask. Lines 13—14 are correspondingly harsh and uncompromising, as Ovid intended. Line 14 is as heavy as a pentameter can be, and, following it, Ovid abruptly changes course in the poem as a whole, now in its last lines, with an effective coda in which the suggestion that Augustus might suppress his just anger is floated for the first time in the poem.

Questions

1 Is there a contradiction in lines 1 and 2? What does Ovid really mean?

2 What is Ovid's attitude to Rome? What is the evidence?

3 Do lines 11–12 explain why Ovid develops his picture of Rome at such length?

4 Do lines 13–14 add anything to the conclusion suggested by lines 11–12?

5 How might Augustus have reacted to this piece? Is there anything specifically intended to catch his vanity?

6 What would a modern exile remember of your home town? Is it likely to be an accurate picture? Should this make us more circumspect in our treatment of Ovid?

7 Not all Rome's inhabitants could live the leisured life suggested by Ovid. Contrast with our passage Martial, *Epigrams* V.20.

I.3 Martial, Epigrams *III.52*

Language and content

1 **empta . . . fuerat:** Martial makes free use of the pluperfect forms even where we might expect plain perfect. Here we have 'empta fuerat' for 'empta erat'.

tibi: Form C (dative) of the agent.

Tongiliane: the same name appears in Martial, *Epigrams* XII.88, credited with 'nasus' (i.e. 'nose', 'sharp wit') and nothing but 'nasus'.

ducentis: 200,000 *sestertii.* Cicero paid 3,500,000 *sestertii* for Crassus' house on the Palatine (*ad Atticum* I.13; *ad Familiares* V.6) and Clodius' house cost 14,800,000 *sestertii.* Suetonius (*Iulius* 38.2) quotes *c.* 2,000 *sestertii* as an annual house-rent for ordinary people. The extravagant Caelius was supposed to have paid rent of 30,000 *sestertii*, though Cicero imagines 10,000 to be nearer the mark (*pro Caelio* 17). Some comparative rebuilding costs can be found in Duncan-Jones 160–2. It is worth noting that 'the annual rent of a dark abode in Rome would buy the freehold of a fine house and garden at a nearby town' (Duncan-Jones 345, on Juvenal *Satires* III.223ff.). See also Yavetz on prices and conditions. Tongilianus seems to have bought at a bargain price for Rome, if it is possible to assume some stability of price levels.

2 **nimium casus . . . frequens:** Rome was 'a city of tall buildings and narrow streets . . . and fire (was) a constant hazard from timber buildings and oil lamps' (M.W. Frederiksen in Balsdon, 1965: 167). Juvenal (*Satires* III.193ff.) says:

> 'We live in a town supported, much of it, by flimsy props. That's how the landlord steadies his tottering property. He covers over the gape of an ancient crack, and tells the tenants to sleep sound as the building threatens collapse. Come and live in the country, where there are no fires, no night-time frights.'

Discussion

This sharp and well-constructed little poem picks out a theme which may already be familiar to pupils (*CLC* Unit III *Attainment Test* 7).

The poem starts with 'empta domus' (1) and is completed by 'domum' (4): first and last lines both focus on Tongilianus and his house. Symmetry is confirmed by the second halves of lines 1 and 4, where 'tuam' picks up 'tibi', the lengthy name is repeated, and the last word starts with 'd'. The repetition of the long and rather barbarous 'Tongiliane' is no doubt calculated to suggest distaste (see *CLC* Unit IV *Teacher's Handbook* 152 on Martial, *Epigrams* VII.3). Key words are brought to the beginning of the four lines, with 'empta' (1) contrasting wittily with 'incendisse' (4), and the destructive 'abstulit' (2) set against another 'ferre' compound, the positive 'conlatum' (3). The power of the crucial 'deciens' (3) is enhanced (i) by a certain ambiguity between its root meaning ('ten times' *sc.* the original price) and the monetary idiom ('deciens' = 'deciens centena milia sestertium'); (ii) by the jingle 'casus in urbe frequens. / conlatum est deciens'. Finally, we come to realise the full significance of 'nimium' (2): of course such fires are far too frequent if the rewards are on this scale!

The progression through the tenses is managed so as to jerk the reader from a recital of past history to a vivid direct question in the present, with Martial in the rôle of prosecuting counsel. The question itself is utterly predictable, of course, and the wit of the poem lies in the way Martial expands the predictable to fill one-and-a-half verses out of four — 'calculated, perhaps rather heavy, irony' assisting this effect: 'Pray, Tongilianus, is it not (just) possible that (some uncharitable persons might think it looked as if) you . . . ?' (Kenney).

Juvenal explores the same theme at greater length (*Satires* III.198— 222). A brief comparison might be fruitful, not least for any light it might shed on the differing demands and restrictions of epigram and satire.

Questions

1 How has Martial patterned his poem? Is this important?
2 What seems to be Martial's attitude towards Tongilianus? Would it affect your reaction to the poem if it could be proved that Martial had invented Tongilianus?
3 How might Tongilianus have replied to Martial's question (3—4)? Write a matching four lines or so (in English).
4 Why were fires such a frequent occurrence in Rome? What was done about preventing them? (See note on line 2; *CLC* Unit IV 'Bithynia' section IV, with *Handbook* 74—5 and slide 48; Carcopino 44—5; Earl 88, 97—9; Martial, *Epigrams* XI.93; etc.)

I.4 Martial, Epigrams *IV.8*

Language and content

1 For the programme of a client's day, see also Juvenal *Satires* I.127—34.
On the shape of the Roman day, see Balsdon, 1969, Ch. 1, and Carcopino, Part 2: in each there is the following comparative table of Roman
and modern time-measurement:

	Midsummer	Midwinter
Hour 1	4.27— 5.42	7.33— 8.17
Hour 2	5.42— 6.58	8.17— 9.02
Hour 3	6.58— 8.13	9.02— 9.46
Hour 4	8.13— 9.29	9.46—10.31
Hour 5	9.29—10.44	10.31—11.15
Hour 6	10.44—12.00	11.15—12.00
Hour 7	12.00—13.15	12.00—12.44
Hour 8	13.15—14.31	12.44—13.29
Hour 9	14.31—15.46	13.29—14.13
Hour 10	15.46—17.02	14.13—14.58
Hour 11	17.02—18.17	14.58—15.42
Hour 12	18.17—19.33	15.42—16.27

2 **tertia**: the courts sat early, sometimes even before the third hour.
raucos: may be proleptic — they become hoarse as a result of 'exercitio'.
3 **in quintam**: it is between the third and fifth hours that the miserly
Titullus of Martial *Epigrams* VIII.44 collects his debts. These are Rome's
prime business hours.
4 **quies**: seems to imply an early siesta — usually taken in the seventh
hour. Presumably the sense of this line is that some may stop work early,
but no one continues after the seventh hour.
lassis: colloquialism.
7 **Eupheme**: assumed to be a *structor* ('carver') of Domitian, but the name
is reminiscent of Greek 'euphēmeite' requesting silence in the presence
of a god.
9 **aetherio**: a title of Jupiter. For Domitian's palace, see *CLC* Unit IV
slide 28.
10 **pocula**: the dinner appears to have reached the drinking stage or
comissatio (Balsdon, 1969: 44).
parca: Suetonius (*Domitian* 21) and Statius (*Silvae* V.1.121—2) both
refer to Domitian's abstemiousness.
11 **gressun metire licenti**: the manuscripts have either 'gressum metire' or
'gressu metire'. With our conjecture, Martial is asking his Muse whether
she makes provocative advances to Jupiter in the morning. The question
technically is left open ('gressun' = 'gressune') although the answer is
clearly to be in the negative. See further, Discussion below.

Discussion

Martial's poem changes course in line 7, when he begins to focus on his
own circumstances after what promises to be an impersonal survey of
town life after the manner of Juvenal (*Satires* I.127—34).
In lines 1—7 Martial provides an hour-by-hour catalogue of social
activity in Rome. Unless carefully managed, such an approach is liable
to bore the reader, who waits with increasing impatience for each stroke

of the hour. Martial avoids this by (i) varying the number of hours mentioned in each line, and in fact devoting half the poem to a single hour; (ii) varying the position of the numbers in the lines; (iii) omitting mention of the fourth hour, and not working remorselessly through eleven and twelve; (iv) producing several vivid effects despite the numerical straitjacket.

The *salutatio* is described with some bitterness, probably founded on personal experience. The harsh 't'-alliteration (though predictable in a poem with so many number-adjectives) is particularly marked in the first line, and emphasised by the repeated '-ter-' in 'altera conterit'. The root sense of 'conterit' ('pound to pieces') must be in the reader's mind: 'hora' is personified in a reversal of the usual phrase ('diem conterere') as grinding the clients to powder for two whole hours. The 't'-alliteration runs through into the second line; and the assonance of '-er-', '-au-', '-os', repeated on either side of the caesura, completes the picture of the noisy lawyers. Again 'hora' is presented as a taskmaster keeping the lawyers busy, and the choice of the word 'caus*idic*os' brings to the fore the speechifying which makes them hoarse. Furthermore, their tedious activity is underlined by the metrical heaviness of 'ēxērcēt raūcōs'. The next line (3) is similarly heavy (except in the second foot), and the long 'ō' is repeated on the verse ictus. The impression of unremitting tedium thus carries over from line 2. As we arrive at the sixth hour (4), the accent is on leisure rather than work, and this is reflected in the lighter feel of the pentameter with colloquial 'lassis'. As 'sufficit' (5) undercuts 'finis' (4) and the commendatory 'nitidis' (5) betokens relaxation, a note of optimism begins to make itself felt in contrast with the rather dour beginning. 'hora' (understood with 'nona' in 6) is again strongly personified: the ninth hour gives the order for the *cena* to start. Two things weld lines 1—6 to what follows: (i) the dinner-party, which provides the backcloth for the second half, is introduced in line 6; (ii) the last of the hours ('decima') is mentioned in the first line of the second half (7).

Line 7 is resonant with '-ōr-' sounds, but not intrinsically heavy; in fact, the alliteration of 'l' and 'm' gives it a softness which contrasts with the 't'-alliteration of line 6. The tenth hour is described, not unreasonably, as the hour for books to be read. The introduction of Euphemus marks the change from general to particular, and 'meorum' is very striking at the end of the line. Not only does the poet introduce his own personality into the poem, but he does so with the amusingly arrogant implication that the only books read at the tenth hour are his books. In fact, as we discover in line 8, the main clause of this sentence merely defines the time of the more significant events of the 'cum'-clause. The inverted 'cum'-clause is typical of epic (cf. I.1.24; IX.2.20), and together with the mention of ambrosial feasts it helps elevate the reader to a superhuman sphere of activity parallel with epic Olympus (see note on line 7). We are in the imperial court ('Caesar', 9) — a point the reader may have taken with the mention of Euphemus, if historical, in line 7. Domitian is described hopefully as 'bonus' (regularly used of gods), and the sense of divinity and calm is confirmed by 'aetherio laxatur nectare' (9), in clear contrast with the frenzied extremes of the ordinary inhabitants of Rome (1—6). The Emperor's hand is large — the words 'ingenti . . . manu' enclose the rest of line 10 — as befits a god; but his drinking — albeit of nectar — is restrained, as befits the *censor perpetuus*.

'tunc' in line 11 opens the final couplet. It is an effective means of tying together and concluding all the references to time without going full circle back to 'prima . . . hora'. The point of the poem is now made clear. Line 7 is seen to be more a suggestion of what ought to be the case than descriptive of an existing situation. Now, in line 11, the request for better-timed exposure is made with a bluntness which only escapes censure by being sandwiched in flattery. (It is unfortunate that textual uncertainty makes the second half of line 11 insecure. Our text involves a rather abrupt rhetorical question and change of addressee, and an awkwardly absolute use of 'metiri'.) We rise to a yet higher plane in which Jupiter himself is approached by Martial's Muse. 'Do you approach Jupiter in the morning "gressu licenti"?' Martial asks his Muse. Although the question is left formally open, there is no doubt about the answer (see note on line 11), and the implication is clear that Martial's poetry should be served up to Jupiter's earthly representative at an appropriate hour. The question is ponderously phrased (eight long vowels between 'iocos' and the four-syllable 'matutinum'), presumably to give it emphasis, and is the only occasion in the poem where the sense runs on across the end of the line. Two final points are worth mentioning: (i) there is a clever play on 'gressu licenti', where 'gressu' can be taken either as 'gait' or (in the light of 'nostra Thalia') as 'metrical foot'; (ii) Martial seems in line 12, with the juxtaposition of 'Thalia' and 'Iovem', to establish his own talent as something of sufficient value to entitle it to a place in the charmed circle of Domitian's mini-Olympus.

For a poem in similar vein, but without such extravagant flattery, see Martial *Epigrams* X.19, written to Pliny the Younger. For further examples of adulation, see X.6 and Martial *Epigrams* Book VIII, with its prose dedication.

Questions

1 Produce a timetable of the Roman day as described by Martial. What has he left out, and why?

2 Does Martial manage to avoid monotony in his catalogue (1—7)? If so, how?

3 What attitude does Martial express towards Domitian (7—12)? What is the implication of 'ambrosias . . . dapes' (8) and

'aetherio . . . nectare' (9)? Can you find anything else making the same suggestion about Domitian?

4 What precisely does Martial want when he says: 'tunc admitte iocos' (11)? Does line 7 make the same point? If so, why does Martial repeat it? 'tunc admitte iocos' is very blunt; how does Martial protect himself against accusations of rudeness?

5 Discuss the sound of lines 1—4.

6 Does this poem fall apart too easily into two distinct halves? Is there any attempt to weld the two halves together? Are lines 1—6 really necessary?

7 Write a poem, in similar vein to Martial, which starts with a catalogue of the school day and finishes with a personal request to the head teacher.

I.5 Martial, Epigrams *VII.61*

Context

See the preceding poem (Martial, *Epigrams* VII.60) for the extremes of adulation to which Martial could sink.

Language and content

1—2 The first two or three lines of the poem may prove perplexing; pupils should be encouraged to work out the surface meaning, and return to these lines after the precise description of line 4.

2 **in . . . suo nullum limine limen erat:** i.e. shops spilled out (with projecting stalls, etc.) beyond their original thresholds to create new thresholds in the roadway. On Roman shops see Paoli 12—13, 33—5; *CLC* Unit I slides 33—5, 37; Liversidge 101—2 with illustrations.

3 **iussisti:** Domitian's edict is dated A.D. 92.
Domitian took the title 'Germanicus' after his expedition against the Germanic Chatti in A.D. 84. See *CLC* Unit III slides 70, 73—4.

5 **catenatis:** much as modern retailers chain, e.g., bicycles on display.

6 **luto:** i.e. in the roadway between the pavements — cf. the function of Pompeii stepping-stones (*CLC* Unit I slide 29).

7 **caeca novacula:** pupils may like to speculate about the sense of 'caeca'. 'novacula' must mean 'razor' rather than cut-throat's knife, and the picture is of a barber shaving in the street. The razor is 'caeca' (i) because as a mere instrument it does not discern whom or where it cuts; (ii) because it is concealed from the view of those who are slashed by it; (iii) because the epithet is also transferred from the barber who draws it from its case — he is so crowded-in that he has to rely on feel.

8 **aut:** following 'nec . . . nec . . . ', equivalent to a third 'nec'.
nigra popina: on *popinae* see Balsdon, 1969: 152—4; Casson, 1974: 212—18; cf. Ward-Perkins and Claridge, illustration 227. 'nigra' must indicate that this one is dirty and disreputable.

Discussion

Martial introduces his picture of a Rome choked by ambitious retailers with an alliterative couplet which is provocatively indirect in its

expression. He describes the shopkeepers as 'temerarius' in order to
capitalise on the inevitable resentment against them, though the full
significance of the word appears only in line 3, where Martial is seen to
have thereby aligned himself with imperial policy. The same effect is
achieved by the forceful first word ('abstulerat') and the exaggeration
of 'totam' (1), 'nullum' (2) and the singular for plural 'institor' (1).
There is no doubt whose side Martial is on. He seems to take pleasure,
too, in the artful construction of line 2: 'limen' has escaped its adjective 'nullum' and is physically outside 'suo . . . limine', creating an ear-
catching repetition. The assertive 'iussisti' (3) leads us directly to the
addressee, Domitian, who is flattered with his military title prior to
being congratulated on domestic policy. The decision to clear the streets
was hardly earthshaking, but Martial portrays it in almost magical terms:
only a god could order streets to grow — an event which is perhaps
suggested by the insertion of seven syllables between 'tenues' and 'vicos'
(3).

Some street scenes follow. It is interesting that Martial's snapshots,
excluding the generalisations of lines 9–10, are all of pre-edict Rome.
Presumably there was more to catch the writer's eye in the bustle and
confusion; the new Rome would have been far less rich in material. He
may also have been tempted either by the technique of negative enumeration, common in rhetorical literature (cf. VIII.1), or by the wish to
make a smaller-scale parallel with the contrasts drawn by Virgil and
Ovid between contemporary Rome and the city as it once was. In any
case, the effectiveness of these pictures (they are entirely visual conceptions) depends mainly on the keenness of observation and variety of
scene — the important magistrate set next to the wineshop doorpost
and the barber's razor. There is also some technical cleverness in the
way 'pila' (5) and 'novacula' (7) are appropriately embraced by
'catenatis . . . lagoenis' (5) and 'densa . . . turba' (7); in the keeping of
'luto' (6) till the end of the line, against expectation for 'road'; and in
the carefully chosen 'caeca' (7) — see note.

Line 8 is another such street scene, with its 'nigra' redolent of greasy
snackbars of all ages. At the same time, Martial uses the line to prepare
for the end of the poem. Lists of examples are always difficult to close
without appearing arbitrary. Martial draws his to an end by a subtle
reflection of the first line of the poem: 'occupat aut totas' picks up
'abstulerat totam', adjective and subject follow in the same order, and
both lines are concluded by a reference to the city. The same technique
is used in line 9, where 'sua limina' takes us back to line 2. But now we
are given a glimpse of the new order. The various traders are neatly
arranged one after the other. Any further reference to the edict (3) is
now out of place, since the results of the change are a perpetual
reminder of Domitian's wisdom. The final line, therefore, is modelled
on line 4, but this time the present is before the past, so that lines 4 and

10 together form a chiasmus. The first half of the pentameter is insistently spondaic and the final amusingly gross exaggeration shows us how terrible a fate Rome has escaped.

Questions

1 What is the problem? Why does it arise? What evidence for it is supplied by lines 5—8? Who solves it?
2 What is Martial's attitude to (a) shopkeepers, (b) Domitian?
3 What do you think Martial means by the word 'caeca' in line 7?
4 How effectively does Martial use (a) exaggeration, (b) selected examples, (c) word-order?
5 Find out what you can about Roman shops (cf. notes on lines 2 and 8).

I.6 Martial, Epigrams *XI.96*

Context

The surrounding poems display a morbid obsession with a full range of sexual activity. For the modern reader at least, this imparts a certain irony to our poem's assumption of Roman superiority.

Language and content

1 **Marcia:** the Aqua Marcia was one of the most important Roman aqueducts. It was built in 144 B.C., cost 180 million *sestertii,* ran about 90 km into Rome (often on arches) and was high enough to supply water to the Capitol. Remains of it are still to be seen. Agrippa and Augustus made repairs and additions. Nero upset public opinion by bathing in its springs (Tacitus, *Annals* XIV.22).
   salit implies water under pressure, presumably a fountain feeding a street watertank (*CLC* Unit I slide 28).
   Germane: a German slave.
2 **divitis:** probably best taken as 'precious'. Pliny the Elder (*Natural History* XXXI.24.41) remarks on the exceptional coldness and salubrity of the Aqua Marcia's water. There may however be a suggestion of plenty for all, giving an ironic slant to the German's unwillingness to share ('prohibes').
3 **ministro:** Form C (dative) — 'for the benefit of a servant'.

Discussion

'Marcia' establishes the epigram firmly in the city of Rome, and 'salit hic' (1) and the direct speech make a vivid beginning. The Aqua Marcia, splendid though it was, is clearly less impressive than the Rhine (chosen as a typical German river), and the contrast was no doubt intended to be hurtful to the German. Martial has introduced himself as a character in the poem, a Roman onlooker who with nationalist zeal supports a young fellow-countryman in a squabble at the drinking-fountain. His 'Germane', sounding out of place in a Roman context, is also intended to wound (contrast I.5.3).

In the second couplet, the rhetorical question gives place to a strongly worded suggestion, and the issue widens from a German in Rome preventing a local boy getting a drink, to a native slave slighting a Roman citizen and indeed the whole conquering might of Rome. The contrast is heightened by the juxtaposition of 'cive' and 'ministro' (3) and 'captivam' and 'victrix' (4). 'victrix unda' (4) is a bold use, and 'captivam . . . sitim' (4) effectively depersonalises the German. If this poem reflects a real incident or attitude of mind, one can only wonder that slave revolts were not more common.

Questions

1 Martial creates a vivid little scene in the first couplet. Is the reader left to fill in any necessary background, or does Martial provide all the details?
2 How does Martial show his attitude to the German slave?
3 How does Martial point up the contrasts in his second couplet?
4 By the time of Frontinus (A.D. 97) the nine major aqueducts supplied Rome with just over 1,010 million litres daily (Dudley 41). (In 1976, the British Severn—Trent Water Authority was able to supply Birmingham, a city roughly comparable in terms of population with Frontinus' Rome, with just over 486 million litres daily, most of it transported some 120 km from Mid-Wales along the Elan Aqueduct.) Do some research on the Roman system of water-supply. The following books are among those which may be helpful: Dudley; Singer *et al.* II: Ch. 19; Forbes I: 161—73; Liversidge 32—4; Platner and Ashby; Lewis and Reinhold II: s.v. 'aqueducts'; Carcopino Ch. 2; Brunt and Moore on *Res Gestae* 20.2; and see *OCD* bibliography, s.v. 'aqueducts'. See also note on I.2.10 and *CLC* Unit III slides 31—2.

Section II

Section II is concerned with wealth and with the system of patronage which was encouraged by the vast difference between rich and poor in Roman society. Ovid in II.4 launches a withering general attack on the craving for wealth, establishing the viciousness of contemporary society by contrast with the relative simplicity of the Golden Age: some memorable visual details establish his portrait of early Roman society, while the complexity and greed of Augustan Rome are suggested by a series of rhetorically complex, sententious remarks. Horace, on the other hand, in his sketch of the miser Opimius (II.2), relies largely on the accumulation of exaggerated detail, partly on the vividness of dialogue, for his realisation of Ovid's 'opum furiosa cupido'. Opimius condemns himself because he fails to get possessions into proportion.

Catullus' lines to Furius (II.1) are much gentler. It may be that Furius, driven by the fashion, has taken on a greater mortgage than he can cope with. But Catullus' primary intention is neither to criticise Furius for this nor even to sympathise. The facts of the case are taken for granted: the point of the poem is its word-play. Far more polemical than this are the treatments of *clientela*. Tiresias' advice to Ulysses (II.3) is so outrageous that it cannot be taken at face-value: it is intended as a strong attack on the institution, spiced with humour and detailed observation of the life of a client. Its superficially Homeric characters throw into strong relief its Roman and contemporary reference. Martial's handling of a similar theme in II.6 is equally humorous and has a similar collection of persuasively realistic details. However, the nature of epigram and the demands of the elegiac metre impose a greater formality of structure on the Martial poem, and furthermore the poet has a personal involvement in this situation and his criticism is not so exaggerated as that of Horace: Martial wants to remain a client, but on his own terms. Similarly in II.7 Martial regrets Afer's failure to receive him, and there is no suggestion that being a client is degrading *per se*. The criticism is perhaps more general in II.5, where Tuccius is so outraged by the *sportula* that he cannot bear to enter Rome despite his long journey. But in both II.7 and II.5 the point of the epigram is not essentially its attack on *clientela*. The wit of II.7 resides largely in neat patterning, word-play and the surprising way in which the initiative is taken by the client; while II.5 relies for its effect on exaggeration and an unusual angle of attack.

II.1 Catullus, Poems 26

Language and content

The metre is hendecasyllabic. The scheme is as follows:
Fŭrī, / vīllŭlă vēs/tră nōn ăd Aŭstrī
Final *anceps* is common. See Raven section 136.

1 **Furi:** referred to in *Poems* 11, 16, 23, 24; possibly the poet Furius Bibaculus.
    vestra: the plural may suggest Furius' family home — his father and stepmother occur in *Poems* 23. One manuscript has 'nostra'.
3 **aut:** following 'neque ... nec ... ', equivalent to 'neque'. For the technique of negative enumeration, see I.5 Discussion.
    Apheliotae: the recondite, Greek word for 'East Wind', in place of 'Euri'.
4 **milia quindecim et ducentos:** on house prices, see note on I.3.1. As far as can be judged from scanty evidence, mainly appertaining to property in Rome itself, Furius' mortgage would not have been thought extraordinarily high, except perhaps by the indigent Furius.

Discussion

Poets are conventionally short of money (see III.1.5 Discussion), and Furius' poverty has already been remarked on in *Poems* 23 and 24. With this in mind, we are surprised to find him in possession of a piece of property, modestly dismissed in the diminutive 'villula' (1), which seems ever more desirable as we progress through lines 1–3. For the importance of siting a villa in line with a healthy wind, see Varro *Res Rusticae* I.12.1–3: an unhealthy wind could carry with it from nearby marshes invisible organisms ('animalia quaedam minuta, quae non possunt oculi consequi') which penetrate mouth and nostrils and occasion disease. In general, Varro prefers a villa to face the east wind. Presumably Catullus' readers expect him also to fix on the east wind, after ruling out the other three points of the compass with the aid of loaded 'flatus' (2) and 'saevi' (3). Instead, Catullus completes the circle, flouting geographical possibilities, with a mannered, scholarly word taking end-of-line stress (like 'Austri' and 'Favoni') and intended to draw his reader's attention to the oddity of a house facing in no direction. This oddity is resolved in line 4 as the second, and less usual, sense of 'opponere' is activated by the sum of money. This is the wind which Furius' property faces. Just as a real wind may make you shiver (cf. 'horreo') with cold or fever ('pestilentem', 5), so this wind is 'horribilem atque pestilentem' in the senses of 'dreadful' and 'detestable'. This exclamatory line, dovetailed into line 4 by means of shared 'nd'/'ent' assonance, dispels 'the atmosphere of measured statement' (Quinn, 1973) and recalls the literal winds of lines 1–3, so rounding off the poem satisfactorily.

Questions

1 Why does Catullus list each wind individually, rather than saying 'Furius' house "opposita est" to no wind, but . . . '?

2 Is it possible to catch the ambiguity of 'opposita est' in English? Fordyce has 'exposed to the elements' / 'exposed to a mortgage'. Jay (1963) has 'wind' / 'windfall'. Whigham has 'draughts' / '*over*draft'.

3 What circumstances might have caused Catullus to write this poem to Furius? (See Fordyce 156 for speculation.) Is Catullus necessarily attacking Furius, as many commentators have assumed? 'Exaggeratedly abusive language is not uncommon among friends, particularly if they are of Catullus' violent temperament, and there are hints in the Furius poems, and in other violent poems, that the abuse was not meant to wound' (Quinn, 1969: 45).

II.2 Horace, Satires *II.3.142–57*

Context

This lively scene comes from a long satire devoted, not too seriously, to maintaining the Stoic proposition that everyone is afflicted with madness except the Stoic wise man. Horace presents himself as under attack

from Damasippus, a recent convert to Stoicism, who repeats for
Horace's benefit an address delivered by the Stoic Stertinius: he exposes
as madmen all who are driven by avarice, ambition, luxury and superstition. The story of Opimius rounds off the treatment of avarice.

Language and content

1–6   The teacher's reading should emphasise, e.g., the thread of the main
clause and the final syllables of 'Campanā' and 'trullā'. It could be
supplemented by suitable comprehension questions and graphic illustration of the sentence structure.

1   **Opimius:** Mr Moneybags (cf. 'opes' and 'opimus') – see Note on I.1.1.
positi intus: either 'although he had heaps of it at home', or 'a poor
man for all his heaps of silver at home'.

2   **Veientanum:** a red wine described disparagingly by Persius (*Satires* 5.
147) and Martial (*Epigrams* I.103.9 and III.49.1), as also by Lejay
('petit vin rouge peu agréable') who claims that its modern successors
are no better. Opimius will not stretch to anything more palatable even
during holidays.

3   **Campana . . . trulla:** Campanian ware was plain enough for Horace himself to use in *Satire* I.6.118. The *trulla* seems to have been a ladle for
transferring wine from the mixing-bowl to the cup. These could be
exceedingly precious: Cicero (*In Verrem* II.4.27) refers to one made
from a single gem with a golden handle. Opimius is apparently not even
going to the expense of a cup, but drinking a miserly quantity from a
plain ladle.
vappa: when the grape-juice ('mustum') had fermented, producing
'vinum', there was occasionally a second reaction converting the wine
into a form of vinegar ('acetum'), which on exposure to air became
even less drinkable and was known as 'vappa'. On the wine-making process, see e.g. Forbes III: 115–22; Liversidge 140–1.

4   **lethargo:** Celsus (*De Medicina* III.20.1) says of 'lethargus': in this condition there is languor (*marcor*) and an almost irresistible need for
sleep'. He quotes various remedies, including nasty smells and 'three or
four amphoras' of cold water over the head. The shock technique is
similar to that employed by the doctor in this context, as is the recommended diet – 'sorbitio', broth.

6   **medicus:** on doctors, see Liversidge 82–7; Balsdon, 1969: s.v. 'doctors',
'medicine'.
multum: colloquially with adjective, meaning 'very'.

7   **hoc pacto:** a prosaic expression (Lejay on *Satires* I.4.99).

12–13   Problems may arise from the complex structure or from the boldness of
the building metaphor (see Discussion). The notes in pupils' text should
assist with the former.

14   **tisanarium oryzae:** 'tisanarium' (L&S s.v. 'ptisanarium') is generally
barley-gruel, but here stands for any such decoction without reference
to its basic ingredient – supplied by 'oryzae' (from which word 'rice'
derives). Both are Greek words, though 'oryza' is of Asiatic origin.
Pliny the Elder (*Natural History* XVIII.13.71) refers to the Indians'
passion for rice 'ex qua tisanam conficiunt quam reliqui mortales ex
hordeo (= barley)'.

Discussion

Our central character is introduced immediately by name. At first glance we appear to have a poor man, 'pauper Opimius'. But there are distinctly wealthy overtones about our poor man's name, and although we may first interpret 'pauper . . . argenti . . . et auri' (1) as meaning 'badly off for silver and gold', there is something awkward about this. With 'positi intus', Horace's intentions are fully revealed. We have a neatly paradoxical situation — 'badly off for the silver he kept stacked away at home' — and are driven into a reassessment of 'pauper'. Either Horace intends us to view Opimius through the man's own eyes (however much he has, he still considers himself 'pauper'); or we are to adopt the superior viewpoint of the Stoic sage and see him as poor because lacking 'sapientia'; or we are to take the practical view that he is effectively a poor man because he spends none of his money and lives the life of a poor man.

With the next line (2), Horace's hexameter becomes drearily heavy, the cumbersome four-syllable 'Vēiēntānūm' giving the reader early warning of this. The heaviness is only remitted with the heir's racing about and the entry of the 'medicus . . . celer' in line 6. Opimius drinks his abysmal Veii wine on red-letter days, and for him this is a considerable concession. He makes up for such extravagance, however, by drinking it from a Campanian wine-ladle — 'trulla', against expectation for 'cup', being neatly held back till after 'solitus'. If Opimius saves 'Veientanum' for feast-days, Horace's audience must be thinking, what could he possibly sink to for everyday? The answer is 'vappa', the vinegary drink resorted to by the boatman in IX.2.16.

Lines 2 and 3 have kept us in suspense for the main verb which will reveal what Opimius is doing. 'quondam' in line 4 takes us into the story proper. Opimius, we now discover, is not up to anything, but merely lying ill. The humour of this passage resides partly in the fact that Opimius' only activity, apart from a few virtually monosyllabic utterances, is his strong verbal reaction (16) to the idea of 8 asses being spent to save his life. He is ill with lethargy (see Notes) — not just an ordinary dose, but 'grandis' ('serious', 'extreme'). The hexameter (assisted by the sustained double consonants of 'oppressus') is as solemn as metre allows, and the amusingly swift appearance of the heir before the line is out suggests that this may well be a death-bed.

Our attention is now taken first by the heir's high jinks and then by the efficiently down-to-earth character of the doctor. The only contents of Opimius' home worth Horace's mention are the money-boxes and keys: one imagines bare rooms full of nothing but chests like the 'arca' of *CLC* Unit I slide 22. We are distinctly surprised by 'laetus ovansque' and the re-emergence of dactylic rhythm, which Horace means to jar with 'oppressus' and 'grandi'. The doctor is 'celer' both because the revival of Opimius is swiftly effected and because he arrives swiftly on the scene. (The doctor, like the heir, stood to benefit, but from a different outcome; though doctors with fewer scruples were no doubt expecting to be well rewarded by Regulus the heir in Pliny, *Letters* II.20,

abridged in *CLC* Unit IV 'domi' section I.) With the initiation of the
cure, and as the doctor barks out his instructions, the clauses become
staccato. The solemnity of the first half of the story is recaptured as the
cherished coins are poured ceremoniously onto the table: line 8 is as
heavy as it can be, and has no fewer than four words with double consonants (cf. 'oppressus' in line 4). The implication of 'plures' is no doubt,
as Palmer suggests, that many pairs of hands are necessary for counting
such a vast sum of cash. The effect is immediate. For the miser, this is
shock treatment with a vengeance (see Notes on 'lethargo', 4). The
doctor presses home this advantage with a remark well calculated to
produce a reaction (10). He suggests that Opimius is failing to achieve
the object on which his whole attention has been centred, *viz.* protecting his money. The term 'avidus' is nicely, and very pointedly, applied
to 'heres' (kept till late for maximum effect). 'avidus' in fact sums up
the attitude of mind underlying 'ni tua custodis', and we naturally
anticipate it being applied to Opimius.

At line 11 Opimius takes his first active part in the proceedings. (It
is perhaps worth noting that almost every syllable he utters is heavy:
there are just two dactylic feet, both in his last line, and one of these is
necessitated by the hexameter.) If Rudd is right (1973) in translating
'men vivo' as 'over my dead body!', then the humour is obvious —
though not intended by Opimius. Horace's word-play with the syllable
'vi-' compounds the fun, as does the implication in the curt 'vigila' and
'hoc age' that the miser is dropping off again, now that the conversation
has shifted from money to mere self-preservation. In line 12 there is
further irony in the description of Opimius as 'inopem' (cf. 'pauper
Opimius' in line 1). The doctor has lapsed into medical talk, and his
mention of the pulse, 'venae', guarantees the limited sense of 'inopem'
without destroying its overtones. After 'cibus' (12), the reader expects
a salubrious alternative to 'vappa' and 'Veientanum' (2 and 3). Instead
Horace offers a huge prop such as might be used for holding up a wall.
The adjective 'ingens' appears to confirm that Horace intends the reader
to have in mind the usual concrete sense of 'fultura'. (*OLD* cites only
one classical parallel — and that from Pliny, *Letters* I.9.4, and not
exactly comparable — for the noun being used metaphorically, but see
Palmer on 'fulcire'.) With the participle 'ruenti' (held back) we are certainly in the realm of civil engineering. Nothing short of a pit-prop will
restore Opimius' ruin of a stomach.

What the doctor offers in line 14 is the magnificently outlandish
'tisanarium oryzae', two Greek words meaning a rice-based gruel. (Might
the doctor himself be Greek?) Opimius' first thought is for the price,
and in pressing for the exact amount he is in a sense only carrying out
the doctor's command 'tua custodire' (10). It is a technical triumph to
include four remarks and part of the fifth in a single hexameter (15).
The pace has quickened in anticipation of the climactic line 16, as the

miser begins to suspect the financial implications of his gruel. The episode only has point, of course, if 8 *asses* is really a trifling amount. (For some general remarks on wages and prices, see Balsdon, 1969: 354, and Cowell 104ff.) Rough calculations show that 8 *asses* would have bought about 5.5 litres of wheat, about five times the daily ration for one of Cato's slaves; but this should be compared with the price of a peacock at about 500 *asses*. It would take much of the bite out of this ending if rice were an imported luxury, but I can find no evidence for Roman farmers growing this crop: 'irrigation was not the strong point of the . . . Roman farmer' (Forbes III: 88). However, it is grown in Italy today, e.g. in the plain of the Po. The story of Opimius is concluded with his outraged ejaculation in line 16: in order to upstage 'morbo', the scale of the alleged theft is exaggerated by the repetitive 'furtis' and 'rapinis', while its implications are grossly and amusingly distorted by the enclosed 'peream'.

The particular virtues of this piece are its humour both subtle and slapstick; the liveliness and pace of the dialogue; and the virtuoso deployment of metrical contrast. Comparable humorous studies of the miserly condition by Horace and by other authors are not difficult to find.

Questions

1 In what sense is Opimius 'pauper' (1)?
2 Could Horace have omitted mention of the heir from this story? What would have been lost and what would have been gained?
3 Why is the heir 'laetus' (5) and in what sense is the doctor 'celer' (6)? What is it that certainly motivates the heir and probably motivates the doctor? Is this significant? What is Horace attacking in this passage?
4 What are the methods employed by the doctor to cure Opimius, and how successful are they? Is lethargy the real disease Opimius is suffering from?
5 What, in Opimius' view, constitutes 'rapinis' (16)?
6 How does the metre of line 4 reflect the sense? Can you find other examples?
7 This is a light-hearted passage: find or compose a serious attack on the same target.
8 Do people today act like Opimius (or Scrooge)? If not, is this passage irrelevant to its twentieth-century readers? Why might Horace have selected such an extreme case here?

II.3 Horace, Satires II.5.93–104

Context

Satire II.5 adopts the setting of Homer *Odyssey* XI, where Ulysses

makes contact with the souls of the dead, and in particular with the soul
of Tiresias the prophet. Horace conjures up a latter-day Ulysses, whose
only concern is how to restore his vanished fortunes when he arrives
back in Ithaca. Tiresias gives an uncompromising recommendation for
legacy-hunting (on *captatio* see *CLC* Unit IV *Teacher's Handbook* 129f.
and Rudd, 1966: 224–7), illustrated by a number of amusing instances
– from the last of which this passage is excerpted. That one is not to
take Tiresias too seriously is indicated by the credentials he flaunts
earlier in the satire (*59):

> o Laertiade, quidquid dicam aut erit aut non.

'Son of Laertes, whatever I say will, or will not, come to be.'
Our passage sets out some practical advice from Tiresias to the intend-
ing *captator*: hence the run of imperatives. The victim's name is Dama
(9).

Language and content

1 **grassare**: often used of hostile or predatory behaviour.
2 **velet**: with a fold of the toga (see Note on IV.2.12).
3 **aurem substringe**: Ulysses is to hang on every word. 'substringere
  aurem' here probably means 'to compress the ear from underneath' in
  an attempt to concentrate the sound. Rudd (1973) translates 'cup your
  hand to your ear'. Other scholars prefer to interpret in terms of pricking
  up one's ears: Kiessling and Heinze, e.g., looking to the basic sense of
  'to fasten from below', see it as a comic exaggeration of 'erigere aures'.
  loquaci: the Form C (dative) means 'to' or 'for (the benefit of)'. A more
  concrete example from *CLC* Unit I *Stage 9* might help: 'coquus Quinto
  cenam parabat'.
4–5 Perhaps use a series of questions like the following:
      What is Ulysses told to do in line 5?
      Why might the old man say 'ohe!' in line 4?
      When is Ulysses to stop flattering the old man?
      What will the old man be doing by this point?
5 **manibus sublatis**: a gesture of astonishment.
6 **infla**: once seen as parallel with 'urge', there should be no problems with
  the wine-skin image. Try suggesting 'windbag' as a retrospective translation of 'loquaci' (3).
8–9 The actual wording on the document would be 'Ulixes heres ex quarta
    parte esto'.
9 **Dama**: a typical slave-name. Ulysses' patron would be a freedman.
10 **nusquam est**: euphemism for 'mortuus est'.

Discussion

Ulysses, in the first of a series of imperatives from Tiresias, is urged to
act like a slave. He is by this late stage of the satire so fully persuaded
by Tiresias that he raises no objections. The old prophet is a thoroughly
devious character, as appears both from the nature of his advice and the
way in which it is expressed, hurtful 'grassare' being juxtaposed with
commendable 'obsequio'. Line 2 is thrown into prominence by marked
alliteration and a bucolic diaeresis. It also contains the tendentiously

ambiguous 'carum', which, like 'precious', oscillates between 'beloved' and 'expensive' (*OLD* s.v. 'carus' 1). Tiresias raps out his advice in four curt commands (1–3); the last three being practical illustrations of the more general 'obsequio grassare', and together flashing before us three vivid portraits of Roman private life. Dama's appetite for a listener ('loquaci', 3: placed at the end of the line for emphasis) is matched immediately by his greed for listening ('importunus': placed for emphasis at the very beginning of line 4) when his own praises are being sung. Verbal flattery is accorded more verses than Tiresias' other suggestions: flattery 'runs through the satire like a thread of gilt' (Rudd, 1966: 232). The victim's pomposity is underlined by the vivid little picture of him in lines 4–5. Ulysses has to achieve the almost impossible by sating Dama with self-praise, and the situation is only deflated (as Dama is not) by the unexpected and colloquial 'utrem' at the end of line 6, laying retrospective stress on the literal sense of 'tumidis . . . sermonibus' – these puffed-up words being literally contained within 'crescentem . . . utrem'.

In lines 7 and 8, we move with great speed through a glancing reference to Dama's death, into a clearly-imagined depiction of the scene at the reading of the will. The *servitium* of Ulysses is made explicit again (see above) in line 7 – which is triply ironical: (i) the real *servus* was Dama, Ulysses only figuratively so; (ii) in death-bed contexts 'cura' normally denotes a wholly praiseworthy devotion, whereas here the sinister overtones are clear; (iii) Ulysses the slave is to receive metaphorical manumission on the death of his master, yet one of the points of this satire is that *servitium* to the trade of *captator* becomes a way of life which cannot be thrown over. In line 8, 'certum vigilans' hints at the obsessive dreams of the corrupted *captator*, who has savoured this hour of triumph so many times in fancy. The legal phraseology which it introduces makes a good contrast with the *sermo cotidianus* of most of this extract. 'Ulixes' is kept for the strong position at the end of the line, and 'heres' is neatly isolated for emphasis. Further variety is provided by the direct speech of Ulysses' hypocritical remarks (9–10). The alliterative 'tam fortem tamque fidelem' is hackneyed (cf. Trimalchio's gravestone, Petronius *Satyricon* 71). In case the reader is tempted to take these utterances at face value, Tiresias adds (held back for greater effect) 'sparge subinde', suggesting a cool, calculating approach – with 'sparge' looking forward to the tears of 'illacrimare'. Tiresias amusingly assumes that under no circumstances will Ulysses be able to raise many tears, but may manage a token display. The monosyllabic final 'est' (11), following a strong sense-break, marks the depth of his certainty: you may or may not be able to raise tears, but you will definitely be able to conceal the joy in your expression. At which point the reader realises that the *captatio* procedure is beginning again for Ulysses. Otherwise, with Dama dead, all pretence could be dropped. A whole new career is opening out before him, rather than a short-term means of replenishing his fortunes. As McGann puts it (in Costa 84): 'this madness is a *perpetuum mobile* as the death of one quarry leads to the pursuit of another'.

There are two tensions worth noting in this passage. The first is that between the Greek and Roman elements both in these lines and in the satire as a whole. There is no doubt that the setting is overwhelmingly Roman (see Rudd, 1966: 232): the legal terminology and the attendance danced by the *captator*-client guarantee this. Why, then, does Horace select Tiresias and Ulysses, with all the inescapable reminiscence of Book XI of the *Odyssey*? There is much to be said for the view that Horace is using Greek literature, and in particular the highly esteemed epic tradition, to point the contrast. *Captatio* must seem infinitely more debased if advocated and practised not by a Regulus but by such grandiose characters as Tiresias and Ulysses. Ulysses, with his glib tongue and teeming brain, is incidentally a first-rate choice for the rôle, and it is ironic that the ready-witted Ulysses is the one who receives instruction throughout the satire. The second tension resides in a larger-scale irony. This satire is unique in that Horace nowhere obtrudes his own satirist's persona. At face value, then, the satire is an exhortation from Tiresias to make money like Ulysses by disreputable means. At the same time, the audience is aware that this conflicts totally with the high moral tone adopted in Horace's other satires; and this, coupled with the *reductio ad absurdum* effect of Horace's choice of characters, keeps the reader perpetually challenging the apparent message of the poem.

Swift's *A modest proposal for preventing the children of poor people in Ireland from being a burden to their parents or country, and for making them beneficial to the public* may prove a useful parallel for the ironical tension between author's statement and author's belief. The following is a representative quotation:

> 'I shall now therefore humbly propose my own thoughts, which I hope will not be liable to the least objection.
>
> I have been assured by a very knowing American of my acquaintance in London, that a young healthy child, well nursed, is at a year old a most delicious, nourishing, and wholesome food, whether stewed, roasted, baked, or boiled; and I make no doubt that it will equally serve in a fricassee or a ragout.'

Questions

1 List the various activities required of Ulysses. Do you find any of these activities, taken individually, acceptable ways of behaving? Are they the sort of activities you would expect of an epic hero? If not (but see Rudd, 1966: 235ff., on the

rascality of Ulysses), why do you think Horace invents a scene where Tiresias recommends such activities to Ulysses?

2 In what sense is Ulysses to endure *servitium* (7)? When will it end for him?

3 Why should Ulysses bother about what he says and does after the reading of the will?

4 Metre apart, is there anything to choose between 'crescentem tumidis infla sermonibus utrem' (6) and 'utrem crescentem infla sermonibus tumidis'?

5 'Whereas other vices often only degrade one person, *captatio* degrades hunter and hunted alike. Thus . . . the vain and gullible old man is only one degree less contemptible than Ulysses himself' (Rudd, 1966: 239). Does Horace in our passage make any attempt to colour the old man's character?

6 Horace never sets the moral record straight in this satire: Tiresias' views are never combatted, except briefly and feebly by Ulysses. Is there anything to stop Horace's audience from taking what Tiresias says as what Horace thinks?

7 Why does Horace choose Ulysses and Tiresias rather than two contemporaries?

II.4 Ovid, Fasti *I.193—218*

Context

Ovid had only half completed the *Fasti* when banished to Tomis in A.D. 8, and the work was never to be finished. What survives is a poetic interpretation of the Roman calendar from January to June, with all its accompanying rituals, traditions and festivals, and numerous fascinating digressions. Our passage is loosely related to the festival of Janus on 1 January. A feature of the festival was the gift to one's friends (and one's patron) of dates (often gilded), figs, honey and coins; and Ovid questions Janus about this. The fruit and honey is given, says Janus, so that the rest of the year may be as sweet as its beginning. Prompted further by Ovid, he goes on to say that cash is even sweeter ('dulcius': picked up in line 2) than honey, and he develops this theme in our excerpt.

Language and content

1 **Saturno . . . regnante:** during the Golden Age. Later in this book (*235— 8) Janus says, 'I remember how Saturn was welcomed in this land after expulsion by Jupiter from the heavenly kingdoms . . . The land was called Latium because the god hid here ("latente").' According to Macrobius (*Saturnalia* I.7.21), Janus was the original ruler of Italy and agreed to share his kingdom with Saturn in exchange for the knowledge of husbandry. The Golden Age was supposed to be a time of innocence, peace and leisure. So far were the inhabitants from a concern for money-making that Ovid's more traditional account (*Amores* III.8.36) has 'omne lucrum' still buried in the earth.

2 **forent:** subjunctive in a generic relative clause — Woodcock sections 155—8. Cf. III.1.20; III.2.1; X.4.11—12.

4 **progrediatur:** subjunctive in a final (purpose) relative clause — Woodcock section 148.

7 **casa:** there was on the Palatine Hill a hut known as the Hut of Romulus preserved as an ancient relic and still extant in Ovid's time. It was built of sticks and reeds (Dionysius of Halicarnassus, *Roman Antiquities* I.79.11). Vitruvius (*De Architectura* 2.1.5) mentions a competing 'casa Romuli' on the Capitoline!

Martigenam . . . Quirinum: Romulus became identified with the ancient Sabine deity Quirinus after mysteriously disappearing at the end of his forty-year reign. Ovid seems to have coined 'Martigenam': Romulus was son of Mars and Rhea Silvia — see Livy, *Ab Urbe Condita* I.4, with Ogilvie (1965) on I.3.10—14.

9 **angusta . . . in aede:** possibly (Frazer, II: 116) the cramped and ancient temple of Iuppiter Feretrius on the Capitol, said to be the first temple dedicated in Rome (tentatively dated to 650—550 B.C. by Ogilvie 1965 on I.10), but there is no good reason to suppose Ovid had a specific building in mind; the idea is closely paralleled by Tibullus, *Elegies* I.10.20.

10 **fictile:** Pliny the Elder (*Natural History* XXXV.45.157) records how Vulca of Veii made for Tarquinius Priscus a painted terracotta statue of Jupiter to be consecrated in the Capitol.

11 **gemmis:** Augustus dedicated in the shrine of Iuppiter Capitolinus 16,000 Roman pounds (over 5,000 kg) of gold, with pearls and other precious stones worth 50 million *sestertii.*

15 The contrast between the hardy veterans of old and their degenerate descendants was a well-worn topic. There is a glancing reference here to Cincinnatus: when he was appointed dictator in 458 B.C. the messenger found him at work on his farm.

16 **crimen:** Publius Cornelius Rufinus, ex-consul and ex-dictator, was struck off the senate list by the censor in 275 B.C. for having 10 Roman pounds (just over 3 kg) of silver plate in his possession. Contrast the silver hoards from Pompeii and *CLC* Unit I slide 24.

17 **fortuna loci . . . huius.** 'Gods were presumed as and when the need for them arose' (Ogilvie, 1969: 12), and in particular different aspects of the same divine power were isolated: Le Bonniec (1965) instances 'Fortuna huiusce diei' which had a temple at Rome, and 'Fortuna huius loci' and 'Fortuna balneorum' on inscriptions.

18 **tetigit summo vertice:** proverbial Greek expression for supreme good fortune, introduced to Latin by Horace and imitated by Ovid (Le Bonniec, 1965).

22 **vices:** i.e., the ups and downs implicit in line 21.

23 The comparison of the miser to a man with dropsy is found, e.g., in Horace, *Odes* II.2, but is again an inheritance from the Greek tradition. Cf. II.2.4.

25—6 The theme was a commonplace of debate in the Roman schools of declamation (cf. Seneca the Elder, *Controversiae* II.1.17).

Discussion

The god Janus is speaking about money. This is highly appropriate, since his two-headed portrait appeared on one side of a common type of *as*: a ship's prow was on the other side, and Roman boys used to shout 'capita'

or 'navia' when they tossed a coin (Macrobius, *Saturnalia* I.7.22). The
bronze *as* was not minted in Rome after about 80 B.C., but the old coins
were still used for token presents at New Year in the time of Martial
(*Epigrams* VIII.33) — cf. maundy money. Furthermore, Janus' temple
was on the north side of the Forum at the entrance to the Argiletum,
the banking centre of Rome. Janus and money would have been securely
linked in the minds of Ovid's audience. They would thus have found it
both amusing and appropriate that Janus should have displayed the
jaundiced attitude towards the Golden Age which appears in the first
couplet (cf. note on line 1). There is a further touch of humour in the
way Janus can casually reminisce with Ovid at first hand about the
Golden Age: we are, so Ovid would lead us to believe, being given the
inside story.

The *locus communis* is to start from virtuous poverty and to work
towards vicious luxury. But Ovid's Eden is corrupt from the start, and
the literate reader is intrigued to see how Ovid will develop his theme.
Line 3 is particularly skilful: (i) the isolation of 'amor' leads one for a
split second to think of a further distortion of the usual story, the
growth of love rather than greed; (ii) the delayed 'habendi' acquires
weight from its position; (iii) the protracted phrase 'amor, qui nunc est
summus, habendi' is very powerful, not least because of a metrical
heaviness which contrasts strongly with the line's dactylic start. Ovid's
originality, then, lies in his move from 'it was bad under Saturn' to 'it's
far worse now'. Apparent ubiquity of Golden Age greed ('vix quemquam',
1) is used to exaggerate the plight of contemporary society, which is
many stages worse ('crevit', 'summus', 3). Similarly, line 4 — a pentameter acting as backwash to the wave of the hexameter — projects the
graph of avarice into the future largely as a means of highlighting the
awfulness of the present. There is a nice irony in the conscious repetition of 'habet': 'amor habendi' has acquired almost everything,
except room to expand.

Ovid has now worked himself into a position where he can after all
produce his own version of the traditional theme of ancient poverty.
Line 5 summarises his attitude, and facilitates the transition: the so-
called greed of Janus' Golden Age must be viewed in perspective and set
against the excesses of Augustan Rome. Janus now characterises early
Rome in a tricolon crescendo. The final leg of the tricolon brings us
down to detail. There is a humorous contrast between the simplicity of
'casa . . . parva' (7) and the little reed-bed (8) and the grandiosity of
'Martigenam' and 'Quirinum', juxtaposed with 'casa' and 'parva' respectively, in a sub-Golden Line (AbcaB).

The next couplet presents a yet more gross disparity — Jupiter
hunched in a tiny shrine, with the spondees of 'angusta vix totus stabat'
showing the effort required to squeeze himself upright, and 'angusta'
(like 'casa' and 'parva' above, 7) put next to the word with which it

contrasts. The 'Iuppiter'/'Iovis' repetition enhances the power of Jupiter, set against which is the amusingly alliterative 'fictile fulmen' (10). We have now, incidentally, lapsed imperceptibly from the pre-sculptural times of Romulus to the good old (historical) days when terracotta statues were in vogue. So far, adjectives have done most of the comparative work ('pauper', 'parva', 'exiguum', 'angusta', 'fictile') — one belittling epithet in each of lines 6—10. In lines 11 and 12, Ovid establishes the contrast by means of nouns. 'frondibus' is set against 'gemmis', and just as these two are at opposite ends of a rhetorically complex sentence, so the tension in line 12 is between the last two words ('senator oves') in a simply-structured sentence. In the next couplet, the contrast is not made explicit, though 'pudor' (13) hints at the elegant alternative. The separation of 'pudor' and 'fuit' seems distinctly awkward. Ovid concludes his list of examples with a couplet adumbrating two well-worn moral instances. He avoids the predictable by keeping these instances general, and consciously steering clear of the obvious remarks which would specifically identify Cincinnatus and Rufinus. Again, the contrasting words are set together ('praetor'/'aratro', 15; 'lammina'/ 'crimen', 16); and the lines are quite heavily alliterative. 'levis' in line 16 simply reinforces the sense of 'lammina', which means a thin sheet of metal.

Lines 17—18 open with adversative 'at', and sweep us forward to Augustan Rome from the simplicity of the good old days. The Greek idiom of hitting your head on heaven warns of a distinct increase in rhetorical complexity to balance the increased sophistication of life in the Empire. Lines 19—26 display a self-conscious cleverness and artifice. 'creverunt' (19) picks up 'crevit' from the initial summary in line 3. The assimilation to the same verb of both 'opes' and 'opum . . . cupido' is neat, and the juxtaposition of 'et opes' and 'et opum' catches the ear. The apparently gentle 'amor' of line 3 has now been transformed into a 'furiosa cupido' (19). The 'p'-alliteration just audible in line 19 is unmistakable in line 20. The assonance of 'et opes et opum' is mirrored by 'plurima, plura', in chiasmus with the two verbs. There is a paradox too in the superlative 'plurima' being ousted by the comparative 'plura'. Line 21 provides a third repetition ('absumant, absumpta'), again in chiasmus (with 'quaerere', 'requirere'). The image of consumption carries over into the self-nourishing vices of line 22 and then the belly and the drinking of lines 23 and 24. Thus the grecism of the dropsical miser, a striking simile, is fitted snugly into the narrative. The paradox of line 24 makes a strong impression with its heavily spondaic first half, the balance of its two halves across the caesura and the unusual passive of 'sitire'. All these lines (19—24) are contrived, but memorable for their artifice. Ovid concludes Janus' speech with three sharp *sententiae* worthy of Juvenal, each following on from its predecessor. Again we observe repetition and chiasmus. The very simplicity of their verbs ('est', 'dat', 'iacet') is effective in contrast. The final clause for the first time switches the emphasis from the rich men obsessed with the creation of wealth, to the poor man who suffers from their success. The image is simple and the message bleak.

In this complex piece of poetry, Ovid seems at first to be debunking through Janus the notion of an ideal age, but is then seen to be following so many other Roman authors in mounting a strong attack on the rapacity of his own time. The picture of early Rome (6—16) may have looked faintly comic, but after the devastating attack of lines 17ff. with its picture of a society obsessed with money-making, we are better able to look back and appreciate the concern for religion and the goods it brought — peace of mind, simple self-sufficiency and doing one's duty to the community. Rome has now touched the gods (18) in the sense that rapacity has ousted worship. Janus of course is an interested party in the restoration of religion to its proper place, and Ovid no doubt saw that as part of the function of the *Fasti*.

Questions

1 What does Janus say about the Golden Age of Saturn (1—2)? Do his remarks make a good introduction to the criticism of Augustan Rome which follows?

2 What view of primitive Rome does Ovid intend the reader to gain from Janus' remarks (5—16)?

3 Augustus was keen (a) to restore the ancient religion and encourage a more demanding morality; (b) to make modern Rome a sparkling architectural improvement on the old city. What sort of view is he likely to have taken of this piece?

4 Analyse the poetic effects of lines 17—26. It could be said that the description of ancient Rome looks simple by comparison. Might this be intentional on Ovid's part? Can you see any artifice in the ·earlier parts of the passage?

5 Write an alternative piece extolling Augustan society at the expense of primitive Rome. Cf. Ovid, *Ars Amatoria* III.113—28.

6 Is this an effective attack on materialism? If not, why not?

II.5 Martial, Epigrams *III.14*

Language and content

The metre is alternating iambic trimeters and dimeters:

> Rŏmăm / pĕtē/băt ē/sŭrī/tŏr Tŭc/cĭŭs
>   prŏfēc/tŭs ēx / Hīspā/nĭă.
> ōccŭr/rĭt īl/lī spŏr/tŭlā/rŭm fā/bŭlă:
>   ā pōn/tĕ rĕdĭ/ĭt Mūl/vĭŏ.

1 **esuritor**: apparently coined by Martial, from 'esurire'.

3 **sportularum**: on the *sportula* (25 *asses*, = 6¼ *sestertii*), see Balsdon, 1969: 22—4. Pupils may be reminded of the narrative of *CLC* Unit III *Stage 27*.

4 **ponte . . . Mulvio**: the Mulvian Bridge carried the Flaminian Way across the Tiber some 3 km north of Rome.

Discussion

Martial contrives both to establish the plight of Tuccius as extreme ('esuritor', 1), and to suggest by the novelty of the coinage that he is not writing a serious attack on malnutrition: he writes 'esuritor Tuccius' as if starving were Tuccius' profession (cf. III.7.1, 'Eutrapelus tonsor'). The short line (2) develops the idea of journeying implied in line 1, and finishes the first half of the epigram with a stress on distance — all the way from Spain (Martial's own birthplace, of course). 'occurrit' in line 3 suggests a personal subject, but Martial deceives the reader's expectations with something quite insubstantial — talk. The short line (4) again develops the trimeter. The reaction is sharpened by the lack of a connective, and the tribrach in the second foot sends Tuccius skipping away. The humour of the poem depends partly on the ludicrous notion that someone who had journeyed from Spain would be diverted home from the very suburbs of the Italian capital; and partly on the wry supposition that a professional starveling would react so violently against a dole which was designed to benefit people in his situation. Martial has contrived to mount a snappy attack on the inadequate *sportula*-system without even taking his reader within the walls of Rome.

Questions

1 Why is Tuccius described as 'esuritor', a newly-formed noun?

2 Why does Martial mention Spain?

3 How does Martial defeat the reader's expectations in the last two lines?

4 Why does Martial refer to the Mulvian Bridge, giving it the prominent final position in line 4?

5 What is the object of Martial's attack? How effectively does he mount this?

6 Find out what you can about the *sportula*. What was so bad about it?

II.6 Martial, Epigrams *III.46*

Language and content

1 **operam . . . togatam**: see note on III.8.3. Clients had to wear a toga while doing duties for their patrons.

4 **lecticam subsequar**: a regular duty of the client.

5 Cf. II.3.2—3. The clause, like many in this piece, is expressed paratactically: the syntactical equivalent would be 'si . . . incideris, . . . repellet'. This omission of 'si' is frequent in Martial.

8 **sophos:** technically a Greek adverb, here apparently treated by Martial
as a neuter noun with 'tergeminum' in agreement.
9 **lis erit:** implies personal involvement in a quarrel or brawl.
10 **vetuit:** 'has forbidden'.
12 **Candide:** cf. Martial, *Epigrams* II.43 for the great wealth of Candidus
and his claim that friends have all things in common. Martial writes him
into five of his poems.

Discussion

Martial establishes very early that he is attacking (cf. implications of
'exigis', 1) the patron—client system, and more particularly the patron—
client nexus between himself and a specific patron, not to be identified
until the very last line. 'exigis a nobis' (1) makes an arresting start, and
the 'operam . . . togatam' phrase is appropriately stretched by the
insertion of 'sine fine'. The answering pentameter (2) provides Martial's
response: 'non eo' corresponds to the abrupt 'exigis' (1), and the
molossus 'lībērtŭm' (2) is brought before the conjunction to make the
audience aware that the word is crucial. The direct speech of line 3
keeps the epigram lively, and provides a target for Martial to shoot at.
He makes his case with four arguments, carefully arranged so as to avoid
monotony. They have in common their paratactic construction (see note
on line 5), which gives them a polemical sharpness. Two scenes are
envisaged: the escort through the streets, and support in disputes. In
each case, the final pentameter (6 and 10) suggests that Martial's breeding prevents him physically (6) and temperamentally (10) from providing the patron with effective assistance. Only once is the contrast
between Martial and his freedman contained in a single line (4). Otherwise, Martial rings the changes by having the patron followed by the
freedman in line 5 and by Martial in line 7, and the freedman as a lone
personal subject in lines 8 and 9. The spondaic 'cunctos umbone' (5),
following dactylic 'incideris', gives a vivid picture of the freedman
wading slowly through the crowd. 'invalidum' (6) is set in contrast with
the superlative implications of 'cunctos' (5) and the large area of 'latus'
(6) with 'umbone' (5). 'ingenuum' (6) has a certain ambivalence, as
suggested in the pupils' text. The irony is that a patron was as much
concerned with the social standing of his clients as with their efficiency
as crowd-dispersers. The patron, as Martial well knew, was anxious to
show off a train of *ingenui*, not *liberti*. Such a snobbish attitude was not
likely to defer to the practical considerations raised by Martial, for
whom his free status was in reality a matter of pride and not something
to be excused (as in line 6).

The note of irony continues to be heard in the next couplet (7–8).
The surface meaning of line 7 is that Martial's 'pudor' (10) prevents him
from cheering, however good his patron's speech. But it can also imply
that his patron's efforts, however excessive, will not be good enough to
earn any words of praise from Martial. The only applause will be from

the uncritical, beast-like freedman: 'mugiet' (8) is particularly expressive. Lines 9–10 are arranged in chiasmus with lines 7–8, so that line 9 keeps up the picture of the bellowing freedman. In both lines, alliteration adds to the aural effect. Martial's choice of the moral quality 'pudor' in line 10 casts a strong note of criticism over the patron who is prepared to employ such methods. 'fortia' (10) is a neat reminder of 'invalidum' (6), and the couplet finishes with 'mihi', one pole of contrast, just as the first argument had opened with 'vix ego' (4).

The last couplet balances the introductory first couplet. Martial has the patron play into his hands by asking what he *will* do, and then wittily defines this as what a *libertus cannot* do. The highly emphatic placing of 'amicus' (11) is intended by the patron to remind Martial that this status does have duties attached to it. In his reply, Martial lets slip for the first time the patron's name, and the reader can cast his mind back to the earlier poem (see note on line 12) where Candidus says with great emphasis, and in Greek, that we are all friends together. Martial wants Candidus to live up to his hollow promise and treat him as an 'amicus' deserves. He will then, so line 12 implies, immortalise Candidus in verse — a final irony.

Questions

1 Has Martial selected examples to fit his case? What other use would a patron make of his clients?
2 Write a curt note of reply from Candidus.
3 Is there any evidence for ill-feeling against Candidus on the part of Martial? Is irony used to suggest this?
4 How does the *libertus* emerge from the comparison?
5 Examine the structure of this poem. To what extent is the epigram symmetrical? How successfully does Martial relieve pattern with variety?

II.7 Martial, Epigrams *IX.6(7)*

Language and content

1 **Afer:** mentioned in seven of Martial's epigrams, but otherwise unidentifiable.
2 **have:** in Martial *Epigrams* IV.78.3–4, Afer is described as an aging social climber who makes a point of saying a daily 'have' to all the notables.

Discussion

Martial's long wait is amusingly recreated by the extraordinary separation of 'dicere' (1) and 'have' (2). The African detail acts as a foil to Martial's 'reverso' (3); the mighty Afer returning once from exotic lands, while the lowly Martial returns several times from down the road. 'continuis' (2) is used to strengthen the effect of 'quinque'.

The impersonal 'dictum est' (3), balancing 'dicere' in line 1, matches the brusqueness of Martial's reception, vividly caught in the reported speech with its dental alliteration. The punch-clause (4), following the first colon, is particularly neat. 'non vis', caught between the colon and the caesura, reflects 'volui' in 2, and both are closely associated with 'havere'. The word 'Afer' is now seen to create humorous assonance with 'havere'. Martial's determined 'vale' (4) is set off by its neighbouring 'havere', and balances the final word of the first pentameter, 'have' (2). The curt phrases, further dislocated by the apostrophe of Afer, perhaps hint at the depth of feeling which Martial wishes to suggest.

A further point to this little epigram is afforded by awareness of the earlier reference to Afer's propensity for saying 'have' (note on line 2). The urgency is transferred in our poem to Martial, who is clearly not sufficiently significant for cultivation by Afer.

Questions

1 Why was Martial upset?
2 Can one detect a balanced construction in such a short poem?
3 How does Martial build up to his final punch-clause?

Section III

The poems in Section III touch on various types of occupation. Catullus and Horace explore the rewards (III.3) and pitfalls (III.1) of creative writing. III.3 ('exegi monumentum') is intensely serious and uses symbol, rich ambiguity and a fascinating breadth of reference to broadcast the confident claims of its author. Catullus' purpose is very different, and his poem is light-hearted (except at the end), highly specific about the tools of the trade, and colloquial rather than poetic in diction. Despite the biographical detail of III.3.10—14, the character of Horace is largely irrelevant to the poem, while for III.1 the character of Suffenus is the crucial ingredient. III.3 can help the reader understand why a Roman was moved to write poetry. III.1 can tell him how some Romans fell short, and can stimulate incidental interest in writing-materials and methods of publication. The other lines from Horace (III.2) are prescriptive in tone, suggesting a recipe for literary success — rejected by Suffenus, but one which even today has much to offer. Ovid (III.4) is merely using various lowly occupations as parallels for his own exile. Nonetheless, the details he selects create a strong series of portraits which may inspire questions about boatmen and shepherds, chain-gangs and slave-girls. In III.6—8, Martial has in mind the specific occupations of lawyer, barber and teacher. In III.6 and III.7, the occupation is incidental to the wit. In III.8, the tone is more serious, giving the impression of a rebuke actually delivered to an over-enthusiastic teacher. All three poems provide suggestive details about Rome and the occupations concerned. Martial's fourth poem (III.5) is different in that it relies solely on word-play and makes no attempt to characterise effectively the life of, e.g., the muledriver. It does, however, illustrate an obsession with work — paralleling, perhaps, the obsession with wealth of II.2 and II.4.

III.1 Catullus, Poems 22

Language and content

The metre is a scazon, or limping iambic trimeter (Raven section 42*A*). The scheme is as follows:

Sūffēnŭs īs/tĕ, Vārĕ, quĕm / prŏbē nōstī

The trimeter is said to limp because the final metron is always $\cup - - \times$ (against expectation for iambic $\cup - \cup \times$), giving an accumulation of heavy syllables at the end of the line. Furthermore, because the Latin stress accent always falls on the penultimate syllable if this is heavy, the last foot of each line is necessarily accented on the penultimate syllable. Since the metrical ictus in an iambic line is on the second element of the foot, there is a perpetual clash between accent and ictus at this point in the line. Several lines here have final *anceps*. The first foot is an iambus ($\cup$-) in 2, 4, 6, 7 and 15. The first foot of the second metron is a spondee (- -) in 3–11, 13, 14, 17–21. The second foot of the first metron is resolved into a tribrach in 19 ('ĭn ălĭqua').

1 **Suffenus**: listed with other bad poets in Catullus, *Poems* 14.19: otherwise unknown.
   Vare: no secure identification (but for possibilities see Fordyce and Quinn, 1973: 121).
   probe: colloquial usage.
2 **homo**: with a certain derogatory force — 'individual', 'chap'.
   venustus et dicax et urbanus: words of strong commendation from Catullus (see Fordyce 197).
5 **perscripta**: 'per-' is intensive, suggesting the effort involved.
   palimpseston: see *OCD*, s.v. 'palimpsest'. Papyrus would be washed clean for re-use. (Illustration in Tingay and Badcock 154.)
6 **regiae**: technical term for superlative papyrus (cf. our 'imperial' of paper size). For details, see Fordyce.
7 **umbilici**: these rollers had projecting knobs (often decorated) to facilitate handling. Expensive scrolls might have a roller both at the beginning and the end.
   lora rubra membranae: the roll-cover was often dyed red, so presumably its 'lora' are coloured to match. For the possibility of 'lora' referring to the title tags attached to the end of the roll, see Fordyce.
8 **derecta plumbo**: in order to get straight the margin to the left of his proposed column, a careful scribe would rule out his roll in advance of writing, marking it with a circular plate of lead slid down a straight-edge.
   pumice . . . aequata: the two edges ('frontes') of the roll were thus smoothed, partly for the sake of appearance and partly to guard against tearing of the edges.
9 **cum legas tu**: subjunctive of indefinite second person (Woodcock section 217 n. i) — 'when one reads'. See Fordyce on 'tu'.
   bellus: colloquial; another favourite word of Catullus, often coupled with 'homo' (see line 2). The behaviour of the *homo bellus* marks him as sharp-witted and fashionable (see Quinn, 1973, on Catullus *Poems* 3.14).

10 **caprimulgus:** Pliny the Elder (*Natural History* X.56.115) refers to birds
    called 'caprimulgi', 'looking like a rather large blackbird' which 'fly on
    to the she-goats' udders to suck their milk' thus injuring the udder and
    making the goats go blind! Catullus, uniquely in extant Latin, uses the
    word to mean little more than 'rusticus'.

11 **abhorret:** see *OLD* 5a, Fordyce and Discussion.
    mutat: see *OLD* 8.

12 **hoc quid putemus esse:** deliberative subjunctive (Woodcock section 172)
    — 'What are we to make of this?'
    modo scurra: the second syllable of 'modo' becomes heavy before 'sc-'
    (but see Fordyce on *Poems* 17.24).

13 **hac re:** probably colloquial.

19–20 **quem . . . possis:** generic subjunctive. Cf. II.4.2 and note.

21 **manticae quod in tergo est:** for partitive Form D (genitive), see Wood-
    cock, sections 72 (4) and 77. In Aesop's fable (Teubner edition, 1956–
    9, no. 229), Prometheus created men with two bags hung from their
    necks, one in front full of other people's faults, and one behind full of
    their own faults; so everyone could see other people's faults, but no one
    could observe his own. (Cf. the mote and the beam in St Matthew 7:
    3–5 and St Luke 6: 41–2.) Quinn 1973 quotes Phaedrus' version. By
    'mantica' Catullus seems to be envisaging a sort of rucksack like a pair
    of panniers slung over a man's shoulders, half in front and half behind.

Discussion

The reader's interest is engaged from line 1 as Catullus begins casually
and rather colloquially, putting the reader in the position of one eavesdropping on a gossipy conversation. The expectation of scandal is
reinforced by the metre: limping iambics are associated 'with abusive or
satirical verse' (Quinn, 1973: 116). Line 2 is therefore the more surprising for its trio of voguey compliments. These soon begin to look
pitched a little high, both because there are too many of them and in
view of line 3. The adversative 'idemque' (3) begins the long and delicious
process of undercutting 'venustus et dicax et urbanus' (2), which is
increasingly seen to require qualification. The *poetae novi* followed the
trail blazed by Callimachus towards a poetry which was *doctus* (learned,
full of allusions, demanding) and *tenuis* (fine, delicate, subtle, unbom-
bastic) — so Lyne 2. This approach was essentially incompatible with
the mass-productions of a Suffenus, whose claims to being 'venustus' etc.,
at least in his writings, were thereby undermined. And it is the sheer
quantity of his writings that Catullus dwells on in line 4, marking the
effort involved by means of (i) the extraordinary quintuple elision (presumably calculated to take the reader on relentlessly without pause for
breath); (ii) the ascent from an unusually high base of 'milia' through
'decem' to the open-ended 'plura'; (iii) the striking enjambment with
line 5, being the first of any consequence in the poem so far; (iv) the
force of the prefix in '*per*scripta' (5), together with the strong 'p'-
alliteration of lines 4 and 5.

In line 5, the argument shifts slightly. The poverty of poets was a conventional theme (worked effectively by Catullus in, e.g., *Poems* 13: 'tui Catulli / plenus sacculus est aranearum'). Again, Suffenus is out of step. The Catullan set usually ('ut fit') composed on palimpsests, presumably both from necessity and on the principle that poems would need filing into shape over a period (see III.2) and should not be rushed into a *de luxe* edition. Suffenus lacks both poverty and the ability to criticise his own work; and Catullus clearly enjoys the rich description that follows of Suffenus' scrolls. The language changes to the technical terms of the book-trade, with the turning-point marked by the virtually unmanageable four syllables of prosaic 'palimpseston' in the metrically stressed final position — looking forward to the contrast it provokes with both 'libri' (6) and 'novi' (6 and 7). In terms reminiscent of advertising copy (6—8), Catullus underlines the splendour of the wrappings to such a degree that the alert reader must feel implied the squalor of the contents. Apart from the profusion of words indicating the technical quality of the product (e.g., 'regiae', 'rubra', 'aequata'), the structure is given a degree of bombast by sustained chiasmus and by 'r'- and 'br'- alliteration in lines 6—7.

'haec' (9) embraces all these splendid trappings, but the sting is in 'legas'. We have been encouraged to view the books as purely decorative objects, but we are now duly reminded that people do occasionally wish to read them, and it is in the reading that their inadequacy is exposed. Appropriately, the diction reverts to the ultra-simple, verging on the colloquial. Suffenus' *urbanitas* (which is recalled to our attention in line 9, with 'urbanus' taking the final stress as in line ·2) merely establishes a target for line 10, where it is revealed as totally imapplicable to his poetry. However genuine Catullus may have been in his compliments of line 2, he leaves no doubt in line 10 that these qualities so prized by the new poets do not flow over into Suffenus' writing. The man's name is repeated in the same emphatic position as in the initial complimentary couplet, but now Catullus shows his own wittiness with the expressive terms 'caprimulgus' and 'fossor' — the quintessential occupation of the country bumpkin — activating and contrasting with the root meaning of 'urbanus' in line 9. ('unus' in line 10 merely twists the knife further by suggesting that Suffenus is not even an out-of-the-ordinary yokel.) The whole is summed up by the difficult 'abhorret ac mutat' (11), where Catullus is apparently remarking on the incongruity between how Suffenus (i.e. his poetry) reads and (i) the splendour of the papyrus in which the poetry resides, (ii) the figure that Suffenus strives to cut in the world (2).

After this dénouement, we have a reflection on the implications, introduced for the sake of liveliness by a deliberative question. The terms employed ('scurra', 12; 'infaceto . . . rure', 14) are consciously selected to give variety, but nonetheless operate in the same area as the fashionable epithets of lines 2 and 9. Line 14 is a notably witty description of dullness — with the seven long vowels, slurring effect of the elisions and the rhetorical structure and synecdoche of 'rure'. The reflective approach of lines 12–15 moves towards the new and final point of the poem: Suffenus is blissfully unaware of his shortcomings. The idea is introduced with typical Catullan flair. In line 3, 'idem' is used to set the contrast with 'venustus', etc., in line 2. In line 14, 'idem' is used in the same adversative fashion to set the contrast with 'scurra' (12) and 'scitius' (13). Then a third 'idem' (15) makes yet another contrast: Suffenus may be a dull writer, but at least he is never as happy as when he is writing poems. Thus our attention is transferred to the unaffected pleasure Suffenus takes in his own poetry, and there is at least a flicker of sympathy for Suffenus in line 16 before the barbed qualifications of line 17 excite the 'self-satisfied' nuance of 'beatus' (see Fordyce). The self-centredness of line 17 is well caught by the repeated 'se', symmetrically placed round 'tamque'; and alliteration of 't' and 's' is prominent, perhaps suggesting the scorn Catullus feels (see Wilkinson, 1963: 54).

It is in line 18, as we are revelling in the discomfiture of Suffenus, that Catullus springs on us his biggest surprise. With 'idem' mirroring the hard-worked 'idem of lines 3, 14 and 15, the finger of criticism is turned to point at the reader. No one escapes ('omnes', 'neque est quisquam / quem non', with 'quisquam' at the emphatic part of the line). Each of us is in his own way something of a Suffenus — the proper name acting adjectivally, and in a sense repaying us for all the epithets applied to Suffenus himself. The line is cardinal, and is set in high relief by the tribrach of line 19, unusual in Catullus. There follows the generalising statement of line 20, effectively completed by the boldly allusive line 21 — together explaining fully the initially puzzling reference of 'Suffenus' in line 19. (For an even more abrupt change of tack in a Catullan poem, with a similar move from specific to universal, see *Poems* 51, 'ille mi par esse deo videtur', with perceptive comments by Lyne.) Williams (1968: 584) comments that 'the solemn comedy of Catullus' satiric portrait of Suffenus is intensified in this straight-faced reflection on human frailty and lack of self-criticism (in which the poet includes himself)'.

Questions

1 Why is Suffenus out of favour with Catullus?
2 How does Catullus attract our attention to the beginning of his poem? What scene does the beginning of the poem force the reader to reconstruct?
3 How many parts does this poem fall into? Are any of them distinguished by a particular brand of language? Does any part join uneasily with its neighbour? If so, is this a fault?
4 What do we learn about Catullus' attitudes to poetry and behaviour?

5 Find out what you can about the Roman book-trade and
   books. Use, e.g., *OCD* s.v. 'Books, Greek and Latin'; Paoli Ch.
   16; Balsdon, 1969: 148—9; Hadas 82—3; Tingay and Badcock
   95—6; Singer *et al.* I: 757; II: 187—90; *CLC* Unit II slide 31.
   Draw or make a model of a luxury papyrus roll.

III.2 Horace, Satires I.10.72—7

Context

Horace has criticised his satiric predecessor Lucilius for the diffuse
character of his writing (cf. III.1). Lucilius, says Horace, would write:

ante cibum versus, totidem cenatus $\overset{\text{ducentos}}{}$

'two hundred lines before eating, and as many again after
dinner.'   (*60—1)

By contrast, Horace recommends restraint in composition.

Language and content

1—2 **vertas, ... neque ... labores:** for present subjunctive expressing general
     instructions or prohibitions to an indefinite second person, see Wood-
     cock section 126, n. ii.
  1 **saepĕ:** remains light before 'st-' (contrast 'modo' in III.1.12).
     stilum vertas: the erasing end is just visible in the drawing in *CLC* Unit I
     Stage 10: 12; or see Paoli plate 44, or Tingay and Badcock 96.
     quae digna legi sint: generic subjunctive. Cf. II.4.2 and note.
  2 **neque:** used in preference to 'neve' for connecting a negative command
     to a previous positive command (Woodcock section 128, n. iii).
  3 **contentus paucis lectoribus:** see Introduction 7 on the exclusive
     nature of much Latin poetry since Catullus.
     an: 'or is it the case that ... ?', expecting a negative answer (*OLD* 1b).
  4 **dictari:** the repetition of texts by both *grammaticus* and pupils. Balsdon
     (1969: 99) comments that 'it was an approach which stressed every
     aspect of literature but the aesthetic'.
     malis: potential subjunctive (Woodcock sections 118—21).
  5 **equitem:** the *equites* were great literary patrons, and in the theatre they
     had the right of sitting in the first fourteen rows.
  6 **Arbuscula:** a famous actress (*mima*), referred to approvingly by Cicero
     in 54 B.C. (*ad Atticum* IV.15).

Discussion

Horace's advice begins with a paradox, pointed by the promotion of
'iterum' from the relative clause: keep rubbing out what is to be read
more than once. 'scriptūrūs' is in weighty isolation at the beginning of
line 2, balancing 'labores' at the other end of the line. For Horace,
unlike Lucilius, writing has to be hard work. Furthermore, the inevitable
consequence of concern for detail and the production of highly worked
literary pieces is a depleted audience. The metre is heavy in the first
half of line 3, as if to underline the serious nature of this conclusion,

statement would have been dissipated. The second, more powerful, point of comparison exactly fills the next line, and like line 1 has the key comparative logically late but emphatically placed at the end of the line. 'altius' (2) is at first sight surprising, since height is not an obvious feature of Horace's 'monumentum'. But the notion must be suggested by the point of comparison which precedes it. The pyramids are long-lasting because they are so immense: this memorial will be even higher and hence more durable. Furthermore, 'altus' does also have the sense 'elevated' or 'superior'. Woodman's interpretation of 'situ' (in Woodman and West 117—18) is very compelling (but see note on line 2). He suggests that Horace intended the word to mean 'site' at first reading, but intended the 'decay' sense to be activated as his reader moved on into lines 3—5. In Woodman's first sense, 'situ' seems to add to the notion of royal pyramids a feeling of two-dimensional extension and even permanence (cf. use of the participle 'situs' for towns, etc., 'being situated'). 'altius' adds the dimension of height, which is seen in this context to imply durability — until we read about the wind and the rain, and realise that the pyramids for all their height will crumble. Ambiguities abound in this poem, and I cannot help wondering whether Horace also meant the first two lines to proclaim his rejection of money and politics: 'aes' is, of course, very commonly used in the sense of 'cash' (e.g. IX.2.13), and the political implications of the pyramids are heightened by the choice of 'regali'.

The last leg of the tricolon (3—5) breaks expectation, since it does not provide a third comparison: what, after all, could cap the pyramids? Instead, we have three destructive agents, all proving ineffective, of which the last (Time) is itself divided and spread out in time. The important words in line 3 are 'edax' (just before the sense break) and 'impotens' (in the final position). The elements attack memorials either slowly and insidiously or violently and uncontrollably; the choice of 'edax' and the elevation of wind and rain to the status of grammatical subjects dramatise the situation by making these great enemies of survival personified characters. The third enemy, Time, is introduced with the massive six-syllable 'innumerabilis', and for the first time in this poem Horace runs over into the following line (5) for the noun in agreement, the lengthy effect being compounded by the repetition of '-nn-' in 'annorum'. 'fuga' is surprising, since the stress has been on the slow passage of time, and this change of tempo is marked in the metre: for example, the ending of 'annŏrum' is echoed in the much lighter 'tempŏrum'.

With 'non omnis moriar' (6) we learn for the first time explicitly that the grave-memorial we have been hearing about is for Horace himself. The declaration grows in confidence from the hesitant 'non omnis' through the confident 'multa . . . pars' to the triumphant and now unqualified first-person 'crescam' with emphatic 'ego'. In fact, we have

another ascending tricolon, balancing that of lines 1—5. By the end of
this sequence, Horace has come to identify his own existence with that
of his poetry.

Mention of 'Libitinam', the ancient Roman goddess of burial, injects
in line 7 a specifically Roman flavour — perhaps hinted at earlier by the
choice of the Roman name for the north wind in line 3. The Roman
context becomes overpowering in lines 8 and 9: Horace's achievement
is a Roman achievement and will endure as long as Rome itself. Horace
avoids the prosaic by means of his sharp and accessible image of the
'pontifex' on the Capitol: the very existence of Rome was intimately
bound up with the performance of ceremonies at her central shrine.
Here the measure of time becomes, interestingly, not physical objects
like gravestones and pyramids, but the performance of ritual, the
actions and words ('tacita virgine' implying a vocal 'pontifex') of human
beings. Horace sees his own rôle, 'Musarum sacerdos' (*Odes* III.1.3), as
essentially similar, poet and 'pontifex' alike speaking for the people.

On what does Horace rest these mighty claims? 'dicar' (10) introduces his statement, but the reader is left waiting for 'deduxisse', the
verb which depends on 'dicar', until line 14. The impact is by then considerable. With 'Aufidus' and 'Daunus' (10 and 11), the poem is local-
ised still further. We are now in Apulia, deep in the *mezzogiorno*,
Horace's birthplace. Why should Horace wish to introduce a provincial
note into this important poem? One reason may be that he wanted to
follow the custom of completing a collection of poetry with a personal
reference or 'seal' (see, e.g., Woodman and West 115—16), but in such
cases (e.g., Virgil, *Georgics* IV.559—66) it is customary for the poet to
refer to his own name, and Horace does not do so. The answer does
depend partly on how we understand these lines (see notes). Horace is
proud of his birthplace and wants to be remembered there, but it seems
wrong to take lines 10—14 as an assertion that his lyrics were actually
composed in Apulia. In these lines immortality is again viewed not in
terms of the specious permanence of objects, but through living,
human reaction and experience — in this case, the natural pride of
Apulians in the success of the local man and Horace's appreciation of
their pride. In these resonant lines ('Aufidus . . . pauper . . . Daunus')
there is a paradox: the river is characterised as roaring and violent, but
Daunus is said to have been poor in water. Woodman (in Woodman and
West 122ff.) rightly points out that the river, though equally fierce (cf.
'violens' in line 10 with 'impotens' in line 3), contrasts with the destructive natural elements of line 3, in that it stands for the area where
Horace's poetry will be preserved and spoken of ('regnavit' in line 12
echoing 'regali' in line 2, and thus clinching the comparison). Woodman
goes on to take Horace's references to water as images for literary
inspiration, as often in ancient poetry (see Nisbet and Hubbard on
Horace *Odes* I.26.6). 'King Daunus, despite the region's natural

resources, was helpless (11—12): he could not utilize the river and himself remained *pauper aquae* (a metaphorical way of saying that he lacked
poetical inspiration), while his people remained uncultured (*agrestium*)'
(Woodman in Woodman and West 123). By contrast, Horace does have
the ability to channel the Aufidus, to harness the flow of Italian inspiration. Daunus' power was very limited and is now past and gone; the
tense of 'regnavit' is in marked contrast with that of 'obstrepit' (10),
with which it is in parallel, and is the only aorist-perfect (as opposed to
the true perfect 'exegi') in the piece. Horace is now 'potens' (or will be
said to be; the syntax is, no doubt intentionally, ambiguous). The word
echoes 'impotens' in line 3: like 'regali' (2) and 'regnavit' (12), 'impotens'
and 'potens' are at the same, emphatic point in the line. The strongly
positive 'potens' now highlights the 'powerless' alternative sense of
'impotens': Horace the human poet can achieve positive ends where the
inhuman forces of nature prove inadequately destructive. His boast is to
have been 'princeps' (emphatically placed) 'deduxisse Aeolium carmen
ad Italos modos'. See notes for various interpretations of 'deduxisse';
the root meaning, of course, entails no more than 'to have removed'.
Whether we take the dominant sense as spinning or conducting in triumph, or however else, Horace is boasting (in a phrase which culminates
in noticeable alliteration of 's' and 'd') that he has brought the rhythms
of Greek lyric poetry to Italy. Purposeful ambiguity is inherent in this
poem, and it is one reason why the reader can return to it so frequently.

There has so far been no hint of an addressee. The imperative 'sume'
(14) implies one, and in a poem of such cardinal importance for Horace
it is right that the person addressed should be a deity. (The Muse, herself immortal, is to confirm the immortality of Horace's poetry.) The
poet offers Melpomene his pride to have for herself. This is the final act
of self-depreciation: Horace has earlier seen his own immortality as
depending on that of his verse, but now he withdraws himself completely by dedicating to the Muse even the pride he feels in his own
achievement. The pride has been won by the 'meritis' of someone unnamed, and scholars are divided as to whether Horace is referring to
himself (e.g., Woodman and West 126) or to Melpomene (e.g., Williams,
1969: 152). Once again, the ambiguity is no doubt intentional, but it
only arises at second and subsequent readings: it must surely be the
case that at a first reading, with the implications of 'superbiam' and the
fact that we do not yet know the identity of the addressee, 'meritis'
must be taken as referring to Horace. The reverential 'volens' marks the
less emphatic Horace who has now handed over his pride. He asks to be
crowned like a triumphant general. Could the significance of this comparison lie in the way that a triumph symbolised the culmination of
achievement prior to a return to civilian life? For with this poem Horace
is dedicating his *Odes* to the Muse in a blaze of glory, preparatory to
making a discreet withdrawal from this field of poetic activity. As he

makes this final request, he enlarges the area of discourse from the parochial ('Aufidus') and human to the international ('Delphica') and divine ('Melpomene'); after establishing his *Romanitas*, Horace can now lay claim to a broader reputation. He also once again reverts to the personal image, as in lines 8 and 9. His symbol of immortality is a female deity, and the final word of all, isolated by 'Melpomene', is nothing grandiose or time-resistant like the bronze and the pyramids, but merely the poet's hair (cf. *Odes* I.1.36: 'sublimi feriam sidera vertice').

Odes III.30 clearly underlies the final lines of Ovid's *Metamorphoses* (XV.871–79). Woodman (in Woodman and West 127–8) makes a brief comparison of these lines with our poem, much to the discredit of Ovid. Some pupils may find it interesting to see how Ovid adapts Horace — who has himself been supposed to be drawing here on Pindar, Lucretius and Virgil (see Woodman and West, and Williams, 1969: 150f.). Fruitful comparisons could also be drawn with *Res gestae divi Augusti*, which was designed for inscription on the great mausoleum, finished in 28 B.C. — when Horace's poem may well have been maturing.

Questions

1 What are we meant to understand by this 'monumentum' of Horace? What is its essential characteristic? What kind of Roman would have built a 'monumentum'? (See *CLC* Unit III slides 56–60.)

2 How does the sound of 'innumerabilis / annorum series et fuga temporum' (4–5) match the sense?

3 What does Horace mean by 'non omnis moriar' (6)? Has anything prepared the reader for talk of death?

4 Why do you think Horace refers to provincial Apulia in lines 10–12?

5 What does Horace claim as his achievement (13–14)? Is this the kind of thing you would expect a modern poet to be proud of?

6 What is Horace asking of Melpomene in lines 14–16? Why do you think he may be making these requests?

7 This poem is commonly printed in four-line stanzas. Does this help the reader with the sense of the poem? If not, where would you make the main sense breaks? Summarise what Horace is saying in each of your sections.

8 How serious is Horace? How can we know?

9 The following are some of the words in this poem with a range of meanings which cannot always be expressed in a single English equivalent:

2 'situ'	site, decay
3 'impotens'	wild, powerless

11 'agrestium'   country-folk, rustics
14 'deduxisse'   spin, lead in triumph, found a colony,
                  draw off water

Look at each of these instances, and consider how different
translations affect the overall sense. Are there any other
ambiguous words or phrases in the poem? Why do you think
Horace makes difficulties for his reader? Is there ever a single
right answer?

III.4 Ovid, Tristia IV.1.3—14

Context

Ovid wrote the first book of the *Tristia* on his way into exile in A.D. 8.
By the end of A.D. 12 he had completed another four books. Book IV
was completed by about 10 or 11 A.D. (Dickinson in Binns 179). The
first poem (from which our passage is excerpted) explains why Ovid is
still a compulsive writer of poetry, and paints a sad picture of conditions
in exile (cf. I.2). The first two lines (omitted from pupils' text) are as
follows:

> siqua meis fuerint, ut erunt, vitiosa libellis,
>   excusata suo tempore, lector, habe.
> 'If you find, as you are bound to, reader, flaws in my poetry,
> accept the circumstances of composition in excuse.'

There follows, in our passage, Ovid's view of the exile-poetry as a sort
of psychological poultice. The examples he selects give us a lively look
at some of the less elevated occupations in Roman society. They are
followed, in the full version, by two mythological *exempla* before Ovid
concludes (*19) 'me quoque Musa levat'.

Language and content

1 **exul**: technically, Ovid suffered not *exilium* but *relegatio* (cf. *Tristia*
II.137); see Introduction 2*a*. He uses 'exul' here in order to capitalise
on its powerful emotive force.
eram: probably epistolary imperfect ('I am in exile'). Luck (1967) does
not take it so in his translation, presumably supposing Ovid to be
excusing flaws in his (then past) exile-poetry to a future critic who has
just read the first two lines (quoted above). The point is not worth discussion unless raised by pupils.
mihi: cf. I.3.1 for Form C (dative) of agent.
3 **hoc est cur**: for subjunctive following this phrase see *OLD* s.v. 'cur' 3.
vinctus: Pliny wrote, two generations later, that no landowner in his
locality (Transpadane Gaul) ever worked his slaves in chains (*Letters* III.
19.7), and his uncle is equally disapproving of using chain-gangs from
the slave-prisons known as *ergastula* (*Natural History* XVIII.7.36).
Columella (first century A.D.) refers to a 'subterraneum ergastulum'
(*De Re Rustica* I.6.3) for chained slaves on an ideal estate, and says

(I.9.4) that 'vineyards are generally worked by slaves in fetters ("alligatos")'. It seems clear that most slaves on the land, except those who misbehaved themselves and were condemned to the *ergastulum*, did not work in fetters — which must, in any case, have impaired their productivity.

5 **innitens:** on the hard work of bargemen, see Liversidge 168.

6 **trahit:** see Tingay and Badcock 126 for illustration. Cf. IX.2 for this work done by a mule.

10 **pastor:** see Liversidge 134–5 on sheep-management, with *CLC* Unit IV slide 70.

11 **pensa trahentis:** the slave-girl is assigned her day's weight of wool ready for spinning. The occupations of slave-women were limited largely to domestic service, wool-making and occasionally breeding *vernae*. Brunt (1971 (1) 144) argues that there were therefore fewer *ancillae* than *servi* and thus the proportion of 'married' slaves may have been rather low. Columella (*De Re Rustica* I.8.19) gave women their freedom if they produced more than three sons; and in his instructions to the bailiff's wife he says (XII.3.6) that combed-out wool should be permanently on hand so that when women are prevented by rain, cold or frost from working in the fields there should be plenty of spinning available for them. On the other hand, Columella sees the prime rôle of women in domestic service (XII, Preface 4–5), and the inscriptional evidence for women in such occupations as baking is very limited. On spinning, see *OCD* s.v. 'spinning'; Forbes IV. 149–71.

Discussion

'exul eram' is simple but powerful. Awareness of this circumstance, says Ovid, is crucial for a proper appreciation of his poetry. It is written to dull his suffering senses, to give 'requies' (1), not to secure public acclaim. (That 'requies' might also be interpreted as 'reprieve' was no doubt in Ovid's mind.) Just as 'exul' begins the couplet, so the complementary 'malis' (2) brings it to a close.

The rest of our piece depicts other people under stress finding relief in rhythm and music. The implicit comparison is staggering: Ovid, a distinguished poet and an *eques* by birth, sets himself in company with a chained slave, a man who pulls a river boat, a rower, a shepherd and a slavegirl. The effect in a status-conscious community must be to exaggerate the enormity of Ovid's misfortune. Each occupation has a couplet to itself, and the lack of enjambment in lines 1 to 8 gives the poetry a stark formality. The first picture, of 'fossor' (3), is particularly harsh. Thoughtful Romans felt (see note on line 3) that to put even slaves in fetters was undesirable; here 'compede' merely doubles the force of 'vinctus', and the 'c'/'q' alliteration grates on the ear until the sound softens with the singing of line 4. 'mollit' is carefully chosen to remind the reader of the hard fetters of the previous line, and 'indocili' is a suggestive detail, taking the reader back to Ovid's modest hints (1) at the quality of his own work. The protagonist of the next couplet, not distinguished enough to be characterised by an occupation-word, is given a vivid little picture. 'cantat' (5), picking up 'cantet' (3), comes early — partly for stress and partly to clear the way for the effortful picture which follows. 'innitens', 'pronus', 'adverso', 'trahit' (5—6) all denote considerable effort. 'limosae', 'harenae' and 'tardam' add to the same effect, which is further emphasised by the heaviness of both hexameter (after 'cantat et') and pentameter. The rigidity of the structure (see above) is now seen to be mitigated by the links between couplets. Just as 'grave mollit opus' (4) — applying equally to the circumstances of lines 5 and 6 — prepares for line 5, so the boat and the river at the end of line 6 prepare for the rower (again too humble to be thus identified) in the next couplet. Here the stress is not so much on effort or on the unpleasantness of the job (though 'lentos', 7, probably alludes to the hard work involved) but rather on the contribution rhythm makes to effective operation. The oars are brought back 'pariter' and 'ad pectora' for maximum propulsion, and 'pulsa . . . pulsat' marks the beat of the oars in line 8. As we begin the next couplet, the continuation is so smooth that we could still be reading about the rower, and we do not identify the 'fessus' as 'pastor' (10) until after the enjambment. The 'mala' of the shepherd's life are simply crystallised in 'fessus'. The rest of the couplet is idyllic, with 'carmine mulcet oves' (10) providing an easy introduction to the singing 'ancilla' and her wool. This is Ovid's last example from contemporary life (see Context) and it can hardly be accidental that line 11 reflects so many words of previous couplets: 'cantantis' (3 and 5), 'pariter' (7), 'trahentis' (6), in addition to the wool. The line is rhetorically complex, with repetition and chiasmus, and sums up strongly the analgesic rôle Ovid accords music and poetry.

Questions

1 Why does Ovid list the various occupations of lines 3—12? What is he saying (a) about his poetry; (b) about his exile?

2 Why does Ovid choose the particular occupations in this list? Is it significant that they are all labouring jobs?

3 How effectively does Ovid suggest the idea of hard work in lines 5—6? Is hard work the main theme of the other descriptions?

4 How smoothly does Ovid manage the transition from one occupation to the next?

5 Which words used in earlier lines are picked up in lines 11—12? Why might Ovid do this?

6 Do some research into the use of slaves on large rural estates; water transport; the life of a shepherd; the occupations of *ancillae*. (The following books may be helpful: Liversidge; Brunt, 1971 (1); Brunt, 1971 (2); Lewis and Reinhold I and II; Barrow; Casson, 1971: 329ff.; Varro, *Res Rusticae*, with Tilly 19—22; Columella, *De Re Rustica*.)

III.5 Martial, Epigrams *I.79*

Language and content

1 **Attale:** Attalus is not identifiable.
2 See on II.6.5 for the omission of 'si'. For the subjunctive, see Woodcock section 158. 'Whether or not there's something to do, you're always doing something.'

Discussion

This little poem depends for its effect partly on word-play, partly on patterning and partly on the use of paradox. Martial is exploiting the various idiomatic uses of 'agere', probably impossible to capture in translation. Patterning is most noticeable in the repetition and positioning of Attalus' name. The first couplet too is cordoned off by the repeated 'semper agis' (1 and 2): this establishes the regular behaviour of Attalus, which the emphatic third 'semper' at the end of line 1 marks as intolerable. The first paradox is offered in line 2. Even if there is nothing to 'agere', Attalus 'agit'.

In the second couplet, Martial lapses into fantasy suggested by the various uses of 'agere'. There can be no question of a lawyer and business-man actually working as a muledriver. 'Attale, ne quod agas desit' (4) mirrors 'est, non est quod agas, Attale' (2) in chiasmus, just as line 3 picked up 'res' and 'causae' from line 1, also in reversed order. The humour of this last line resides partly in Martial finding yet another 'agere' idiom ('agas animam', 4), and partly in the paradox that having plenty to keep you busy depends on killing yourself.

The tone is, of course, light-hearted. Martial is not seriously advising suicide. Nonetheless, there *is* a sting for Attalus (if historical) in the first couplet.

Questions

1 What occasions the poem? How seriously is it intended?
2 Does the poem depend entirely on word-play with 'agere'?
3 Should Martial have written this epigram at greater (or shorter) length?
4 'This epigram cannot satisfactorily be translated' (Walter C.A. Ker). Can you disprove this?

III.6 Martial, Epigrams *VI.35*

Language and content

1 **clepsydras:** Pompey was credited with the introduction of *clepsydrae* to Roman courts as a check on lawyers' loquacity. Each water-clock seems to have been set to last for about a quarter of the (variable) Roman hour (Sherwin-White, 1966, on Pliny *Letters* II.11.14, who speaks of four water-clocks in addition to twelve large ones allowing him

to speak for almost five hours). Presumably a speaker would not have
to keep going for the full extent of his allowance — established by agreement with the presiding magistrate (Pliny *Letters* VI.2.7—8).

2 **arbiter**: 'a person appointed or chosen to settle a dispute, having wider
discretionary power than a IVDEX (*OLD*.2). Most pupils will be satis-
fied with the gloss in their text. There seems little need to provide any
more information unless the question of the *arbiter*'s function is raised
directly by the pupils.

Caeciliane:a frequent, but unidentifiable, addressee of Martial.

3 **vitreis**: for glassware, see *CLC* Unit II slides 32—9.

Discussion

The long-winded and loud-mouthed Caecilianus makes a dramatically
spondaic entry (1). The 'arbiter', motivated presumably by considerations of justice rather than personal comfort, allows him his time
'invitus'. The central couplet (3—4) pictures the speech that follows. 'at'
(3) shows how Caecilanus refuses to take the hint implicit in 'invitus',
while 'multa' and 'diu' reinforce one another to suggest excessive length.
Martial now focuses on the detail of Caecilianus drinking tepid water.
'tepentem' (3) and 'semisupinus' (4) neatly indicate the seediness and
wilting heat of the proceedings, while the drone of the orator's voice is
again caught in the spondaic first half of the pentameter (4). The third
couplet looks back to the first as it prepares to round off the epigram:
'vocem' and 'rogamus' in line 5 recall 'voce' and 'petenti' in line 1, while
'clepsydra' and 'Caeciliane' (6) recall 'clepsydras' (1) and 'Caeciliane'
(2). This final couplet contains Martial's ingenious suggestion for killing
two birds with one stone: Caecilianus is invited to drink from the
'clepsydra', both to quench his thirst and to reduce his speaking-time:
'saties' works concisely with 'vocem' and 'sitim' to carry both meanings,
with 'saties' / 'sitim' assonance. 'bibas' (6), the surprise word, is of course
kept for last, and for the sneer implied by the repeated 'Caeciliane', see
Discussion of I.3. Again, the pentameter (6) is as heavy as it can be, with
the punch-word kept for its light second half.

Questions

1 Does Martial intend his suggestion to be taken seriously? If
not, why does he make it?

2 To what extent is it possible to see each couplet as an isolated
component of the whole epigram? Is it possible to characterise
each couplet and suggest a progression?

3 Find out what you can (a) about the *clepsydra*; (b) about
methods of measuring time in the Roman world. (See, e.g.,
Pliny *Letters* II.11.14 and VI.2.5ff., with Sherwin-White, 1966;
OCD s.v. 'clocks'; Paoli 82—4; Vitruvius, *De Architectura* IX.7,
with Plate *N* in the Loeb edition; Carcopino 164—8, 206—7;
Hodges, diagram 205; Singer *et al.* I: Ch. 5.) Why was a more
accurate timing-device not invented?

III.7 Martial, Epigrams *VII.83*

Language and content

1 **Eutrapelus** = (Greek) Dexterous; Twinkle-fingers. Mentioned only here.
   tonsor: see Paoli 108—10, 162—3; Tingay and Badcock 130; and notes
   on line 2.
   Luperci: frequently mentioned by Martial, but unidentified.

2 **expingit**: presumably the application of rouge after shaving (see Martial,
   Epigrams VIII.52.8). Juvenal, *Satires* II.93—5 describes homosexual
   males in make-up. Tibullus, *Elegies* I.8.9—12, has the lover using cosmetics, including rouge ('fucus'). Nero was supposed to have used scent
   even on the soles of his feet (see Pliny the Elder, *Natural History* XIII.
   4.20—5). Ovid, in *Medicamina Faciei Femineae* 25, writes of husbands
   making themselves smart 'feminea lege'. See Singer *et al.* I: Ch. 11 (IV).

Discussion

The barber's name is given full effect by promotion from its subordinate
clause, and the word suggests a top-flight Greek hairdressing artiste. The
point of the epigram seems to be that Lupercus' second beard has grown
before the finicky Eutrapelus has disposed of the first; is it too fanciful
to imagine that Martial may have had in mind the supposed connexions
of 'lupercus' with the hairy 'lupus'? The assonance of 'or', 'er', 'ar' holds
the two lines together. Cf. Martial, *Epigrams* VIII.52.

Questions

1 What effect does Martial obtain (i) by the name he gives the
   'tonsor'; (ii) by the positioning of 'Eutrapelus tonsor'?

2 Find out what you can about the use of cosmetics in the
   ancient world. (See Forbes III: 26—43; and notes on lines 1
   and 2.)

III.8 Martial, Epigrams *X.62*

Language and content

The metre is a scazon, or limping iambic trimeter: for the scheme see notes on
III.1. Several lines have final *anceps*. In all but line 6, the first foot of the second
metron is a spondee ('magistēr pārce'). In line 10, the initial spondee is resolved
into an anapaest ('fĕrŭlaē'). In line 12, the second foot of the first metron is
resolved into a tribrach ('aestatĕ pŭĕri').

1 **ludi magister**: cf. the noisy schoolmaster of Martial *Epigrams* IX.68,
   incompletely reproduced in *CLC* Unit IV 'domi' 8. On the background,
   see *CLC* Unit I Stage 10: 13—14 and *Teacher's Handbook* 101—2; Paoli
   113—14, 167—8, Plate 42; Balsdon, 1969: 95—102, Plates 7*b*, 8*a* and
   8*b*; Hadas 82—3; Carcopino 118—22; Liversidge 76—9; Tingay and
   Badcock 77—81; *CLC* Unit IV slide 25.

2 **frequentes**: the more pupils, the more fees.
   capillati: by contrast with the adult fashion for short hair.

3 **delicatae . . . mensae**: for the transferred epithet (frequent in Martial)
   cf. II.6.1 'operam . . . togatam'. 'mensae', the schoolmaster's table,

comes to mean 'those sitting at the table' (*OLD*.6). Cf. Fraenkel's reference (274) to the Upper Bench at Rugby.

4 **calculator, notarius:** Paoli 168. Martial elsewhere pictures a man affecting to be a celebrated lawyer as crowded round by *notarii* (*Epigrams* V.51.2). Cicero was supposed to have introduced shorthand to Rome, adapting a Greek system (*OCD* s.v. 'tachygraphy'). Martial has a two-line epigram on a *notarius* at work (*Epigrams* XIV.208).

6 **leone:** the zodiacal sign of the lion is associated with the months of July and August.

8 **Scythae pellis:** the 'Scythian's hide' may be a nickname for the *scutica*, a Roman schoolmaster's weapon of last resort, resembling a cat-o'-nine-tails. Herodotus (*Histories* IV.64) has a gory passage about the uses to which Scythians put human pelts. Alternatively, the phrase may be a variant on 'Scythica pellis', referring to the leather imported from Scythia, possibly prefabricated into *scuticae*.

9 **Marsyas:** Athena invented the Greek reed-pipe (*aulos*), but threw it away because it distorted her face when she played it. Marsyas the satyr picked it up, learnt the technique and challenged Apollo to a music contest on condition that the winner could do as he wished with the loser. Apollo won, and flayed Marsyas alive.

10 **paedagogorum:** see Balsdon, 1969: 98, and references in note to line 1.

11–12 For a discussion of these lines, see Paoli 172–3, arguing against the view that there was an official summer break from 1 July to 15 October (but see Balsdon, 1969: 106 and 210). Whether or not the holiday was official, schoolmasters would no doubt have attempted to keep their schools going, both for the benefit of pupils who were not able to escape the intolerable heat of Rome, and in order to collect at least some fees.

Discussion

The first line summarises the epigram: a schoolmaster is asked to spare his flock. At the same time, the reference of 'parce' is kept imprecise, and not until line 11 does Martial finally let us know exactly what he is asking. This blurring of 'parce' excites some curiosity in the reader, and helps to give the poem form.

The vague request is followed (2–5) by the rewards Martial wishes on the schoolmaster, should he comply. The key words of lines 2 and 3 seem to be 'frequentes' and 'delicatae', each isolated by the verb from the word it describes. Martial wishes him plenty of pupils from good families. 'capillati' (2) and 'delicatae' and 'diligat' in line 3 (assisted by soft 'l'-alliteration and assonance) have a sensuous quality suggesting the physical charm of the pupils, and 'chorus' (3) is carefully chosen for its literary associations. In line 5, the alliteration of 'c' and 'q', which has been building up through this whole section, rises to a crescendo; and the line ends strongly with 'coronetur', ambiguous between ringing round and crowning as victor.

Lines 6 and 7 take us back abruptly (as the prominent alliterative letter shifts in line 6 back to 'l') to the present, with an extraordinarily vivid evocation of the scorching July heat in Rome. There is not a single word in this couplet, unless one counts the enclitic '-que', which fails to contribute to the brightness, power and heat of the summer sun: 'Iulius' and 'messem' (7) both recall the high summer; 'albae' and 'luces' (6) connote brightness — 'luces' being a studied alternative to 'dies'; 'leone' (6) suggests power. The other words all suggest power or heat or a combination of the two.

In line 8, there is another abrupt change, the four lines of 8—11 corresponding structurally with the four lines of good wishes for the schoolmaster of 2—5. 'cirrata' (8) is regularly used of children, so there is a certain irony about the application of it here to the teacher's terrible *scutica*, with the double 'r' employed to swell the threatening sound of 'cirrata loris horridis' (8). The following line (9) is precisely the sort of comment that would be in place in an ancient schoolroom. Not only does Martial give us the mythical parallel, but also the sub-reference to Marsyas' place of birth. *Scuticae* are coupled with canes, neatly described as 'sceptra paedagogorum' (10) — a phrase which has mock-flattering implications for the *paedagogus*. In line 11, Martial's request is at last put firmly and precisely, 'cessent' (11) coming in with some force. The canes are to sleep, just like the dozing pupils on whom they are used.

Line 12 takes up from line 1, all the intervening lines being variations and explications on the theme of 'parce . . . turbae' (1). Martial suggests, persuasively, that boys do not need formal schooling in summer. 'si valent', thrown in almost as an afterthought, in fact suggests yet another reason for leaving the unhealthy summer climate of Rome. The tribrach in 'aetate pueri' (see notes) merely underlines the lightness of heart at this prospect.

Questions

1 What is the structural pattern of this poem?
2 What is Martial's attitude towards the teacher? How does he try to persuade him?
3 How effectively does Martial conjure up a Roman summer in lines 6—7?
4 Do you agree with the implications of line 12? Is it right that modern school buildings should (generally) remain unused during the summer? Is there a case for more flexibility, a four-term year, a shift system?
5 Discover what you can about the Roman educational system. (See, e.g., note on line 1.)
6 Should teachers be allowed to administer corporal punishment?

Section IV

Entertainment is the theme of Section IV, and in IV.1 Horace has Nasidienus both striving to provide entertainment for his guests and him-

Discussion

Ovid has contrived to spend sixty lines at the races without describing an actual race (see Context). This gives a good idea of his priorities. He has however given the flavour of the occasion as early as *9ff. with a romantic daydream — told in considerable detail — of himself racing a *quadriga* for his girl. As the elegy works towards its conclusion, he needs an exciting race to finish it off. By using the device of the *revocatio* (9), he contrives to extract the excitement of two races from the description of one. Altogether he has given his audience the impression of several races without lapsing into the repetitive phrases which dog commentators on such events.

The excerpt begins with plain narrative, part of a sustained dramatic monologue technically directed at the girl. In fact, much of what Ovid says is entirely for the benefit of the reader. The girl would hardly need to be told that the race had started (1—2), and it is the reader who is expected to appreciate the balanced assonance of 'aequo'/'equos' and the galloping dactyl of 'quadriiugos' (contrast *quadrigas*). 'misit equos' is retained to the end of the couplet in order to give the horses a good send-off. With the second couplet (3—4) Ovid comes closer to dialogue. His sentences are clipped and the syntax simple to match the excitement of the moment. Typically, his compliments are not particularly subtle: 'if you support him, he's bound to win; even horses do what you want.' However, they are expressed with a rhetorical flourish or two. The apparently simple construction of line 3 turns out to be a neat chiasmus marked out for us by the repeated 'cui'. The 'vi-'/'vi-'/'-ui-'/ '-vē-'/'vi-'/'-uī' sequence of lines 3—4 may well have been intended to add to the excitement. 'equi' is kept for the end, partly because it is a surprising subject of 'scire videntur' and partly to keep our focus firmly on the race.

With the next two couplets (5—8) things get even more lively. The exclamations and repeated 'quid facis?' (6 and 7) create unusual immediacy. The abrupt transition from the runaway victory of line 4 to the self-reproach of line 5 (with its gloomy 'm's and long vowels) seems intended to amuse. Here Ovid becomes the touch-line expert, a type no doubt familiar to Ovid's audience and certainly well known to the modern reader. The advice Ovid offers is either painfully obvious to a charioteer (5) or predictable and unhelpful (6). (Earlier, in his fantasy (see above), Ovid has personally carried out the whole manoeuvre to perfection, just grazing the *meta* with his inner wheel (*12). The repeated 'quid facis?' (7) suggests urgency: Ovid too is competing for the 'bona vota puellae' and we begin to realise more and more that his own success is tied up with that of the charioteer. The advice of line 8 is hardly very subtle, despite the apparent flattery of 'valida'. There is an air of resignation about 'favimus ignavo' (9), though it would be wrong to translate this as 'we've backed a loser!', since 'ignavo' is pur-

posely selected to shift the blame from Ovid and his girl (cf. 'vincet,
cuicumque favebis', 3) squarely on to the charioteer.

Ovid has given up the race for lost, but since his designs on the lady
don't allow him to fail he has to secure a restart. He therefore turns to
the spectators (9) and asks in mock-solemn language for the race to be
stopped. The formal language makes a good contrast with the colloquial-
isms of the previous few lines. That his request should immediately be
granted ('en revocant', 11) is seen by Du Quesnay (in Binns 19) as a misinterpretation of reality, in that 'he assumes that the fact that the
citizens' call for the race to be re-run is due to his demand'. But there
may also be a certain irony about 'en' (*OLD* 2), with such a very prompt
repeat of 'revoca-', which is Ovid the writer's way of smiling up his
sleeve and admitting that the whole operation is fixed by the all-
powerful author in order to make his poem turn out properly.

The waving of the togas is straightaway taken over by Ovid for his
own humorous purposes. This incidentally allows time for the race to
be reorganised. The 't'-alliteration of line 11 perhaps suggests the gusty
wind created by the togas, and in line 12 the girl ('te') is literally hidden
in the centre of the line, while 'in nostros . . . sinus' encloses her. Ovid
will clearly not be waving his own toga. 'sinus' of course is susceptible
of a *double entendre*: it primarily refers to the folds of Ovid's toga, but
it may equally hint at a full embrace or a warm relationship (cf. L&S
II.2a 'in sinu esse').

In line 13, 'iam' (cf. 1) summons the reader's attention with its
immediacy, and the three dactyls carry us into the race. For variety's
sake, Ovid focuses on the starting-boxes — empty before we realise the
race has restarted. The answering pentameter (14) picks out the speed
and colour, neither of which was prominent in lines 1—8, but is
reminiscent of lines 2 and 4 in the way 'equis' is reserved for effect. In
lines 15—16, Ovid gives his charioteer a second chance in a fiercely
alliterative utterance. Ovid's prayer goes up for success, almost as if the
charioteer were a god: the reader senses success in the offing. There is
now (17) a splendid jump-cut over the whole of the rest of the race as
'sint' (16) becomes 'sunt' (17), to great effect. The double sense of
'mea vota' becomes unmistakable now. In line 16 the reader fondly
imagines that both Ovid and his girl wish for no more than the
charioteer's victory. With 'supersunt' in line 17 we are reminded of
Ovid's prime purpose in attending the races. The point is driven fully
home with the balanced pentameter of line 18. Ovid still has to ride his
chariot past the winning post. In the final couplet we at last secure a
reaction from the girl. 'risit' (19) is highly emphatic and highly promising. 'argutis' and the soft diminutive 'ocellis' bode well too. 'quiddam'
is delightfully and provocatively discreet. That the girl should then
speak (as our punctuation implies) is the more devastating for her long
silence and the adequate acquiescence of line 19. What she says is a

model of brevity compared with the assiduous attentions of Ovid. Again 'cetera' and 'alio loco' are archly tantalising. 'redde' may possibly suggest the paying of a bet (cf. Lee, 1968). The deal is done, and Ovid wisely cuts the elegy at this point.

Questions

1 How much of the race can we reconstruct from the details Ovid gives us?
2 To whom are Ovid's remarks primarily directed: (a) in lines 1— 2; (b) in lines 3—4; (c) in lines 6—7; (d) in lines 9 (second half) —10? Is this confusing? Why might Ovid have chosen to do this?
3 How helpful is the advice Ovid gives to the charioteer?
4 Is there sufficient difference between the two descriptions of races starting?
5 How effectively does Ovid end this poem? (Our line 20 is the last line of the whole elegy.) For translations of the whole poem, see Wilkinson, 1955: 57—60; Lee, 1968 — both putting a full stop after line 19 and seeming to give the final line to the lover.
6 Research into the Circus Maximus and the Roman passion for horse-racing (helpful references in notes).

IV.3 Ovid, Remedia Amoris *201—12*

Context

The *Remedia Amoris*, 'Antidotes for Love', was written as a companion piece for the lengthier and better known *Ars Amatoria*. It was published in about A.D. 1, and was taken as a serious aid to chastity in the monasteries of the Middle Ages (Wilkinson, 1955: 383; cf. *CLC* Unit IV slide 7). In our passage, Ovid is recommending devotion to hunting as one of several means of falling out of love.

Language and content

1 **leporem**: 'Wolves . . . , bears, boars as well as deer, hares and wild goats were indigenous' (Balsdon, 1969: 302). For an illustration of a hare and a fox pursued by two mounted huntsmen, a beater (?) and two dogs, see Liversidge, illustration 33.
sectare: on the passion of Roman aristocrats for hunting, see Balsdon, 1969: 159—61, 219—20 and Plate 14a — showing hare-coursing. 'Hunting was a matter of driving game (especially hares) into nets and of detecting, pursuing and spearing deer, boars or bears' (Balsdon, 1969: 219). Large beasts would be carried home in a net suspended from a pole (Toynbee, 1973: 24). See also Liversidge 91; Muir on *Aeneid* IV. 131; *CLC* Unit I slide 12, Unit IV slides 21—3.
2 **retia**: cf. Pliny's well-known letter on combining hunting with writing (*Letters* I.6).

3 **varia formidine:** 'with various-coloured scare'; see note in pupils' text. The abstract sense of 'formido' remains as a powerful overtone.

7 **alite capta:** 'by catching birds'. for the timeless past participle, see 'locutus' in V.1.3.

8 **aut lino aut calamis:** a falcon is shown in a fourth-century hunting mosaic from Sicily (Toynbee, 1973: 24) and a decoy lures partridges on a mosaic from Tunisia (Liversidge, illustration 53), but nets and lime-twigs were the normal means of catching such delicacies as nightingales, blackbirds (as in IV.1.34), and (a special delicacy) thrushes (Toynbee, 1973: 276—8). Modern methods are not markedly different:

'There are two main methods of netting. One is the 60 ft.-long clap net, spring-loaded like a giant mouse-trap and released by the trapper pulling a tripwire from his hide. The other is the mist net, strung up against a dark background of trees or shrubs so that birds are unable to see the fine mesh until it is too late . . . In Friuli-Venezia Giulia . . . there are about a thousand trappers still using birdlime . . . The trapper constructs a number of artificial trees which can be raised and lowered by hand. Twigs coated with tacky birdlime are loosely slotted into the branches. Decoys then lure unsuspecting birds. When they alight on the limed twigs they stick fast. The twig is dislodged, and falls to the ground with the bird still attached, to be collected later.' Brian Jackman, *The Sunday Times Colour Magazine*, 7 March 1976.

9 **piscis:** turbots, bass, sturgeon, gudgeon, sea-eel, the entrails of the wrasse and several varieties of mullet are some of the varieties of fish consumed by the Romans (Toynbee, 1973: 210—11).
devoret: relative clause of purpose, hence subjunctive.

12 **tibi:** Form C (dative) of agent with the gerundive.

Discussion

Ovid prescribes the chase as a remedy against love. He avoids in at least three ways the potential monotony of a discourse on the various types of hunting. First, the choice of activity is intrinsically amusing. Hunting is after all very similar to wenching, and the reader can reflect that Ovid is recommending the same sort of techniques ('abdere sub parvis aera recurva cibis', 10) that brought his reader into trouble in the first place. Second, Ovid structures this little piece so as to keep the object of the exercise perpetually before us (5—6 and 11—12), and incidentally to split the various hunting activities into the first and the second rank and across two days. Third, there is a liveliness of detail about the various pictures calculated to keep the attention of the reader.

Much of the detail in the first couplet is contributed by carefully chosen adjectives. Thus the hare is 'pronum' and the hound 'sagaci', while 'frondosis' economically conjures up the healthy outdoor life which is intended to distract the reader from indoor pursuits. Lines 3—4 vividly suggest the climax of the hunt — the fear imposed by the huntsman ('pavidos', 'terre', 'formidine') and the dying ('cadat', 'fossus'). Any fleeting feelings of sympathy engendered by line 3 are dispelled by the reader's pleasure at being credited with a boar ('aper' held till the end of line 4) as the crowning achievement of the expedition. The boar is

cleanly and thoroughly killed, too: here is no glancing blow or inter-
vention of helpers. The change to a third-person subject and jussive subjunctive ('cadat') provides a welcome change from the string of imperatives.

'studium' in line 7, highlighted by the repetition, looks back to the
lines before our excerpt begins. Ovid has urged his reader to shun
'otium' (*136) by devoting himself either to the 'studium colendi'
(*169), i.e. agriculture, or to the 'venandi studium' (*199). Now he
claims that fowling and fishing, though not quite the noblest of sports,
do nonetheless count. Lines 9—10 are particularly striking. The resonance is immediately apparent — not least, the jingle at the end of line 9.
The greed of the fish is strongly suggested ('edax', 'avido', 'devoret').
The scene is presented from the fish's point of view, in that the eating
is described before the revelation in line 10 of the 'back-curved bronze'
hidden in the food — the words are physically hidden in 'parvis . . .
cibis'. The final couplet follows this well: you have deceived the fish,
and now you will have to deceive yourself — without letting yourself
know anything about it ('furtim')!

Questions

1 Why does Ovid recommend hunting? Where is the evidence?
2 The skeleton of the two hunting sequences is as follows: chase
   the hare, set your nets on the hills, hunt stags or kill a boar;
   catch birds or do some fishing. Examine the ways Ovid fills
   out this framework. Can he be criticised for adding too much
   detail?
3 How does Ovid avoid a dry recital of hunting possibilities?
4 What precisely does Ovid mean by line 12?
5 Contrast Horace's treatment of the same theme in *Epodes* II.
   29—38.
6 Rework (in English) the same illustrative material into advice
   on how to get your girl/man.

IV.4 Martial, Epigrams *III.59*

Language and content

1 **munus:** on gladiatorial shows, see *CLC* Unit I Stage 8 with slides 50—4
   and *Teacher's Handbook* 88—9, Unit II slide 51, Unit IV slide 13; Paoli
   Ch. 23; Balsdon, 1969: 288—302; Carcopino 259—67; Hadas 45, 48—
   51; Liversidge 96—7; Tingay and Badcock 141—4; Grant, 1967; Grant,
   1971 (1) 72—4.
2 **fullo:** see *CLC* Unit I *Teacher's Handbook* 67—8; Forbes IV: 81—94;
   Liversidge 106—8; *OCD* s.v. 'fulling'. Pupils may be reminded of the
   importance of fulling to Pompeii.
   Mutina: famous for its wool, and consequently attractive to fullers. It
   seems reasonable to suppose that Bononia had a strongly entrenched
   leather industry.

Discussion

For a poem with similar sentiments see Martial *Epigrams* III.16, where
Martial makes puns on the tools of the upstart cobbler's trade. Our brief
epigram shows (i) that some artisans were doing exceptionally good
business when Martial wrote; (ii) the resentment felt by the upper
échelons of Roman society against people who bettered themselves
socially; (iii) the relatively low social ranking of 'caupo' as compared
with 'sutor' and 'fullo'. Unless this last point has substance, the epigram
has no bite. There seems to be implied the same sort of distinction as
that between skilled and unskilled worker in our own society.

The poem takes form from the repetition of 'dedit'/'dabit', and from
the initial contrast between 'culta' and 'cerdo' which is understood
throughout. 'munus' is held back for emphasis in line 1, in order to
expose it to the ridicule which Martial clearly feels it deserves. Traditionally, only the local gentry put on *munera* (see Introduction for
Martial's own background).

Questions

1 Why does it matter who pays for a *munus*?
2 Does Martial expect an answer to his question? Is it possible to
   detect his own attitude to these events?
3 What can we learn about Roman society from this epigram?
4 Since a cobbler is by definition a *cerdo*, why does Martial use
   the word?
5 Is the breaking down of class barriers in a status-conscious
   society necessarily a good thing?

IV.5 Martial, Epigrams *XII.82*

Language and content

1 **thermis, balnea**: see *CLC* Unit I *Teacher's Handbook* 95–7, with slides
   55–9. Unit III slide 1; Paoli 221–7; Balsdon, 1969: 26–32; Liversidge
   32, 45–6; Tingay and Badcock 137–9. The distinction between
   'thermae' and 'balnea' is that between the large-scale imperial *thermae*
   and the much larger number of variously-sized establishments, probably
   the result of private enterprise and investment, shoehorned into available building-space (Meiggs 407, 416). By Martial's time, *thermae* had
   been built by Agrippa and Nero near the Pantheon, and by Titus and
   Trajan on the lower slopes of the Esquiline near the Colosseum.
2 **Menogenen**: this parasite is not mentioned elsewhere in Martial.
3 **tepidum . . . trigonem**: *trigon* seems to have been played by three players standing in a triangular formation (Greek 'trigōnos' = triangular) and
   throwing a ball round from one to another or knocking it on. The ball
   was small and stuffed hard with hair. 'tepidum' suggests that the game
   was energetic. Playing the ball with the left hand was a particularly
   prized manoeuvre (Martial *Epigrams* XIV.46).
4 **imputet**: there was clearly some method of scoring at *trigon*. Menogenes
   is scoring his own points to the man from whom he hopes for a dinner.

Menogenes is either one of the three players, acting as scorer and crediting his own catches to his victim; or he is perhaps standing behind his victim as a sort of long stop, and again (more properly) scoring his catches to him.

5 **follem**: a bladder, either inflated or stuffed with feathers, suitable for the old and the young (Martial *Epigrams* XIV.47). Menogenes is now acting as ball boy.

6 **soleatus**: see notes on IV.1.24.

7 **lintea**: Menogenes' victim would have brought his own towels to the baths.

10 **dicet Achilleas disposuisse comas**: 'will say that the hair you have arranged is positively Achillean'. See e.g., the Achilles Painter's name-vase (Boardman, illustration 175) and Pompeii wall-painting of Achilles (Richter, illustration 399).

11 **fumosae**: wine-bottles were stored in the *apotheca* at the top of the house, because the smoke from the fire was supposed to mellow the wine.

ipse: i.e., not a slave.

propin: a Greek infinitive, treated as a noun.

faece: why the dregs? The commentators suggest that they were used either as a cleansing agent or as an emetic before dinner, and in Horace *Satires* II.8.9 wine-dregs are one of several *hors d'oeuvres* intended to whet the appetite. The first interpretation fits better with the answering pentameter (12), and this agreement is evident in each of the preceding four couplets describing Menogenes' activity. If this is correct, 'propin' is being used metaphorically.

14 **'veni!'**: to dinner.

Discussion

A general remark about Menogenes is followed by a specification of the various flatteries used by him (3—12). The epigram is rounded off by another generalisation (13) leading into the climactic invitation to dinner (14).

'effugere' (1) and 'Menogenen' (2) are both positioned for maximum impact; and the second half of line 2 is amusingly pointed, since the poem is devoted to the wiles of Menogenes. 'captabit' (3), with its overtones of courting favour, is well chosen, and 'tepidum' is a choice detail — suggesting the sweaty hands of the players. Perhaps Menogenes' ambidexterity (3) explains the frequency with which he chalks up points ('saepe', 4). Certainly in this couplet both Menogenes and his victim are still at the games-playing stage. By lines 5—6, Menogenes has had his bath and is trying to force the issue by putting on his party-shoes ('soleatus', 6). His prospective host has moved on to softball, and Menogenes is now effusive in his service: 'de pulvere' (5) contrasts sharply with 'iam lotus, iam soleatus' (6), and Martial perhaps expresses something of Menogenes' distaste in the heavy first half of line 6. In line 7, the victim is out of his bath. Menogenes' praise of the towels, worthy of an advertising-copy writer, contrasts amusingly with the scene in the pentameter — which gives us one of our rare glimpses of

Roman domestic life. The assonance of the two opposites 'candidiora' and 'sordidiora' adds to the humour, and the baby's feeder leads on naturally to the dinner which dominates Menogenes' thinking. It also leads into the description of the man's balding head — no more hairs than a baby. The wit of line 9 is increased by the idiomatic singular of 'secto . . . dente' (suggesting that this bald pate requires no more than a single tooth to comb it), and by the mournful 'ō'-sounds that accompany the line. Finally, Menogenes' epic reference (10) points up the contrast between fact and fiction: does he fancy himself as Patroclus, one wonders. 'fumosae' (11) breaks the continuity, jarring heavily with the spruce cleanliness of lines 6—10. Like line 8, however, this alliterative line moves our thoughts in the direction of 'cena' and the drinking that accompanies it, though 'propin' (11) is probably metaphorical (see note). The activity in line 12 is surprisingly intimate: we expect Menogenes to be wiping his own brow, not his victim's. If we now look back over the four couplets (3—12), we see Menogenes gradually homing on his victim, becoming ever closer and more personal. The pressure he has exerted reaches a climax in lines 13—14 with a highly polished couplet. 'omnia' (13) is exaggerated by repetition and set within a chiasmus with 'rhyming' centre. 'donec' (13) is exposed tantalisingly: is it possible even now, we wonder, for the victim to assert himself? The crucial word is kept for the very end of line 14, and preceded by a pentameter first-half of laborious heaviness expressing the notion of 'taedia mille' (14). There is no way of escaping Menogenes (1).

Questions

1 What do you think Menogenes is doing (i) in lines 3—4; (ii) in lines 11—12?
2 Is the order of the four couplets in lines 3—12 significant?
3 Examine Martial's use of contrast in this epigram.
4 Discuss sound and word-order in the last couplet (13—14).
5 What would be the rôle of a modern Menogenes?
6 Find out what you can about Roman games and pastimes. (See notes on lines 3, 4 and 5, and on IV.6; Paoli Ch. 21; Balsdon, 1969: 154—9; Carcopino 273—6; Liversidge 87.)
7 Find out what you can about Roman public baths. (See note on line 1.)

IV.6 Martial, Epigrams *XIV.16*

Context

Martial's Book XIV is a collection of two-line epigrams entitled *apophoreta* ('presents to be taken away by guests'). The couplets describe the presents; most are in pairs, suitable for presentation by rich man and poor man alternately. It is unlikely that our dice-thrower is intended as one of the more expensive presents.

Language and content

turricula: on the Roman passion for gambling, see Paoli 234–7; Balsdon, 1969: 154–6; Carcopino 273–6; Ward-Perkins and Claridge items 235–9; Liversidge 87. The severe laws against gaming were widely overlooked, even by emperors, and the stakes could be high enough to bring about a loss of 100,000 *sestertii* in one night. This sort of dice-box (a bronze version illustrated in British Museum, 1920: 205) was cylindrical and stepped outside to give a firm grip (hence its tower-like appearance).

1 **talos**: The knuckle-bone is part of the ankle joint in cloven-footed animals, and the bones (or representations in metal, ivory or stone) were used for various games. When used like dice (*tesserae*) only the four long faces of the bone were employed. The flat face counted for 1, the convex for 3, the concave for 4, and the 's'-shaped face for 6. The highest score was with a 'Venus', when each of four bones showed a different face and the lowest was 'dogs', when four flat faces showed. (Illustration in Ward-Perkins and Claridge item 236.)

Discussion

The point of this little epigram lies in the ambiguity of the second line. The cheating hand ('manus improba') of line 1 is brought into the clause which describes it, so that (i) it reinforces the sense of 'compositos'; (ii) 'improba' begins to react adverbially with 'mittere talos'. The notion of deceit is thus put over very strongly. The first half of the alliterative pentameter is metrically very heavy, and leads up to the punch-phrase 'nil nisi vota feret'. The surface meaning is that the cheat will have all his wishes fulfilled. The underlying meaning is that the cheat will only win in fantasy, not in reality: his wishes for the dice will remain mere wishes.

Questions

1 What is the point of this epigram? Can you translate it so as to keep the ambiguity of line 2?

2 Find out what you can about Roman games and pastimes. (See notes on '*turricula*' and line 1; and IV.5 question 6.) Make a set of *tali*.

3 'Most people think that men and women gamble to make money. And, without doubt, many do. But some also gamble to lose money' (J.K. Galbraith, *The Listener*, 20 January 1977). Discuss gambling and its motivation.

Section V

The verse in this section is all autobiographical. It is not however autobiography for its own sake and may not even be accurate. We lack alternative evidence to act as a control. These qualifications are particularly important in the case of the passages by Horace and Ovid, for here the reader is deprived of the surrounding context which in all three cases invests the autobiography with a special purpose. Horace uses his

lines (V.1) as part of a general argument about equality of opportunity
(see V.1 note on Context, and Discussion). The extracts (V.2, V.3) from
Ovid's *Tristia* are both aimed at least as much at securing recall from
Tomis as at setting down the facts of Ovid's life. V.2 is an apology,
without loss of face, for inability to measure up to Augustus' political
expectations, and forms part of a larger-scale attempt at self-justification,
calculated not to offend Augustus. The narrative of the departure to
exile (V.3) is set at the same target, but uses pathos both in our excerpt
and in the poem as a whole in an attempt to secure support for the
poet's return. But these three passages are not just to be seen as individual elements from arguments developed at greater length: if that is
all they were, then there would be no place for them in an anthology.
They are, in addition, all carefully composed in poetry of great sensitivity, ranging in style from the colloquial (V.1) to the epic (V.3). Furthermore, they *should* be taken (in the absence of evidence to the contrary)
as reflecting, if possibly with some distortion, the lives of Horace and
Ovid. There was after all little to be gained by falsification when the
results were to be published for scrutiny by contemporary readers, some
of whom knew the facts of the case, and it is worth remarking that both
Horace and Ovid offer gently uncomplimentary observations about
themselves ('singultim', V.1.3; 'fugax', V.2.24; 'torpuerant', V.3.4) —
quite a good pointer to overall authenticity. The writer however must
be selective in the details that he puts on record, and to this extent the
extracts inevitably give a less than complete picture. Also, we should
remember in the case of V.3 that Ovid may have been modelling his
account on Virgil (see Discussion). Martial's relationship with Charidemus
(V.4) has to be extreme to be amusing, but there is no reason to reject
the basic sentiments of the poem — even if we do have to make allow-
ances for the exaggeration in line 9. True to the facts or not, the epigram ought rather to be judged by its wit and technique. By contrast,
V.5 presents facts about an honour bestowed on Martial which could
not have been invented, since part of the poem's point is its praise of
Domitian for this kindness. The existence (or not) of Martial's wife is
much more contentious, but is largely incidental to the effect of the
epigram.

V.1 Horace, Satires *I.6.54—64*

Context

Horace had no advantages of noble birth (see Introduction 3), and in
the complex poem from which this extract is taken he argues that
'humble birth ought not to be an obstacle to success, at least when the
success is of a non-political kind and when the man in question deserves
the honour' (Rudd, 1966: 42). This passage describes Horace's presentation to Maecenas in 38 B.C., and his acceptance into Maecenas' *clientela*.

Language and content

3 **singultim**: probably coined by Horace.
locutus: for the use of deponent perfect participles without strict reference to time, see Woodcock section 103, and for non-deponents cf.
'alite capta' in IV.3.7.
6 **caballo**: the prosaic, colloquial word (cf. French 'cheval', etc.).
10 **turpi, honestum**: the commentators disagree as to whether these words
are neuter or masculine. It makes little difference, and the ambiguity
may be intentional. Cf. Rudd, 1966: 41: 'who distinguish the honour-
able from the base'.

Discussion

Horace is concerned to refute two malicious suggestions: (i) that his promotion was a lucky accident; (ii) that he did not deserve the patronage
of Maecenas.

The first suggestion is attacked directly and forcibly — the emphatically placed 'nulla' (1) being a strong alternative to 'non'. The line is
carefully structured for maximum impact, with 'mihi' and 'te' appropriately juxtaposed but separated from 'fors' by the caesura. Set against
the operations of 'fors' are Virgil and Varius, with Virgil in the place of
honour; 'optimus' presumably refers to the poetic achievement as well
as being a term of endearment. There is a dignified simplicity about this
line, as in so much of this short passage. Horace deliberately passes over
an opportunity for self-glorification, in favour of the restrained 'quid
essem' (2). It may well be (so Rudd, 1966: 41) that Horace was playing
down his talent in order to avoid inflaming people's resentment. But it
could equally be argued that the restraint of 'quid essem' combined
with purposeful selection of sponsors is more suggestive than a catalogue
of achievements, and that Horace realised this.

Line 3 sweeps us into the presence. There is only the merest suggestion of a time-lapse, since it suits Horace's book to imply that no further
consultation or investigation was necessary. The heaviness of the metre
suggests deference and the 'c'/'g' alliteration supports the nervousness
of 'pauca' and 'singultim'. The impression of embarrassed shyness
carries over into line 4, the line being virtually parenthetic within an
increasingly complex and rambling sentence, and the excited, nervy 'p'-
alliteration being very prominent (cf. Fraenkel 104, n.2). 'infans' is
brought forward before 'namque' for considerable emphasis and there is
a nice play on the literal meaning ('not-speaking', hence *a priori*
'prohibebat . . . profari'). It also forces on our attention the picture
Horace wants us to have of him at this interview, still wet behind the
ears and pure as the driven snow. He was in fact just twenty-six. In
what he does manage to stammer out to Maecenas he shows himself not
succumbing to the temptation to create a gilt-edged background for himself. The repeated 'non ego' is forceful: 'others might, but I do not'.
The impression we are left with is of a man of integrity, just the sort of

character to give the lie to the second malicious suggestion. The irony of 'claro . . . patre' (5) obviously lies in the fact that, so far from being famous, Horace's father was no more than a freedman — already strongly emphasised (*45—6). The phrase accentuates the distance between Horace and the noble Maecenas, and also marks off Horace from his aristocratic predecessor Lucilius, who probably did run an estate at Tarentum (Williams, 1968: 454). The horse on which Horace does not ride round his estate is obviously an expensive model (though the descriptive force of 'Satureiano' in part affects 'rura') and the deferred 'caballo' is amusingly denigratory, like describing a Bentley as a banger. Further, the plebeian word prepares the ground for the simple structure — a relief after lines 4—6 — and simple sentiments of 'quod eram narro' (7), vividly placed in the historic present and reflecting the 'quid essem' of line 2 but with the forthrightness of the indicative.

What Fraenkel (104) calls 'the painful reserve' of Maecenas is broken, but this reticence ('pauca', 8, in emphatic position) is specifically characterised by Horace as habitual, unlike his own tongue-tied stuttering. Line 8 compresses much into little: we move from Maecenas' few words, which are no sooner uttered than done, through Horace's exit, to the fateful recall and Maecenas' decision. The first half of the line looks disjointed, but elision makes it flow, and we are so quickly back with Maecenas that the nine-month interval seems a little surprising. Why should Horace include such a detail in this sparse narrative? Maecenas was away on a diplomatic mission at this time and he would doubtless wish to have had observed and assessed by his agents a man who had opted for the wrong side at Philippi; one can thus explain the delay, without throwing light on its inclusion. A cogent explanation is that Horace did not wish to seem in any way thrusting (contrast the pest in VIII.2), but was prepared to sit and wait for an answer; this would again serve to establish his character against the second malicious suggestion. The decision of Maecenas is heralded with 'iubesque' (8) and left in suspense over the end of the line. The privilege achieved is toned down into a simplicity ('esse in amicorum numero', 9) which will offend few, and Horace immediately expresses his thanks in terms which make any objection to the appointment an explicit criticism of Maecenas himself. The passage ends with a further impassioned statement ('p'-alliteration) of Horace's moral credentials, again avoiding mention of his poetic talents.

Rudd (1966: 49ff.) sees this satire as an attempt to redefine and re-establish the old Roman concepts of *nobilitas*, *dignitas* and *libertas*, 'a thoroughgoing critique of the aristocratic-republican system' (1966: 51). Our short passage shows how Horace wants moral values to super-sede the accidents of birth, and informed choice to supersede the ran-dom selection now practised by so many patrons. The options are stated rhetorically by a device which occurs very frequently in the poem as a whole, and three times in our excerpt: 'not this, but that'. In our piece we find 'not chance, but Virgil and Varius' (1—2); 'not nobility of birth, but honesty and simplicity of character' (5—7); 'not a famous father, but purity of life and heart' (11). Nonetheless, the most immediate effect of this passage is to provide an apparent record of a historical event. How accurate it is, we shall never know. Horace is at liberty to mould the event for his own poetic purpose. But it is persuasively realistic, not least the cosy intimacy suggested by the profusion (in different forms) of 'ego' and 'tu'. Fraenkel (103f.) comments: 'This is, on a small scale, a perfect dramatic scene, emotionally strong and rich in undertones. The stifling embarrassment of the young poet, the painful reserve of Maecenas, and the sincerity of the two men come out with forceful directness. The choice of words is as apt as the sound is suggestive.'

Questions

1 What criticism is Horace defending himself against in line 1?
2 What is it that Virgil and Varius do on Horace's behalf?
3 How is Horace's nervousness suggested in lines 3—4?
4 Why does Horace select and place so emphatically the word 'infans' (4)?
5 What sort of picture emerges of Horace?
6 How complex is the structure of the sentences in this passage? Is there any reason why some should be markedly less complex than others?
7 How, in the last two lines, does Horace guard himself against criticism from those who were jealous of his promotion?
8 What, if anything, is the object of Horace's attack?

V.2 Ovid, Tristia IV.10.15—40

Context

Ovid wrote *Tristia* IV.10 in self-justification during his exile, though only the second half of the elegy makes specific reference to this experience. Lines *1—14 are about Ovid's birth at Sulmo in 43 B.C., his equestrian rank and the birth of his brother exactly a year before his own birthday. Our excerpt is virtually the only evidence for Ovid's adolescence (Wheeler 4—11).

Language and content

1 **parentis**: see Introduction 4.
2 **insignes . . . ab arte viros**: these may have included *grammatici* as well as *rhetores* (see *CLC* Unit I Stage 10 and Unit IV slide 25; Paoli Ch. 15; Balsdon, 1969: 92—106; Liversidge 76—80), since Ovid and his brother were clearly in Rome for some time before the assumption of the *toga virilis* (14) which was usually taken between about fourteen and sixteen.

3 **frater ad eloquium ... tendebat:** rhetoric, with a political career as its prime objective, would have been a staple diet of both boys' education. Seneca the Elder had heard Ovid declaiming (esp. *Controversiae* II.2.8–12) and says he was considered a 'bonus declamator' and versified many of his own teacher's *sententiae.* He was taught by Arellius Fuscus and Porcius Latro.

'The kind of rhetoric which made the earliest impact on Ovid was simply the study and practice under professional teachers of the art of effective speech. If this art was taught with especial reference to public *speaking* in all its forms, it nonetheless drew its illustrations from literature at large and from poetry as well as prose, and was therefore also of relevance to effective *writing'* (Higham in Herescu 32).

4 **verbosi ... fori:** 'Orators had to compete with one another in the Forum before a number of equally exacting but otherwise very different audiences: the Assembly, the Senate, and the courts' (Grant, 1970: 15, and see further Ch. 6 and 149).

6 **furtim:** 'without my father realising'.

8 **Maeonides:** the patronymic 'son of Maeon' sounds very grand, and Ovid on twelve other occasions prefers 'Homerus'.

12 Cf. Pope, *Epistle to Dr Arbuthnot,* 127–8:

> As yet a child, not yet a fool to fame,
> I lisp'd in numbers, for the numbers came.

The point is not that 'the numbers came' without effort, but rather that Ovid had a vocation to poetry.

14 **liberior ... toga** = *toga pura* or *toga virilis,* as opposed to the striped *toga praetexta* of childhood. On the Roman equivalent of the *bar mitzvah,* see Balsdon, 1969: 119–21.
fratri, mihi: Form C (dative) of agent. Cf. VI.3.28.

15 **cum lato ... clavo:** '(purple clothed our shoulders) with a broad stripe'. Augustus 'wanted senators' sons to adopt the broad stripe, the *latus clavus,* immediately on assuming the *toga virilis,* to attend meetings of the senate as spectators, to engage quickly in military service' (Balsdon, 1969: 120). Augustus also conferred the *latus clavus* on sons of wealthy *equites* (Syme 359).

16 **et:** 'but at the same time', 'and yet' (*OLD* 14).
studium: reminiscent of line 7, must refer to Ovid's obsession with poetry.

17 **annos:** Ovid's brother died in 24/23 B.C., when Ovid himself was only nineteen.

19 The republican *cursus honorum,* which laid down the order in which (and often the age at which) the various political magistracies should be attempted, was extended in the early principate (see *OCD* s.v. *cursus honorum*).
primos: used punningly to mean both 'first' and 'top'.

20 **viris ... tribus:** as a preliminary to the *cursus honorum* proper, Ovid was one of the *tresviri capitales,* or possibly the *tresviri monetales,* minor officials with (respectively) a policing function or supervision over the mint.

21 **clavi mensura coacta est:** the narrow purple upright stripe (*angustus clavus*) of the equestrian tunic, rather than the *latus clavus* of a senator. 'He might have become a lawyer, a Roman senator, a provincial governor: he preferred to be a fashionable poet — and he paid for it in the end. Through the recalcitrance of P. Ovidius, a certain Q. Varius Geminus

acquired the distinction, proudly recorded on his tomb, of being the
first senator from all the Paeligni' (Syme 363). No doubt such prominent exposure would have been alarming for a man who was temperamentally unsuited.

24   **fugax**: ironical choice of word — 'fuga' = exile.
26   **otia**: the view that writing poetry was the antithesis of work was a tra-
     ditional Roman assumption. We should be cautious about accepting
     Ovid's declaration at its face value. 'otium' is often used to mean merely
     the security of private life. See further, Hubbard in Costa 4—5.

Discussion

In line 1, the stress is on the purposeful thoroughness of the educational
process initiated by Ovid's father ('protinus', 'ex-', 'teneri', 'cura'). Line
2, by contrast, neatly catches the awe with which Ovid and his brother
entered on their Roman schooling. 'teneri' has prepared us for this, and
now the ultra-simple, un-prefixed 'imus' is set against the rest of the line,
heavy with authority and 'r'-alliteration and opened by the metrically
weighty 'insignes'. The brother is introduced in lines 3—4 to provide a
convenient foil for Ovid in lines 5—6. He is colourfully described:
'viridi . . . ab aevo' has a Virgilian flavour, and the military imagery of
line 4, with its repeated 'for-' and imaginative use of 'fortia' is very
striking. If the reader is aware of what Ovid later (17—18) tells us about
his brother's premature death, the parallel phrases 'tendebat ad' and
'natus ad', indicating the promise that precedes achievement, hold a
terrible irony. 'at mihi' (5) warns of the contrast: 'caelestia sacra' and
the periphrasis of line 6 are elevated ways of describing poetry. What
starts as gentle dabbling ('placebant', 5) is to become much more
serious ('trahebat', 6). Poetic inspiration is personified (as so often) and
the poet, under her influence, is shown as not fully responsible for what
he writes. (Was this perhaps intended to weigh with Augustus? Cf.
'sponte sua' in 11.) There is a nice ambivalence about 'furtim' (6),
which in context refers to the 'imperceptibly' growing attractions of
the Muse, but is then seen to lead us on to the following couplet: Ovid
has to write 'stealthily' in order to avoid the notice of his father.

A lesser writer might at this point have proceeded from the divergent
scholastic bents of the two brothers straight to their subsequent careers.
Ovid humanises the narrative with reported speech and the sort of episode from domestic life which must seem curiously familiar to most
adolescent boys. The father's objection (7) is the perennial scourge of
the liberal arts, and no doubt it was a fairly characteristic utterance for
Romans outside the circle of literary practitioners who comprise our
main authority for Roman attitudes. It certainly seems well in character
with a wealthy but careful Paelignian *eques*. (For an approximate
contemporary of Ovid's father, also obsessed with money-making, cf.
Varro in the *Res Rusticae*; e.g. III.2.7—18.) The father is Yorkshire in
his bluntness, and picks an example that suits his case. Ovid however has

the last laugh, for he puts into his father's mouth the grandiose, poetic patronymic. Ovid professes willingness to abjure poetry, but by the end of line 9, with its heightened reference to the Muse and marked sequence of mournful 'ō' sounds, the reader must be a little doubtful of his ability. Then in lines 9–12 Ovid gives the reader close focus on his attempts to break free from the Muse. The several imperfects of lines 10–12 and the repeated 'temptabam', recalling his father's word in line 7, show the extent of Ovid's effort, while the plodding first half of line 12, giving place to the regular dactylic ending, may show a last despairing fling at prose.

Line 13 increases the pace, with several years compressed into a single line. 'labentibus' in this sense is highly poetic, and its suggestion that the years pass without one's noticing is underlined by 'tacito passu'. The first word of line 14, 'liberior', takes a lot of emphasis, since it is kept so far from the 'toga' which it qualifies. Furthermore, Ovid selects 'toga liberior' in preference to the more regular descriptions of the adult garb. Propertius seems to have been the first to use the term 'toga libera', and he applies it to his own coming of age in *Elegy* IV.1.132. Ovid may be consciously associating himself with his literary predecessor; by expanding the adjective into its comparative form, he may be suggesting that the new freedom is only relative to the stultifying influence which his father continued to impose through his ambitious plans for his children. In any case, the new opportunities symbolised by the *toga virilis* are trumped by those springing from the broad stripe of line 15 (see notes). Immediately (16) Ovid establishes that his vocation to poetry is still there: it has not been a mere youthful obsession.

Line 17 moves us quickly forward again. The inverted 'cum'-clause and the poetic periphrasis for 'twenty' ('viginti' *is* used in hexameters) set an elevated, slightly artificial tone — which is broken by the curt 'cum perit' and the simply expressed (but nonetheless emotional) 'coepi parte carere mei'. Alliteration and rhyme add to the effect: with the consonantal structure of 'cum perit et' closely mirrored by that of 'coepi parte'.

The next couplet (19–20) closes a swift shutter on this personal grief (forceful 'cepimus', with no connective). Ovid alludes to his junior magistracies, laying some stress on these achievements of his youth ('tenerae', 'primos', 19) and making the most of the word-play on 'viris . . . tribus' ('tribus' set next to 'una', 20). The politician's progress is interrupted violently at the caesura of line 21. And there is no longer any attempt to shift responsibility on to the Muse, for line 22 generalises about Ovid's own weakness — a point which is amplified in the lines which follow. Ovid confesses that he lacked the mental and physical stamina for political office and thus acted like a runaway slave. Only then do the Muses enter the scene, when Ovid has already committed himself to withdrawal from politics. The Muses persuade rather than order, and the final judgment is Ovid's ('iudicio . . . meo', 26). It would be interesting to know how Augustus might have viewed these excuses. He could hardly have approved of Ovid's action, for the poet had failed to measure up to the demands of a society where '*otium* was suspect' (Hubbard in Costa 5), and a political career was expected of a young man in Ovid's position. Yet Ovid seems to have hoped that an honest confession might secure his recall.

When writing these lines, Ovid would doubtless have been aware of their potential audience in Rome, although the poem is technically dedicated to 'posteritas' (*2). If Dickinson is right (in Binns, 1973: 180) in suggesting that Ovid originally intended *Tristia* IV.10 as a tail-piece to the whole work, then the sentiments of the poem would have been crucial for Ovid's chances of escape from Tomis. In these early lines we have a strong statement of Ovid's position. His conversion to poetry was a slow, spontaneous process against which he struggled. Had Ovid's brother lived, his rhetorical gifts would have taken at least one Ovidius Naso to the senate. Ovid went through the motions of political advancement after his brother's death, but felt himself inadequate for top-level politics. He followed his 'iudicium' and the persuasion of the Muses and achieved (so the poem goes on) immortality through his verse. There is no flattery here, no loss of self-respect: Ovid sets out his failures to please Augustus and counterbalances these with his poetic achievement, in the hopes that Augustus will be moved to clemency.

Questions

1 What picture of Ovid's father do we get (a) from lines 1—2; (b) from lines 7—8?
2 Why does Ovid introduce his brother into this poem?
3 When Ovid wants to say, 'I found poetry attractive', he refers on two occasions (line 6 and line 25) to the Muses. Why do you think he does this?
4 List the various facts Ovid gives us about his early life. Would a biographer have included any other information? Is this really autobiography, or is Ovid's material selected with another end in view?
5 What is the point of studying literature?
6 Find out what you can about (a) Roman education; (b) the ceremony of relinquishing the *toga praetexta*; (c) the various ways in which different types of dress were used to mark status-differences in Roman society. See *OCD* s.v. 'dress', *toga*, *clavus angustus*, *latus*; Paoli Ch. 7.

V.3 Ovid, Tristia *I.3.5—26*

Context

Tristia I.3, recapturing Ovid's last moments in Rome, is justly described

(Dickinson in Binns 163) as 'a carefully constructed work of haunting poetry'. It is composed of four main sections; our excerpt is the first, which gives Ovid's own extreme reaction and that of his wife, friends and household to his impending exile. The four-line introduction (omitted) has established an atmosphere of gloom and foreboding.

Language and content

1 **lux**: Ovid has twice so far (*1 and *3) declared his intention to write about his last night ('nox') in Rome; so 'lux' is the more unexpected (see Discussion). The line is phrased like epic poetry — cf. Virgil, *Aeneid* II.268, just before the fall of Troy (see line 22).

2 **finibus extremae . . . Ausoniae**: Ovid must leave land at the very edge of Italy; and the adjective (cf. line 11) also suggests that this is his last glimpse of the country.

4 **longa . . . mora**: Wilkinson (1955: 313) translates, 'My mind was atrophied by long despair'. 'mora' must be the time between the passing of the sentence of exile and Ovid's departure.

6 **vestis**: on the cold climate of Tomis, see *Tristia* III.10.13–34 (quoted and translated in Wilkinson, 1955: 326–7).

12 **erat**: for the singular verb with 'unus et alter' see, e.g., Pliny the Younger, *Letters* II.13.3. Here it has the effect of emphasising Ovid's loneliness.

13 **uxor**: Ovid's third wife was a member of the 'gens Fabia' and on close terms with Marcia, wife of the influential Paullus Fabius Maximus, and she was also a friend of Augustus' wife Livia. Ovid always speaks of her highly; she stayed in Rome during the whole of Ovid's exile (A.D. 8– c. 17) to protect the family property.

15 **nata**: cf. I.2.4. Ovid had one daughter, whose name he never mentions — perhaps for metrical reasons. Her mother was probably Ovid's second wife. By the time of Ovid's exile, the daughter was twice married and had produced two grandchildren for her father (*Tristia* IV.10.75–6). Her second husband was the senator Fidus Cornelius, who was seen by Seneca the Younger weeping in the senate when Corbulo called him a plucked ostrich ('struthocamelum depilatum', *Dialogus* II.17.1).
Libycis: 'Libya' was used generally for the whole of North Africa. Ovid's daughter seems to have accompanied her husband on a tour of duty to one of the two senatorial provinces (Africa and Cyrenaica).

17 **quocumque aspiceres**: hypothetical subjunctive — 'wherever you might have looked (if you were present)'.

18 **intus**: the wailing at real funerals took place outside during the procession from the house to the place of burial outside the walls.

21 For parallel expressions, see Virgil, *Eclogues* I.23 and *Georgics* IV.176: 'si parva licet componere magnis', 'if one may compare small with large'.

Discussion

The passage gives us a vivid and moving picture of anguished separation. There is no reason to suspect its factual accuracy, but it is important to remember that it was composed after the event, was no doubt intended to create sympathy for the poet, and was primarily a work of poetic creativity and only secondarily reportage.

The approach of day (1) is usually a good sign. For Ovid, the dawn is ominous, while the choice of Virgilian 'Ausoniae' (2) makes the event

rather more than just a private tragedy. With the time of the action
established, Ovid introduces a line or two of flashback (marked by the
pluperfects). 'nec spatium' implies that Augustus had allowed very little
time for preparation; 'nec mens' shows that Ovid had been unable to
make good use of whatever time he did have. 'longa . . . mora' (4) seems
to conflict with 'nec spatium' (3). Does Ovid mean us to suppose that
his psychological state was such as to make any length of time insuf-
ficient for practicalities and yet at the same time impose an apparently
never-ending strain on the emotions? 'torpuerant' (4) suggests a physical
condition associated with illness, and its metaphorical use here looks
forward to the ensuing 'death' of Ovid in lines 17—18. The numbness is
well illustrated by the negative enumeration of lines 5—6. Ovid is too
dazed to make even the simplest preparations. 'vestis opisve' suggest the
harsh environment in store. Thus lines 5—6 build up pity for the writer,
as well as demonstrate the practical results of Ovid's psychological condition. In lines 7—10, he returns to self-analysis. Lines 7—8 are remarkable for alliteration of 'i', mostly long or in a heavy syllable, and mostly
on the beat of the metrical foot. The pentameter has rhyming '-ae': this
sequence of internal rhymes (cf. 2 and 4) is far above the average frequency in Ovid (usually c. 20%: Platnauer 49), and it is likely that it
was intended to contribute to the doleful atmosphere. The image of
'Iovis ignibus' (7) works two ways: it both exaggerates the immensity
of the poet's misfortune, and (at least ostensibly) it flatters Augustus
who was responsible for it. The memorable description 'vivit et est vitae
nescius ipse suae' (8) — cf. Eliot's 'living and partly living' — is the
stronger for 'vivit' being held over from line 7. Again, this picture of
vegetable existence prepares for the funeral imagery of lines 18—19.
Unrelieved depression, however, is no way to keep your reader's attention. Ovid now shows his quality by extracting himself from the depths
of despair without in any way spoiling the air of sadness which lies over
the whole of this piece. Line 9 is a strikingly imaginative conception.
'dolor ipse', personified and contrasting with the immediately preceding
'(ego) nescius ipse', removes the cloud from Ovid's spirit. Ovid's grief is
now so intensified by the imminence of departure that it begins to focus
and clarify his faculties rather than paralyse them. The picture is both
apt and convincing: 'when a man knows he is to be hanged in a fort-
night, it concentrates his mind wonderfully'.

   Ovid's strength returns ('ēt tāndēm sēnsūs cōnv-', 10; 'ēxtrēmūm
maēstōs', 11) and he summons up the emotional energy to speak to his
friends. Lest we misinterpret the significance of this 'recovery', Ovid
includes no fewer than three words to remind us of the sad circumstances of his departure ('extremum', 'maestos', 'abiturus'). Even
'amicos' has a certain poignancy, for there will be no friends travelling
with Ovid (cf. line 5). There is a cutting edge to the answering pentameter (12), and this complaint about his friends' desertion appears in

several of the poems from exile. Ovid has shifted from the self-analysis
of lines 3–10 to the reaction of his friends in lines 11–12. The next
couplet, an earnest of fuller coverage later in the poem, is devoted completely to his wife. Lines 13–14 both have great emotional power and
are technically complex. The repetition 'flens'/'flentem' emphasises the
mood of despondency. 'amans' (13) works both adjectivally with 'uxor',
and verbally: her tears show love in action. 'amans' and 'flens' embrace
their object, Ovid ('flentem'), positioned between the double caesura.
Line 14 provides a gentle variation on the same theme. Though less
rhetorically contrived than the hexameter, the clearly-marked '-gnas'/
'genas' rhyme draws proper attention to the crucial 'indignas'.

   The first word of line 15 shifts the focus to Ovid's daughter. By
pointing up her separation ('procul', 'Libycis', 'ab-', 'diversa'), Ovid
exploits the irony that as he sets off for exile his daughter should be at
the ends of the Empire. At line 17, the reader is drawn (hypothetically)
into the action, as Ovid's focus widens to include the whole household.
'luctus gemitusque' (17) are inescapably reminiscent of funerals, held
by night, and the developing image is finally crystallised in line 18 and
allowed to run on into lines 19–20. 'meo' (19) is sharply cut off from
'funere' in order to isolate a logically startling idea — reporting on one's
own funeral. We have seen the reactions of Ovid, his friends, his family
and slaves: and in line 20 it is as if even the house weeps for his plight.

   The sequence has now progressed towards a conclusion, which Ovid
provides in lines 21–2. He paraphrases an excusatory formula from
Virgil (see note). But in Virgil's estimation the 'parva' were indeed
unimportant (Mantua as compared with Rome; bees as compared with
the Cyclopes). For Ovid, his exile is primary, and 'parvis' is no more
than a deferential nod to the sanctity of legend. Spondees give weight
to 'exemplis in parvis', to which the dactylic 'grandibus' is juxtaposed.
Similarly, the comparison with a besieged town is not unusual. In
Propertius, *Elegies* IV.8.56, e.g., Cynthia bursts in looking as frightening
as the sack of a city. In that instance the tone is light-hearted and the
image, though contrasting markedly with the party which is under way,
is introduced by no apology. Ovid, by contrast, clearly feels that there
is a great similarity between his own plight and Troy, yet even so
apologises for the presumption. The comparison has been written so as
to correspond quite closely with the sack of Troy as described in Virgil,
Aeneid II:

   1 The weeping in Ovid's household is matched by *Aeneid* II.298,
      486–8, 776.
   2 Ovid's state of mind in lines 3–8 corresponds to Aeneas'
      amentia in *Aeneid* II.314, 558, 594–5.
   3 Ovid has to leave the scene at Caesar's decree, just as Aeneas
      follows the command of Hector in *Aeneid* II.289. Ovid is
      blasted by 'Iovis ignibus', just as it is Jupiter ('superi regnator
      Olympi', *Aeneid* II.779) who effectively despatches Aeneas.

4 In both episodes it is night (cf. *Aeneid* II.268, 801–2).

5 Ovid suffers exile, as Aeneas goes off to 'longa exsilia' (*Aeneid* II.780).

6 Ovid is unable to take leave of his daughter, just as Aeneas loses his wife Creusa (*Aeneid* II.738); but embraces his wife, just as Aeneas attempts a tearful embrace of Creusa's phantom (*Aeneid* II.790–4). Ovid was to lack the comfort of an Anchises and a Iulus.

The parallels would no doubt have made themselves felt to Ovid's audience even without the Virgilian feel of the first couplet. The comparison serves to provide our excerpt with a dignified ending on a heroic rather than pathetic level. Ovid preserves his self-respect.

Questions

1 Write your own prose description of Ovid's mental state (3–10). What precisely happens in line 9? How true to life is this?

2 Why were Ovid's friends now so depleted (12)?

3 Discuss the construction of line 13.

4 Why should Ovid mention his daughter if she is not present (15–16)?

5 To what extent has the reader been prepared for the rather extravagant comparison with a funeral (18 and 19)?

6 Consider the structure of this piece. What does Ovid focus on, and for how long? How effectively are the various sections linked together? How successful is this as a self-contained piece, without the support of its context?

7 Read a translation of Virgil, *Aeneid* II. How close a parallel is the capture of Troy to Ovid's departure for exile? If Ovid meant his readers to remember Virgil, what did he hope to gain? Why does he apologise in line 21?

V.4 Martial, Epigrams *XI.39*

Language and content

1 **cunarum**: there can be seen at Herculaneum the remains of a wooden cradle on rockers.
fueras: see note on I.3.1.
Charideme: apparently Martial's *paedagogus*. See note on III.8.10.

3 **sudaria**: (= sweat-cloths) presumably put round the neck to catch the shavings, or for wiping the razor.

5 **tibi**: Form C (dative) of person judging (Woodcock section 65).

10 **ferulis**: see III.8.10.

11 **Tyrios**: on the production of purple, see Paoli 161–2; Muir on *Aeneid* IV.262. The process was associated with Phoenicia (hence Tyre), the first centre of the trade. The actual colour varied, with brown, violet and red predominant.
unxive capillos: a wide variety of fragrant preparations was used for the hair. Capua was a big centre for the production of this luxury item. See note on III.7.2.

12 **fecerat**: see note on I.3.1.
13 **trientes**: technically thirds of a *sextarius*, so that one *triens* would be just less than one-fifth of a litre.
14 **sit**: subjunctive because the possibility is hypothetical (Woodcock sections 250—1).
15 **Catonem**: the claim to unyielding standards of moral behaviour was established by Marcus Porcius Cato, famous for his insistence on the destruction of Carthage in 146 B.C., and sustained by his great-grandson Marcus Porcius Cato Uticensis, the Stoic politician who committed suicide at Utica in 46 B.C.

Discussion

The relationship between Martial and Charidemus is deftly summarised in the first couplet, with just a hint in 'adsiduus' (2) of the tension that is to permeate the rest of the epigram.

Line 3 cuts swiftly to Martial's manhood as suggested by that prime symbol of virility, the beard. It is worth remembering the seriousness with which Roman society viewed a young man's first shave, the *depositio barbae*: Trimalchio was not the only one to lay up the clippings in the household shrine (Petronius, *Satyricon* 29). But there is no suggestion that this is such a serious moment and the next line (4) is light-hearted. Martial is so virile that no sooner do we have him shaved (3) than incipient growth (4) is troubling his girlfriend (cf. III.7). The sound-effect of '*pu*ncta *pu*ella' perhaps assists the humorous quality of the line. 'tibi' (5) comes in smart contrast with 'meis', and the rest of the couplet is heavy (metrically) with the fear engendered by Charidemus. Anxious to make it clear that the fault is not in himself, Martial now cites 'vilicus' (5), 'dispensator' (6) and 'domus' (6) in a neat little tricolon crescendo held together by repeated 'te'. 'ludere' (7) is emphatically placed outside the clause which governs it. Martial at first seems to be harking back to his childhood again, a childhood deprived of play; but the present tense of 'permittis' and the sense of 'amare', the final word of the line balancing the first, spark off in retrospect the secondary meanings of 'ludere' more appropriate for adults — 'to gamble', 'to make love', 'to write light verse' and generally 'to have fun' (see *OLD*). None of these does the puritanical Charidemus allow. He, by contrast, takes all manner of liberties, as the balanced line 8 suggests. Line 9 is more specific and more vivid, the abrupt list in asyndeton suggesting that the critical tutor is ever-watchful. 'ferulis' (10) is introduced to give a further hint of boyhood, but this Charideman view of Martial as a schoolboy is immediately contradicted by the sophisticated portrait of line 11. Martial is being daringly fashionable, and the spondees of line 11 and the first half of line 12 help to build up our anticipation of Charidemus' response: 'Your father never did that'. This is Charidemus' only utterance, a remark carefully calculated, given the prominence of the *paterfamilias*, to deflate the young man about town.

'pater' is of course left till last word. We have now heard about Charidemus' strictures on women and clothes; not surprisingly, the final
descriptive couplet (13—14) deals with drink. This gives us a memorable
and highly credible picture of the old retainer putting on the moral
pressure (13). He is spurred on by intense feelings of responsibility for
the family property, the legacy of many years' service.

Martial's growing irritation explodes in the sharp 'desine' (15), followed by the heavy, deliberate 'nōn possŭm lĭbērtŭm fērre' and the
mention of Cato, personification of old-fashioned temperance and
rigidity. Martial therefore decides to confront Charidemus with a witness to his virility, in the hopes that this will at last bring the old slave
to a sense of proportion. No doubt the girlfriend, an outsider to the
family, will be better able to get home to Charidemus. She can at least
testify to Martial's sexual prowess (cf. Ovid *Amores* III.7.20), if not to
the fact that he is now grown up: 'esse virum' can mean both.

Questions

1 What can we learn about the character of Charidemus?
2 What picture of himself does Martial present? How old and
   how experienced does he want us to imagine him?
3 Find out about the functions of the *paedagogus*, the *vilicus*
   and the *dispensator*. (See, e.g., Paoli 122; Duff 90 and 93.)
4 Is it possible to imagine the same sort of conflict arising today?
   Consider occasions when you have felt like saying 'sed tibi non
   crevi'.

V.5 Martial II.92

Context

In the previous poem (*Epigrams* II.91) Martial has requested from
Domitian the rights of a father of three sons (see note on line 1) either
in return for the pleasure his poetry has afforded the Emperor, or in
consolation for the displeasure it has caused!

Language and content

The metre is hendecasyllabic. See notes on II.1.

1 **natorum . . . ius trium**: Augustus, most completely in the *Lex Iulia et
   Papia Poppaea* of A.D. 9, was the first to confer special privileges on the
   fathers of three children. Later, the privileges were often given to child-
   less or unmarried people, thus vitiating the aim of stimulating child-
   bearing in the upper classes. Martial was given the privileges by both
   Titus and Domitian. They included the right to receive inheritances
   bequeathed to bachelors (debarred from inheriting) and preferential
   treatment when standing for political office — including the right to
   anticipate the stipulated age-limit or reduce the prescribed interval
   between offices. See Lewis and Reinhold II: 253—4.

3 **solus qui poterat**: the addressee of the previous poem (see note on Context) is 'Caesar', at this time (? A.D. 86) Domitian.
valebis: a colloquial, familiar alternative to 'vale!'.
uxor: there is no conclusive evidence for Martial being married. This
passage may imply that he was not (see Discussion).
4 For the sense of this line, see Discussion.

Discussion

The placing of 'natorum' and 'Musarum' and the similarity of their end-
ings set up a connexion between them. Martial's poetry is the equivalent
of other men's children; it is his contribution to the perpetuity of the
Empire. The end of line 3, where Martial turns from honorific address
of Domitian to familiar address of his wife, is even more witty if Martial
were generally known to be unmarried. If not a bachelor, then he is pro-
posing (none too seriously) a separation from his wife. If unmarried,
then he is saying goodbye to the possibility of marrying and hence of
having legitimate children. Both interpretations tally with line 4, where
Martial is saying that he must not slight Domitian by now producing
three children and thus nullifying the Emperor's special concession. The
merit of the poem, such as it is, lies in the way Martial contrives somewhat wilfully to interpret this special concession as a positive veto on
his producing children — hardly Domitian's intention.

Questions

1 What is the sense of line 4?
2 Should poets expect to be rewarded by the state?
3 What right has the state to control the production of children?

Section VI

The subject of this section is Death. Only one of the poems (VI.2,
'diffugere nives') has no specific reference to a dead individual, although
Martial's epigram on the boy killed by the icicle (VI.4) shows very little
involvement with the subject of this misadventure, if factual. Martial
uses the tragic accident, carefully detailed, to provide the basis for some
stirring remarks about the uncertainty of life. Horace, in VI.2, is also
concerned with the universal circumstance; but he draws his conclusions
not so much from examples of the permanency of death as from cross-
reference to, and contrast with, the naturally recurring cycles of nature.
Where he does use human examples, they are — with the exception of
the still-living Torquatus — either antique or mythical. This gives a uni-
versality to his poem which the Martial epigram never aspires to; and
the Ode is in other respects richer and of infinitely greater range. The
Ovid piece on the death of Tibullus (VI.3) and the Catullus poem (VI.1,
'si quicquam mutis gratum') are, like VI.2, sophisticated literary pro-

ductions. Both poems rely very heavily on the works of other authors: neither is properly intelligible without some appreciation of this background. Both poems adopt a highly serious tone, obviously appropriate for the death of a friend, but from time to time lapse into markedly lighter material. Both end optimistically. Martial's epigram for Erotion, VI.5, reflects perhaps the closest-felt sorrow. The sadness is evident, despite the conventional nature of several of the themes: the poem's very simplicity makes a good contrast with the relative complexities of Catullus and Ovid.

VI.1 Catullus, Poems *96*

Language and content

1 **mutis:** cf. 'mutam cinerem' in *Poems* 101.4 ('multas per gentes' = *CLC* Unit IV 'odi et amo', poem IX).
2 **Calve:** C. Licinius Calvus Macer, orator, poet and friend of Catullus. See *Poems* 14; 50 ('hesterno, Licini, die otiosi' = *CLC* Unit IV 'odi et amo', poem XI); 53.
3 **desiderio:** picks up and defines 'dolore' (2).
5—6 **non tanto . . . dolori est . . . quantum gaudet amore tuo:** 'brings less sorrow than your love brings joy' (Williams, 1968: 188).

Discussion

'The six lines form a carefully constructed, strangely impressive periodic sentence' (Quinn, 1973). The first couplet establishes the protasis of the conditional: 'if our grief makes any impression on the dead'. It links directly with the final couplet of apodosis, introduced (as frequently) by 'certe' (5): 'the dead *will* be cheered by the affection displayed'. The central couplet, crucial to the success of this little poem, merely fills out the reference of 'dolor', picking up 'dolore' in line 2 and looking towards 'dolori' in line 5.

The first two lines rehearse a commonplace of Roman consolatory writing — that the dead are saddened by their own deaths and appreciate the sympathy of the living. Catullus adopts this convention in order to put himself and his readers within the same frame of reference as that in which Calvus wrote. For we are in this poem directed towards a specific elegy of Calvus, written on the death of his much-loved Quintilia. It was clearly a distinguished poem, for Propertius (*Elegies* II.34.90) refers to how Calvus 'caneret miserae funera Quintiliae'. Two fragments of the original survive:

(1) cum iam fulva cinis fuero . . .
(2) forsitan hoc etiam gaudeat ipsa cinis.

The first of these seems to show the dead Quintilia talking about her posthumous state, in line with the convention. The second one ('perhaps her ashes actually find pleasure in this') suggests that Calvus puts for-

ward as a possibility something which is to be duly confirmed by
Catullus — that the dead Quintilia is impressed by Calvus' devotion. The
temptation to place too much weight on brief quotations from the original must be avoided. What we can posit with some confidence is that
Catullus follows Calvus in adopting the convention that the dead not
only grieve for their death but are also open to the feelings of the
bereaved. The grief of line 2 is described as 'nostro'. This is at first
taken as a generalised use (all of us on this side of death) in common
with the generalised sentiments of line 1; but after the revelation in the
next word of the addressee, when Catullus' educated readership may be
supposed to recall Calvus' Quintilia elegy, it is seen to link Catullus with
Calvus in his grieving — and it may not be coincidental that the comfort-
ing shared grief encloses Calvus in the centre of the line. There is, of
course, a tangible link between the two: both have expressed their feelings in verse.

In the second couplet Catullus continues to use the first person
plural, again associating himself with Calvus. The brief lightening of the
metre in line 3 (contrast lines 1, 4 and 5) reflects a lightening of subject
matter as Catullus talks of reliving in the imagination past love-affairs.
The informed reader is now thinking of the relationship of Calvus and
Quintilia, but Catullus deliberately keeps the reference unspecific at
this stage. Equally unspecific is line 4, in which the love-affair started
in line 3 is concluded by the lover, to be regretted later ('flemus'). But
Calvus had a reputation for promiscuity (associated with that of
Catullus, in Ovid *Tristia* II.431–2), so again the reader would tend to
apply line 4 to Calvus, abandoning one love in favour of a newer fancy.
Fraenkel 'drew the conclusion that, when Calvus represented his dead
wife as speaking, he made her reproach him with these infidelities.
Catullus takes this up in the second couplet and generalises it as a normal human characteristic not only to feel regret when it is too late but
also to have so acted as to have good cause to feel regret' (Williams,
1968: 189). Catullus can give Calvus comfort by saying (i) he is not the
only man to have been unfaithful to his loved one; (ii) even those of us
who have not lost a loved one in death can share his nostalgia for past
love and his regret for affection trampled on.

The heavy metre of line 5 is intensified by the shortness of the words
and the double caesura in the first half, while the assonance of 'mors
immatura dolori' is happily picked up by 'amore' in the final line. The
gloom of 'mors immatura' is dispelled by the sudden sharp focus of
'Quintiliae' and the surprisingly strong 'gaudet' (6), coupled with the
singular 'tuo' in effective contrast with 'nostro . . . dolore' of line 2: the
universal sentiments and the shared grief give way to a specific and personal love. The outward expression of this love is Calvus' poem, for love
is now paradoxically presented as the product of grief, with which it
should have so little in common. 'The grief which Calvus put into her

mouth in the elegy is less than the joy she will feel at the love which he expressed in the same poem' (Williams, 1968: 189). The poem is thus not only consoling but also highly flattering to Catullus' friend.

Questions

1 What precisely is Catullus saying to Calvus? Summarise each couplet in your own words.
2 What contribution does metre make to sense?
3 How essential is the central couplet? Would the poem be (i) intelligible, (ii) impoverished, if it were excised?
4 How vital to our understanding of the poem are the fragments of Calvus' own poem and Propertius' reference to it (see Discussion)?
5 Examine Catullus' use of first person plural and second person singular. Is it far-fetched to suppose a progression?

VI.2 Horace, Odes IV.7

Context

Odes IV was written after the *Carmen Saeculare* of 17 B.C., and possibly not 'published' until about 8 B.C. (Williams, 1972: 46). One of the themes of this collection is the poet's age and the approach of death. The pessimism of our poem is muted by the pieces which flank it, saying (i) that Horace is a substantial poet, thanks to Apollo, (ii) that poetry provides immortality for distinguished men. It seems to follow that Horace's own immortality is assured in the survival of his writings (cf. III.3).

Language and content

The metre is unique in Horace. Hexameters alternate with a short line like the second half of a pentameter:

ārbŏrĭbūsquĕ cŏmaē

3 **decrescentia**: the melting snows caused floods, now subsiding.
7 For alliteration of 'm' in a gloomy context, see Catullus *Poems* 101 ('multas per gentes' = *CLC* Unit IV 'odi et amo', poem IX).
13 **damna . . . reparant**: mercantile language (Fraenkel 420, n. 1).
    lunae: i.e. the different phases of the moon.
14 **decidimus**: pupils may recognise the echo of Catullus *Poems* 5 (= *CLC* Unit IV 'odi et amo', poem VII):

    soles occidere et redire possunt:
    nobis cum semel occidit brevis lux.
    nox est perpetua una dormienda.

15 **Tullus**: Tullus Hostilius, reputedly the conqueror of Alba Longa and the Sabines. His wealth is confirmed by Dionysius of Halicarnassus (*Roman Antiquities* III.1).
    Ancus: Ancus Marcius, the successor of Tullus, supposed to have built the first bridge over the Tiber, colonised Ostia and enlarged Rome.

21 **cum semel occideris**: see note on line 14, above.
23 **Torquate**: there is no convincing identification of Torquatus – also the
addressee of Horace *Epistles* I.5.3.

Discussion

Horace begins with a spring-song and a note of optimism ('diffugere
nives'). The opening words are like a cry of victory, their strength lying
in the personification of natural events, the bringing forward to initial
position of an assertive verb, and the poetic plurals. (The personification,
observable throughout the first half of the poem, looks forward to the
contrast in the second half between the natural order and Man.) The
emphasis, appropriate for the time of year, is on change and movement.
Even the rivers change ('decrescentia', 3). Horace then takes personification a stage further, with the Nymphs and Graces in an unmistakably
light-hearted vignette. 'audet' is in a position of emphasis, as if portend-
ing some great achievement. This turns out to be no more than braving
the cold in customary undress for the first time in the year.

The quantitative heaviness of 'immortalia' (7) strikes a serious if not
sombre note, and the introduction of an unnamed addressee ('speres')
also helps to set apart the phrase 'immortalia ne speres', which is to
become a key motif. The phrase strikes the reader sharply, but it has in
fact been neatly worked into the flow of the poem, which sets the
immortality of Nymphs and Graces against human mortality. The
alliteration of nasal 'n' and 'm', foreshadowed in line 5, gives the line a
distinct resonance and solemnity, and the *joie de vivre* (*pace* Quinn,
1963: 19) of lines 1–6 is quickly deflated. 'almum' ('nurturing', 'life-
giving') is brought forward and exposed at the end of line 7, only to be
destroyed by the sinister and violent 'rapit' (8). The personified 'hora'
is placed next to its victim 'diem'. Now the full significance of 'annus'
(7) is clear. Just as the hours (the smallest Roman unit of time) gobble
up the days, so the days gobble up the years; and the (as yet) unspecified addressee grows older and closer to death. 'almum' is revealed as
ironical: if the hours are sinister, *a fortiori* so are the days. There is an
implicit *parallel* here between Man and the seasons, in that both are
subject to Time: the *contrast* has yet to be developed.

After the premonitory chill of lines 7 and 8, we return to the revolving seasons; but there is a bitterness about lines 9–12 quite out of keeping with lines 1–6. The year moves away from spring towards winter,
the accent is on completion and obsolescence, and the message is that
nothing survives indefinitely. What is striking now is the increase of
pace. Instead of four lines devoted to the coming of spring, we have the
whole cycle of the seasons in four lines, and this acceleration provides
an excellent illustration of 'rapit' (8). Each brief clause contains within
it the seeds of its own season's destruction. The cold is losing its bite,
spring is being trampled on, summer is moribund and autumn will soon

have ceased production ('effuderit', 11, future perfect). The most vivid example of this swiftness of pace is perhaps in the second clause, into which two seasons are crammed: 'ver' is taken as subject of the clause until violently ousted by 'aestas', and before the end of the clause even summer is 'inter*it*ura' in a clear sound-echo of 'pro*terit*', the death of spring (and cf. 'effu*derit*' in line 11). Winter rushes back in line 12, recalling 'diffugere nives' in line 1, and rounding off this section of the poem. After all the bustle of the previous lines, 'iners' is a masterly epithet. Set at the end of the line and at the end of the section, it carries great weight. Juxtaposed with 'recurrit' it seems paradoxical, but (i) the inactivity is really human; (ii) the word-order suggests an initial turn of speed followed by a sustained torpor.

The depression engendered by 'bruma . . . iners', and indeed by the sense of time rushing past in lines 9—12, is lifted briefly in the dactylic line 13. The financial turn of phrase (see notes) is allowed to establish itself before the introduction of 'caelestia' and 'lunae' at the end of the clause. Only then can we appreciate the suggestive reference to the phases of the moon, the clearest possible image of the self-renewal and perpetual recurrence of the various seasons of the year.

'nos' (14) is boldly placed outside its clause and without any connective to 'lunae'. The echo of Catullus' poem (see notes) warns of a similarly black conclusion about death (though Catullus at least gathers rosebuds, while 'Horace moves to a still darker view' — Commager 280). This pessimism duly arrives in line 16, all the more powerful for the simplicity of its expression. Horace began (1—6) with distanced description, then (7) involved himself more closely by means of a (then) unnamed second person; and now, with 'nos', he includes himself and all mankind in his statement. (There is to be a parallel withdrawal from such full personal commitment in the second half of the poem.) In line 15, he further includes the legendary and semi-legendary heroes of the past. These are names of great strength. The suggestion that such men, like us, will be no more than 'pulvis et umbra' is no less forceful for being something of a literary commonplace.

Another financial metaphor occurs in line 17, the two being balanced symmetrically round the centre of the poem. By contrast with the swift, optimistic 'damna . . . celeres reparant . . . lunae', this one is hesitant and foreboding. So far are we from immortality that today may be our last — the present tense of 'adiciant' making the gods' activity actually in progress. The rhetorical question of lines 17—18 provides relief from a series of statements, more of which are to come, and creates just the right atmosphere of uncertainty.

This hesitancy is in strong contrast with the optimistic assertion which follows, the setting being now the death-bed itself. In fact, the one thing a first-century Roman could not be confident about was that his property would escape the grasp of his heirs (cf. I.2 and II.3). Yet here (19) we are offered a certain remedy: you *can* take it with you when you go, all of it — emphatic 'cuncta'. 'amico', completing line 19 and moved forward out of its clause, is naturally interpreted as a noun, and for a moment Horace deludes us into thinking that his remedy is to give away our goods to a true friend. But 'animo' (20) provides an extra-ordinary reversal. 'amico' has to be adjectival after all, and the sense appears to be (see Rudd, 1960: 383, on its difficulty) that only by self-indulgence ('carpe diem') can the *captator* be foiled — or perhaps that all you can take away are the abstract qualities of *facundia, pietas* etc., to be exemplified in lines 23ff. There is, after all, no way of taking your possessions with you when you die. Several commentators (e.g. Fraenkel 421) have felt uneasy about lines 19—20, and there is certainly quite a marked change of gear after line 18. But these lines can be defended. (i) They demonstrate in the sphere of human society the sort of change and succession Horace has stressed in the seasons of the year: 'manus avidas' (criticised as a 'weak verbal cliché' by Woodman 766) is prob-ably meant to remind us of 'rapit' in line 8. (ii) They provide an effec-tive introduction to the pointed remarks of the final eight lines: you can't in fact take anything physical with you, and even the virtues and abstract qualities which do pass over will do you no good at all. (iii) The defeat of expectation, of which they are such a good example, is very much in accord with the depressed conclusion of the poem and with the implicit relegation of the mighty Aeneas, Tullus and Ancus to 'pulvis et umbra' (15—16).

There is an ambiguity about 'cum semel' (21). Normally the 'semel' would indicate no more than 'the simple antecedence of an occurrence' (L&S), but in this context (and with the echoes of Catullus *Poems* 5 still resounding) it must remind us of the unrepeatable nature of death. The gloominess is enhanced by the collection of heavy syllables in the last four feet: for the second time in two lines the second-person singular ending of the future perfect indicative is given its optional but rare final long vowel (Plessis lxxvi). The unexpected 'splendida . . . arbitria' both is highly poetic and by giving us a glimpse of the prosecution sets up an effective contrast with the naked soul in the dock. It introduces the most potent couplet in the poem (23—4). The late arrival of an addressee initiates a new tension, underlined by the repetition of 'non' and 'te' and the prevalence of heavy syllables. Three of the most power-ful weapons in a Roman's social armoury — birth, eloquence and *pietas* — are now ranged against death, to no avail. In the last four lines, Torquatus' hopes are finally and forcefully crushed, as Horace parades more big names in an epic magnificence, at the same time developing the hints in line 16 about the unpleasantness of the life to come. If not even celestial heavyweights can save their special favourites, Torquatus cannot hope to get away. The snows escape and the grass returns (line 1), but no one escapes the bonds ('vincula', 28) of the Underworld.

A.E. Housman's translation of this poem (to be found, e.g., in Balme
and Warman 92) may well be used to provoke discussion. Horace *Odes*
I.4, 'solvitur acris hiems', makes a fascinating contrast — see Wilkinson,
1951: 39—43; Fraenkel 419—21; Quinn, 1963: 4—7, 15—28; Woodman
(a severely critical analysis of our poem); Easterling 324—7.

Questions

1 'Horace is clearly talking about spring, but the observation is
   without life or colour' (Woodman). Is this a fair comment on
   lines 1 and 2?

2 In which aspect(s) of spring is Horace particularly interested
   (1—6)?

3 Is there any hint in lines 1—12 of the mood of lines 21—8? Is
   there any recapitulation of the mood of lines 1—6 in the rest
   of the poem? Draw a graph to illustrate these changes of
   mood, with optimism/pessimism on one axis and line-
   references on the other.

4 Why does Horace introduce so many gods and heroes into a
   poem which is about the essential condition of ordinary
   human beings? Can the poem mean anything for a reader who
   does not believe in Diana or a historical Aeneas?

5 There are relatively few adjectives in this piece. Are they all
   used to good effect? Try experimenting with alternatives.

6 Several commentators find lines 19—20 an awkward intrusion.
   Do you agree? Do they merely state the obvious? Are they
   wittily contrived?

7 What is the effect of the late introduction of Torquatus (23)?
   Would Horace have done better to write him into the first few
   lines, to prevent the reader taking the poem as addressed to the
   world in general?

8 What is the effect of repeated 'non' in line 23? What is meant
   by 'genus', 'facundia' and 'pietas'? Why does Horace select
   these three qualities? What might be their twentieth-century
   equivalents in a comparable poem?

9 Could it be argued that the ending of the poem is an anticlimax and that Horace would have done better to omit the
   Greek mythology? See Quinn, 1963: 26—7.

10 Read Catullus *Poems* 5 (*CLC* Unit IV 'odi et amo', poem VII).
   Does Horace seem consciously to be referring to this poem?
   What is the effect of drawing on a largely optimistic poem in
   the pessimistic context of lines 14ff.?

VI.3 Ovid, Amores *III.9.29—60*
Context

For Ovid's *Amores*, see note on Context of IV.2. *Amores* III.9 was written by Ovid when he was about twenty-four. It is a lament, technically an *epicedion*, over the dead Tibullus. This traditional literary form has a long ancestry (cf. e.g. Catullus, *Poems* 101 'multas per gentes' = *CLC* Unit IV 'odi et amo', poem IX, and see Thomas, 1965 (1): 600), but Ovid exploits it with his own special finesse and ingenuity. Our excerpt follows the introductory address (*1–16), bidding Elegy, Venus and Cupid mourn the dead poet, and an indignant complaint that poets should be subject to death while their poetry survives it (*17–28). There are some explicit reminiscences of Tibullus, *Elegies* I.3, especially lines 23–6 (see Discussion).

Language and content

1   **durat opus vatum**: on this theme see III.3, 'exegi monumentum'.
    vatum: the grand word (cf. 13). 'It means to participate in knowledge that is denied to the "profanum vulgus". This knowledge is revealed to the poet by Apollo and the Muses. He is their "sacerdos", priest and prophet in one' (Luck, 1969: 133).

1–2 A reference to Homer's *Iliad* and *Odyssey*. For Penelope's unravelling by night the shroud she had woven for Laertes, in order to defer the attentions of the suitors, see Homer *Odyssey* II.93–110.

3   **Nemesis**: Tibullus' girlfriend in his second book of Elegies, as was Delia in the first book.

5   Ovid extends the association with Isis to both girls ('vos'), although Tibullus (*Elegies* I.3.23) refers only to Delia. For Ovid, such a distinction between the two girls would have distracted from his main theme. On Isis, see *CLC* Unit II *Teacher's Handbook* 88–91; *OCD* s.v. 'Isis'; Lewis and Reinhold II: 575–8 (quoting Apuleius); Witt 143ff.; Ferguson 23–6, 74, 106–8, Plate 55; Liversidge 207–8.

6   **sistra**: *CLC* Unit II slide 27, Unit III slide 68. They usually consisted of 'a "u" shaped piece of bronze attached to a long handle. Wires were stretched between the two sides and bits of metal of various shapes were attached to them which rattled when shaken' (Putnam, 1973: 78). They were no doubt intended to ward off evil spirits.
    vacuo . . . toro: ritual cleanliness and abstinence from sexual intimacy, which would have been particularly frustrating for the passionate elegist. Propertius, refused by Cynthia, refers to the 'tristia . . . sollemnia' of Isis and remarks 'utinam pereant!' (*Elegies* II.33a.1–3).

7   **ignoscite**: the subject of this imperative seems to be 'di', understood from line 8.

9   For Ovid's choice of words, see Tibullus *Elegies* I.3.25: 'quidve, pie dum sacra colis . . . ?'

10 **busta**: see on line 12.

11 **Tibullus**: he published his first book of *Elegies* when Ovid was about sixteen. The second book was probably unfinished at the time of his early death in 19 B.C. while still a *iuvenis*. He was, like Ovid, an *eques* and the client of Messalla to whom *Elegies* I.3 is dedicated; and, like Ovid's, his poetry is elegant, witty and carefully constructed. The self that Tibullus projects in his poems is a man of intense, uncomplicated religious feeling: hence Ovid's line 9. (See Lee, 1975: Introduction.)

12 **urna**: the body on its bier was placed upon a pyre, burnt, and the ashes placed in an urn, usually made of marble, alabaster or terracotta and usually either square or round with an appropriate inscription

(Paoli Ch. 11; Toynbee, 1971: 43ff.; *CLC* Unit II slide 36, Unit III slides 56—60.) The urn was then placed in a tomb (*bustum*) either a *columbarium* or a purpose-built monument, often with land attached and frequently abutting a main road (*CLC* Unit I *Stage 7*: 16).

15 **potuissent**: the subjunctive is potential — see Woodcock section 118.

17 **Erycis**: Mount Eryx (now Monte di San Giuliano) in north-west Sicily had a famous temple of Venus on its summit. Since 216 B.C. there had been a temple of Venus Erycina on the Capitol at Rome. For illustrations of Venus, see *CLC* Unit II slide 18; Unit IV slides 8—9; Unit V slide 2.

19 **Phaeacia tellus**: in *Elegies* I.3.3, Tibullus writes:

> me tenet ignotis aegrum Phaeacia terris
> 'I am held, an invalid, in Phaeacia's unknown land.'

Tibullus had set out with Messalla on an expedition to the east. Odysseus spent time on Phaeacia after being shipwrecked there (Homer, *Odyssey* V.388—XIII.80).

20 **humo**: it was apparently customary to throw some earth over the bones after the body had been cremated (Cicero *De Legibus* II.22.57); but Ovid may have in mind a degrading un-Roman form of burial.

21 **fugientis**: the first extant example of 'fugere' = to die. Ovid may well have in mind Propertius' use of 'euntis' in *Elegies* IV.7.23.
    pressit ocellos: the nearest relation attempted to catch the last breath with his mouth, removed the dying person's ring, closed the eyes and mouth, and called upon the deceased by name. The corpse was then prepared by the undertakers before being laid out feet to the door in the *atrium* or *vestibulum*, with the necessary coin in its mouth and clothed in its best toga.

22 **mater**: Tibullus (*Elegies* I.3.5—8) mentions the lack of mother and sister at his anticipated funeral.
    ultima dona: perfumes, oil, clothes, weapons, food, etc., were thrown into the flames of the pyre in the belief that they would be of use in the next world; the ashes were in due course cooled with wine; and then the bones were put in oil or honey before being placed in the 'urna'. Such ritual was best carried out by a near relative.

24 **inornatas dilaniata comas**: see Woodcock section 19; if pupils are puzzled by the gloss in their texts, it should be enough to say that 'dilaniare' is here used like a deponent in imitation of a Greek construction describing actions done to oneself. See Fordyce 287. The reference is to the funeral procession (see *CLC* Unit IV slide 51), where (uncharacteristically) sons walked with heads veiled and daughters with heads bare and hair dishevelled. The women lamented, beat their breasts and tore their cheeks.

25—6 Strongly reminiscent of Tibullus *Elegies* I.1.61:

> flebis et arsuro positum me, Delia, lecto,
>   tristibus et lacrimis oscula mixta dabis.
> 'You will weep for me too, Delia, when I am placed on the bed of burning, and you will give me kisses mixed with sad tears.'

26 **oscula**: just before the pyre was lit, the dead man was given a last kiss.

28 **tibi**: Form C (dative) of the agent. Cf. V.2.14.
    ignis = 'loved one' may well be modelled on the only clear prior usage, Virgil, *Eclogues* III.66; but the general association of love with fire is very common.

30   These words of Nemesis about herself reflect Tibullus *Elegies* I.1.60: 'te teneam moriens deficiente manu', addressed to Delia!

31–2   Propertius (*Elegies* II.34.53) writes: 'si post Stygias aliquid restabimus undas'.

32   **in Elysia valle**: in *Elegies* I.3.57–66, Tibullus writes lyrically about the Elysian Fields — to which he will be led by Venus.

Discussion

An *epicedion* (see note on Context) traditionally included (i) an introduction, (ii) a passage devoted to the praises of the dead and regret that he should have died (*laudatio/lamentatio*), (iii) a description of his illness and death, (iv) a description of the funeral and (v) a consolatory section (*consolatio*). The poet's originality was displayed in the way he treated individual themes, and the way in which he structured them within the poem. Our piece contains part of the *laudatio/lamentatio* (1–18), the death-bed scene (19–30) which includes references to the funeral, and the beginning of the *consolatio* (31–2), showing Tibullus happy in Elysium. In his treatment of the form Ovid writes with even closer reference than usual to his elegiac predecessors; in particular, he has taken Tibullus *Elegies* I.3 as his starting-point. Tibullus had shown himself as on the brink of death in Corfu, where he had come in the *cohors* of Messalla on his way to the east. He was about to die without the ministrations of his mother and sister, or of Delia who had been loath to see him leave Rome. Tibullus asks for help from Isis, Delia's chosen goddess, before composing his own epitaph and fantasising about the Elysian Fields (where he will go) and Tartarus (where he won't). The poem concludes with a plea to Delia to remain faithful and expect a sudden, unannounced return by Tibullus. It is only appropriate that Ovid should make the most of this poem when writing Tibullus' actual obituary.

Our excerpt opens (1–4) on a note of hope: Tibullus is a *vates*, and his work will last for ever. The seven heavy syllables in the middle of line 1 and the periphrastic descriptions of the *Iliad* and *Odyssey* give it a ponderous solemnity. Also, the deadly implications of 'laboris' (1) and the identification of the *Odyssey* by means of Laertes' shroud are well in tune with the theme of the poem. Tibullus' girlfriends Nemesis and Delia are then introduced, following appropriately on the reference to the faithful wife Penelope, and act as a witty shorthand for *Elegies* Book II and Book I. (The reversal of order, amusing to the alert reader, allows Ovid to make the prominent repetition of 'sic'. The record is set straight in the pentameter, 4.)

The tone becomes more urgent with the series of rhetorical questions in lines 5–6. This is a traditional element of the *epicedion*. Here they are given a special flavour through the implicit reference to Tibullus. Ovid has particularly in mind Tibullus *Elegies* I.3.23–6:

quid tua nunc Isis mihi, Delia, quid mihi prosunt
   illa tua totiens aera repulsa manu,
quidve, pie dum sacra colis, pureque lavari
   te, memini, et puro secubuisse toro?
'What help is your Isis to me now, Delia? What use to me are
those bronzes rattled so often in your hand? What use to me
was your washing yourself pure in pious observation of the
ritual, I remember, and lying apart in a pure bed?'

Ovid's adaptation results in a witty irony. Tibullus' questions, though
asked in apparent disbelief, turned out to demand an affirmative answer:
he did get better, and Delia's prayers paid off. But when Ovid puts virtually the same questions, the opposite is the case: all this frenzied
religious activity could not preserve from death even a distinguished
poet. Tibullus' works may achieve immortality (*laudatio*), but there is
no way for Tibullus himself to escape his fate (*lamentatio*). The tricolon
(5—6) builds up to a crescendo, starting with the colourless 'sacra',
moving to the more clearly visualised and characterised 'sistra', and
concluding in line 6, where 'vacuo' and 'se-' both make the crucial point
about separation, with a fate for the elegiac poet worse (almost) than
death. With 'vacuo . . . toro', also, we are pointed towards the funeral
pyre, for this too is unshared and 'torus' is used for 'bier' by both Virgil
and Ovid (L&S) — cf. the 'arsuro . . . lecto' of Tibullus *Elegies* I.1.61, a
passage very much in Ovid's mind (see note on lines 25—6).

    There follows an 'indignant outburst against an envious and unjust
fate' (Thomas, 1965 (1): 601), another traditional *topos* of the
epicedion. Neither poetic talent nor piety preserve against death (1—6).
So Ovid now declaims against piety (7—10) and against expecting too
much of one's poetry (11—18) — the reversed order of subject matter
allowing continuity from line 6 to line 7. The simplicity of the contrast
between 'mala' and 'bonos' in line 7 enhances the violence of 'rapiunt'.
Tibullus was only a *iuvenis* when he died. Such scepticism (re-echoed
briefly in lines 31—2) must have been unusual in a poem dedicated to a
dead believer (see note on line 11). 'ignoscite' (7) is prospective, as the
punctuation suggests, and the notion that the gods of whose existence
you are doubtful must be asked for pardon (as a sort of fail-safe
insurance policy) strikes at least the modern reader as amusing. But that
Ovid's tone is still serious is indicated by the outcry which follows (9—
16). The starkness of these sentiments has led Ovid to asyndeton and
extreme economy of expression. The first antithesis is extraordinarily
abrupt. The second, expanding and defining it (Thomas, 1965 (2): 150),
promises to be equally abrupt — with 'colentem' picking up 'cole' like
the repetition of 'pius' — but surprises the reader with a full-blown
image of death at work. Line 11 seems particularly bitter; certainly the
hard 'c'-alliteration helps. Again a tricolon (this time the three antith-

eses) works to a climax — assisted by the vivid 'ecce' as if we were present at the funeral — a climax which is marked by the first mention, at
the end of the line, of Tibullus. Line 12 lends a note of pathos, with
'toto' placed for effect next to 'parva'. A strong reaction follows, with
Tibullus' stature re-established in line 13 with the powerful phrase 'sacer
vates' in rhetorical apostrophe. The alliteration of 'rapuere rogales' (cf.
7) is paralleled immediately in line 14 with 'pectoribus pasci nec
timuere tuis'. The harsh crudity of this idea is made even more pointed
by the associations of 'pectora' for an elegiac poet (see, e.g., Ovid *Ars
Amatoria* I.756 and 759 for 'pectora' as the seat of the affections). That
flames should be afraid ('timuere', 14) is nonsense; but the image
strengthens our appreciation of Tibullus, and the next couplet (15–16)
continues the process. Tibullus' corpse is set directly in parallel with the
golden temples of the gods, 'sanctorum' (15) picking up 'sacer' (13).
'aurea' (15) suggests the value of the temples, and hence, by extension,
of Tibullus. Not only is it sacrilegious to destroy Tibullus' body, but it
is large-scale sacrilege ('tantum'; suggestions of weightiness in 'sustinuere',
16). This section concludes on a similar note, but with an abrupt change
of reference, in lines 17–18. 'avertit vultus' (17) introduces a third
party, identified in mid-line as Venus. It is appropriate, of course, that
she should mourn a professional lover, but this reference also takes us
back beyond our excerpt to the last couplet of the introduction (*15–
16) where Venus is pictured at Tibullus' funeral, grieving as she grieved
for the dead Adonis. In lines 17–18 of our excerpt, her reappearance
(i) signals the end of a section; (ii) further confirms the importance of
Tibullus; (iii) steers the reader away from recriminations towards the
funeral scene which is to follow. The last comment applies particularly
to line 18, which not only presents Venus but also suggests ('sunt
quoque qui') the crowd of mourners watching her. The social observation is acute: most people, if they are honest, admit to a mawkish
curiosity about how celebrities behave under stress.

As Ovid launches into his new section with 'sed tamen hoc melius,
quam si Phaeacia tellus . . . ' (19), the reader is prepared for a reworking
of the near-fatal illness on Corfu, already described by Tibullus.
'Phaeacia tellus' (19) does two things. First, with 'ignotum' (20), it provides an explicit cross-reference to line 3 of Tibullus, *Elegies* I.3 (see
note on line 19). Secondly, it reforges a link between Tibullus and
Homer (cf. line 2 and note on line 19). Now, in line 20, Ovid imagines
the fearful obscurity that would have attended Tibullus' burial on
Corfu. The effect is intensified (i) by the contrast ('ignotum vili . . .
humo', 20) with the pre-eminence of Tibullus the celebrity established
in lines 13–18; (ii) by the way Ovid capitalises on the language of
Tibullus *Elegies* I.3.3 — Tibullus merely says he is ill and abroad,
whereas Ovid changes the reference of 'ignotum' and imagines a common burial, abroad, with the poet's greatness going unrecognised. Lines

19—20 can also be seen as providing an excellent bridge between the
lyric fantasy of lines 17—18 and the grim reality of lines 21—30.

Ovid continues to ring the changes on his Tibullan original. Tibullus
is sad because his mother cannot gather up his bones and his sister cannot pour perfume on his ashes:

> non hic mihi mater
> quae legat in maestos ossa perusta sinus,
> non soror, Assyrios cineri quae dedat odores
> et fleat effusis ante sepulcra comis.
>
> 'There is no mother for me here to collect my cremated bones
> to her sad breast, no sister to grant Assyrian perfumes to my
> ashes and weep, with hair flowing, before my tomb.'
> Tibullus, *Elegies* I.3.5—8

Ovid's 'hic certe' (21), heavily spondaic, is a triumphant rebuttal of
Tibullus' 'non hic'. Tibullus' mother *was* with him at the very moment
of death; the poet's eyes were still wet ('madidos') with tears as his life
'escaped' (on this vivid detail, see note on line 21). Tibullus draws a
picture of mother and daughter in separate grief; Ovid adds a hint of
Tibullus' own emotion ('madidos', 21) and makes it a grief which is
shared ('in partem', 'cum', 23). In Tibullus' poem, his sister merely
unbinds her hair; Ovid's selection of 'inornatas dilaniata comas' creates
a much more violent picture, possibly assisted by all the long vowels in
these words, and he confirms the cross-reference by concluding line 24
with 'comas' just as Tibullus had concluded with 'comis'. In mid-
sentence Ovid now glances at more lines of Tibullus (see notes on lines
25—6). Again (cf. 5) he takes the liberty of extending the reference
from just Delia to both girls. There is a distinct lightening of tone here,
reflecting the relative light-heartedness of Tibullus, *Elegies* I.1 and preparing for the happiness of Elysium in line 32. Ovid makes his reader
wait for the object of 'iunxerunt' (25). The rhythm of line 25 is most
unusual in Ovid, who generally contrives a caesura in the third foot of
such lines (as in line 19): here the anomaly gives prominence to
'iunxerunt', the notion of co-operation and sharing being important at
this stage of the poem. 'oscula' seems to be positioned so late, following
Nemesis and Delia, in order to steer the reader away from the funeral
kiss and towards the notion of sexual encounter. 'The combination of
love and death is an elegiac commonplace . . . The attributes of love . . .
are transferred to the instant of cremation' (Putnam, 1973, on Tibullus
Elegies I.1.59 and 62). Tibullus makes the suggestion with 'lecto' and
'oscula'. Ovid (26) highlights 'oscula' and then gives an unmistakable
back-reference to 'in vacuo secubuisse toro' (6): there is no question of
Delia and Nemesis deserting Tibullus' bed now (the possibility of a
threesome spicing the imagination); but the bed, anticipated from
'lecto' (Tibullus *Elegies* I.1.61), is turned back by unlooked-for 'rogos'

into a funeral pyre and the reader is reinstated at the funeral by the four mournful 'ō' sounds in this line (26). Delia and Nemesis are now given a couplet each as Ovid concludes his death-bed scene. The reported speech gives the incident a welcome immediacy, and the four lines are reminiscent of the sort of amoebaean form explored by Horace in VII. 2. Delia's 'felicius amata' has a deliciously catty ring to it. 'vixisti' (28) is obviously intended in its strong sense (cf. I.1.20), the implication being that Tibullus only lived life to the full during his liaison with Delia; the past tense, however, also serves to remind us that Tibullus is now dead. 'ignis' (28) is equally two-edged: while the notion of 'old flame' is uppermost, it is impossible (see note on the novelty of this usage) to dissociate the word from its affinity with the destructive flames of the funeral pyre (cf. 'flammae' in line 13). Nemesis replies crushingly. The loss is not Delia's but hers. She was Tibullus' last love. Line 30 (see note) is the closest imitation of Tibullus' diction that Ovid gives us. Only two changes are made, though these are crucial. The wish, 'teneam', is replaced by the fact, 'tenuit'; and 'te' (= Delia) is replaced by 'me' (= Nemesis). Tibullus' protestations of undying love for Delia are simply updated by Ovid to cater for his latest love, the lady of Book II. The effect is transparently witty and entertaining; reverence and morbidity are not long acceptable at the funeral of a love-poet.

The switch to the last section (*consolatio*) is now straightforward. After the traditional expression of doubt about the afterlife, clearly reflecting the doubts of lines 8ff., Ovid presents us with the confident assertion that Tibullus, if anyone, will indeed go to the Elysian Fields as he had predicted (see note on line 32). Pronounced 'l'-alliteration underlines our excerpt's peaceful conclusion.

Questions

1 Summarise the logical structure of this passage and show how you would divide it into separate sections. Does Ovid attempt to bridge the gaps between sections, or are they clearly differentiated?

2 What evidence are we given for practice at Roman funerals? What can you add to this (a) from other Latin pieces that you have read; (b) from modern reference books? (See notes above, especially on line 12.)

3 Investigate the worship of Isis. (See notes on lines 5 and 6, above.)

4 To what extent is Ovid here optimistic about death?

5 What picture of Tibullus does Ovid wish us to take from this poem?

6 One might well expect a poem about death to be universally serious. Are there any areas where Ovid is being less than serious? Why might this be? Conversely, are there any lines

which seem to be marked by a particular intensity of feeling?
Do you know any other literary treatments of death in a
lighter vein?

7   What use does Ovid make of Tibullus *Elegies* I.1 and I.3? Does
his willingness to draw on his predecessor suggest a lack of
imagination?

VI.4 Martial, Epigrams *IV.18*   ·

Language and content

1   **Vipsanis:** the reference is probably to an arch of the Aqua Virgo (see
notes on I.2.9 and 10; Ashby 175 with n. 1) near the Campus Agrippae
or the Porticus Vipsania (see plan in pupils' text 3). The Campus
Agrippae was part of the Campus Martius, laid out as a sort of park by
Marcus Vipsanius Agrippa and finished and dedicated by Augustus in
7 B.C. The Porticus Vipsania, begun by Agrippa's sister Polla and
finished by Augustus, was at the north-west corner of the Campus
Agrippae (Platner and Ashby).
porta: used for 'arcus' ('arch'), perhaps because a right-of-way passed
beneath the aqueduct.

7   **voluit:** generalising, gnomic aorist — what has been and will be the case.

Discussion

We are given an exact topographical reference, nonetheless puzzling to
later commentators, in order to set the scene. The unusual application
of 'pluit' (1) to an archway focuses our attention on the dripping water
which alliteration of 'p'/'b'/'d' and the watery 'madet', 'lubricus' and
'imbre' (2) reinforce. At this stage, of course, the reader is ignorant of
the senseless tragedy to come, and 'lubricus' (2) lays a false, though
apparently ominous, trail — the expectation that someone will fall over
on the stone pathway. 'iugulum' (3) is equally sinister (cf. 'iugulum
dare' and 'iugulare') and 'pueri' gives us our protagonist. The lovely
epithet 'roscida' (3), rare in this metaphorical sense, appears to set the
balance straight, but in retrospect is seen to be used with a terrible
irony. The full force of the pentameter (4) is reserved for the final word
'gelu', though 'praegravis' points to a disaster as its metaphorical sense
is activated. Above all, the abrupt placing of 'decidit' (4) at the beginning of its clause provides a sharp conclusion to the lengthy scenic construction of lines 1—3 and, in juxtaposition with 'subibat' (3), suggests
the simultaneity of the two coincidental events. After such precise
description, Martial moves briefly into a periphrastic phrase (5), exploiting the ambiguity of 'peregisset' (see pupils' text), before another closely
observed and macabre description (line 6) which explores the apparent
paradox of a weapon that 'tabuit' and is as 'tener' as the boy it killed.
A couple of rhetorical questions take the interest outwards from the
details of the individual tragedy to universal issues. Martial muses on the

omnipotence of 'saeva Fortuna' (cf. X.1 question 7) and the ubiquity of death. The delivery becomes almost declamatory now, with the rhetorical questions, the reference to the goddess Fortune, and the personification, poetic plural and apostrophe of water. The final point lies in the apparent paradox of 'iugulatis aquae' (8): Martial gets away with this because (i) 'iugulare' has moved away from its association with 'iugulum' towards a generalised notion of killing; (ii) 'iugulatis' (8) is now seen to pick up the mention of 'iugulum' in line 3.

Questions

1 What does Martial want us to conclude from the epigram? Is it significant that the boy is only mentioned twice (3 and 5)?
2 Why does Martial take such pains over the setting of this poem?
3 How seriously are we intended to take this epigram?
4 Death by icicle would make excellent material for a detective story. Sketch out the outline of a story which includes two conflicting versions of the cause of death.

VI.5 *Martial,* Epigrams *V.34*

Context

This is one of three poems written by Martial in memory of his slave-girl Erotion, who died just before her sixth birthday. The other poems are *Epigrams* V.37 and X.61.

Language and content

1 **Fronto, Flaccilla**: our only evidence for the names of Martial's parents.
3 **Erotion**: (Greek) = Loved One, Sweet Child.
4 **prodigiosa**: because triple
5 **sextae**: for the tombstone of a six-year-old boy, see *CLC* Unit III slide 64. On life expectancy in the Roman world, see Liversidge 221.
7 **patronos**: Martial's parents are to act as her protectors.
9 **tegat ossa**: on burial, see notes on VI.3.
10 **fueris**: jussive subjunctive.

Discussion

The epigram opens rather formally, with the chiasmus of 'Fronto pater, genetrix Flaccilla' and the use of the elevated word for 'mother'. This formality is immediately broken down by the diminutive 'puella' and the affectionate and familiar words of the pentameter (2). At this stage, there is no hint of gloom: the couplet merely states that Martial is sending his parents a new young slave-girl, and the initial formality can be attributed to a natural deference to parents. The full situation is revealed in the following couplet. The diminutive 'parvula' (3) links this portentous Golden Line (see I.1.27, Discussion) with the endearments of (2), but the tone changes dramatically with the heavy 'ne nigras horrescat', the black ghosts, Cerberus and the resonance of repeated 'r' and 'ō' — set against the sweetness of 'parvula' and 'Erotion' (3). There is a degree of empathy in the way that Martial has selected just the sights that might terrify a little girl. Her exact age follows, contrasting with 'veteres' (7). She was nearly six when she died. Martial adds melancholy to the detail by suggesting (i) that she only failed to achieve her sixth birthday by a day or two; (ii) that she had almost escaped from the cold of winter, with its metaphorical associations, into the summertime — though 'bruma' is frequently found in such contexts meaning little more than 'year'. The spondees and the long 'ō' sounds of the next couplet (7—8) show that Martial's hopes for Erotion's life after death are not of the brightest, despite her natural advantages. She is to have protectors, necessary for her playful character ('ludat lasciva'), who will keep her in check just as 'ludat lasciva' is physically surrounded by 'veteres . . . patronos' (7). Furthermore, her endearing chatter with its fetching lisp will continue to be heard, but she will still be calling for Martial who cannot be with her. The epigram concludes with the traditional prayer that the earth may lie light. Pathos is extracted from the unusual circumstance that her young bones are softer than the turf which covers them, and 'nec illi' is exposed at the end of line 9 to contrast with the Form C (dative) 'tibi' which brings the poem to a close. The repetition of 'fueris'/'fuit' across the caesura of line 10 lends a formal symmetry reminiscent of line 1.

Kenney (1964: 78) has described the poem as 'charming but conventional'. It is important to realise that many of its themes can be paralleled from elsewhere. For example, the *Greek Anthology* sepulchral epigrams provide parallels for the mention of Cerberus (VII.66); the age of the deceased, as on real gravestones, (VII.467); a child playing in Hades with Persephone (VII.483); earth lying light (VII.632). Friedlaender quotes numerous Greek and Roman epitaphs containing the formula *sit tibi terra levis*, and to this one could add the final couplet of Ovid *Amores* III.9 (the poem from which VI.3 is excerpted). To such a conventional substructure Martial has added (i) a vivid personal connexion; (ii) the detailed artistry outlined above.

Questions

1 Is this poem effective for those who do not know the people involved? Is its attraction purely sentimental?
2 What evidence is there for a close relationship between Martial and Erotion? Is there any evidence for Martial understanding how children think?
3 What sort of sound-effects does Martial achieve in lines 3—4?

Section VII

If it seems surprising that a section devoted to love and sex should lack a reference to married love, then this should be taken as reflecting the assumptions and conventions within which our authors (in common with many poets of different eras) wrote. Sympathetic treatments of marriage are very rare in Roman literature. The poems by Catullus, Horace and Ovid all describe rather stormy relationships; this too was part of the tradition. Horace's poem to Lydia (VII.2) is highly formal in structure. Its language also is formal, until quite near the end; but it is the change of tone in the last few lines that roots it in real experience, softening the gem-like quality of what precedes. The Ovid diptych (VII.3, VII.4) is less formal, and is centred remorselessly round a single incident. It appeals for various reasons, but in particular the reader must contrast with the Horace ode the witty assurance with which Ovid avoids direct description of Nape's meeting with Corinna or even the detail of his letter, and yet contrives to suggest the contents of both. Catullus' poem (VII.1) is epigrammatic in its use of paradox and word-pattern, techniques which it shares with that of Martial (VII.5). Catullus seems to rely on the reader's familiarity with his love for Lesbia; similarly, Martial may well have expected his readers to associate certain attitudes with Safronius Rufus (see note on VII.5.1). Whether or not Lesbia was actually loved by Catullus (or Lydia and Corinna by Horace and Ovid) is as immaterial to the quality of the poetry as whether Safronius Rufus actually displayed the qualities with which Martial invests him.

VII.1 Catullus, Poems 92

Language and content

2   **dispeream nisi**: a colloquial phrase, hard to parallel in modern English. The use of the prefix 'dis-' to intensify 'peream' is also apparently colloquial (*OLD* s.v. 'dis-'). There seems to be some punning reminiscence of 'perire' meaning 'be desperately in love' (L&S II.B.2). Cf. IX.3.3.
3   **sunt totidem mea**: a colloquial usage (see Fordyce).
4   **deprecor**: the direct object may be (a) that from which relief is sought; (b) that for which appeal is made; (c) the person to whom appeal is made (Fordyce). See Discussion.

Discussion

Catullus is again exploring the fluctuating feelings in his apparently tempestuous relationship with Lesbia. The first couplet thrusts Lesbia uncompromisingly into first place in both cola, and the object of her attack, repeated 'me', is placed in vulnerable proximity. Displaying his usual economy, Catullus sketches with a crisp five words the essential background — himself regularly under attack from Lesbia. 'nec tacet umquam' seems merely to repeat this, but in fact (i) stresses the tenacity of her attack; (ii) suggests clearly that the reference of 'semper' is to 'dicit' rather than 'male'; (iii) sets up the witty exposure of 'de me' at the beginning of line 2, when the reader has just felt a logical close at the end of the first line. 'nec tacet umquam / de me' also gives advance warning, at least for readers who know *Poems* 83 ('Lesbia mi praesente viro mala plurima dicit' = *CLC* Unit IV 'odi et amo', poem III), of the neatly paradoxical conclusion of line 2. We expect the pentameter to develop the sense of the hexameter with a further example of Lesbia's nastiness. Catullus establishes such an expectation by 'Lesbia me' before the caesura. We anticipate something like 'vituperat' but finally hit upon the astonishing final word of the couplet, 'amat'.

The question 'quo signo?' retains our interest. How *can* such a paradox be explained? This time Catullus keeps no surprises in store. 'quia sunt totidem mea' (3) comes pat in answer: 'because it's just the same with me'. But this vague generalisation demands more details, and these are supplied, with predictable wit. 'deprecor illam' can carry (*pace* Fordyce) any of the senses outlined in the note on line 4, even (b). Only as we read on do we narrow down its meaning into sense (a), and even then there is always half a suggestion that Catullus is begging Lesbia for freedom from the agony of loving her, rather than the more obvious freedom from being shouted at by her. 'assidue' (4) is a wry reminder of the persistent nagging of Lesbia ('semper', 'nec . . . umquam', 1). 'dispeream nisi' is a curious expression to attach to 'amo': it is 'as though one's own feelings were a matter for conviction, rather than certainty' (Quinn, 1973). The phrase is only tolerable because of the amusing symmetry with line 2.

The poem is attractive largely because of the tension between the colloquialism of its language and the artifice of its organisation and wit. As so often, too, we see Catullus both involved in the action as distraught lover, and standing back as poet for some cool analysis of what is going on.

Questions

1 How economically does Catullus establish the background for this poem?
2 Is the element of surprise important?
3 Why do you think Catullus uses so many colloquial words and phrases?
4 Is it true to say of Catullus that 'he is far from exultant in these lines; instead, there is a hint of pathos' (Quinn, 1973)?

VII.2 Horace, Odes III.9

Context

See on III.3. Perhaps illustrate with *CLC* Unit IV slides 10, 11.

Language and content

The asclepiadic metre is based on the choriamb (- ᴗ ᴗ -). Here we have couplets of the following pattern:

> dōnēc grātŭs ĕrăm tĭbĭ
> nēc quīsquăm pŏtĭŏr // brācchĭă cāndĭdaē

In both lines the final syllable is *anceps*.

4 **Persarum . . . rege**: a regular paradigm of worldly success.

11 **metuam**: probably intended (cf. 'patiar', 15) as future indicative, not present subjunctive, since a forceful assertion seems required.

12 **animae**: refers to Chloe ('she who is my life', 'my darling').

17ff. The present tenses have a distinctly future feel to them, while implying that things are starting to happen here and now: 'what if love is in process of returning?'

19 **excutitur**: both out of mind and out of house.

20 **Lydiae**: either Form C (dative) making the poet leave the door open for Lydia, or Form D (genitive) with Lydia leaving open her own door. But (i) the emphatic 'reiectae' makes the former much more likely, since it is up to the poet to initiate a reconciliation; (ii) at the end of line 19 the reader's mind is fixed firmly on the poet's door, making an abrupt cut to Lydia's door the less likely.

21 **sidere pulchrior**: a Homeric image (*Iliad* VI.401).

22 **improbo**: it may be necessary to stress (*pace OLD*) the masculinity here of 'Hadria'.

24 **amem, obeam**: the subjunctive is occasioned by the conditional effect of 'quid si . . . ?' (17ff.). Lydia's reply is somewhat less open and confident than the poet's hypothesis — which he sets out briskly in the present indicative.

Discussion

The poem purports to be a conversation between the poet and his girl-friend Lydia. The reader has the privileged position of the fly on the wall, and is able to indulge his curiosity by listening in. And it is the reader who must make any judgments that are to be made, for the writer does not comment directly (cf. II.3).

The personal nature of the poem comes over clearly in line 1: it is to be a dialogue between 'you' and 'me' (juxtaposed). It also emerges that the two have had a relationship at some time in the past, though 'gratus' implies that the relationship was not unduly close. By line 6, this will appear in retrospect as the ironical understatement of a man who is feeling his way back towards an affair but, sensing himself vulnerable, understates his former passion. In line 1, before 'tibi' is even sexed by the reader, 'gratus' entails no more than 'just good friends'. In lines 2 and 3, it becomes clear that we have an ex-lover addressing his girl, and the possibility of a preferred rival is raised only to be dismissed. There is a calculated uncertainty about 'nec quisquam potior'. Horace seems both to be denying the existence of any other lover ('and no one usurped my place') and to be suggesting that there were other lovers but 'none such an attractive embracer as I'. And Horace thereupon creates a word-picture of an embrace, with 'candidae cervici' encircled by 'bracchia' and 'iuvenis' (2–3). 'candidae' is striking because separated from its noun by the line-break. (Of the strictly comparable lines 6, 10, 14, 18 and 22, only line 22 is similarly enjambed.) It is a compliment casually dropped, but with latent sensual impact. At this early stage the lover is careful not to presume too much. His ardour burns a little hotter than in line 1, but this is merely the first stage in a progression, and Horace with 'bracchia . . . dabat' (2–3) seems purposely to avoid at this point hints of anything more passionate. The conclusion (4) of the 'donec' clause turns out to be no more than a lover's commonplace, with its well-worn reference to the king of Persia and the play implicit in the Latin word 'beatus'. Nonetheless, it is clearly intended to be complimentary.

As we progress with lines 5 and 6, we realise that Lydia is now granted right of reply. She neatly and humorously caps the remarks of her former lover. 'arsisti' is intrinsically powerful. The lover has pussyfooted with 'bracchia . . . cervici . . . dabat': Lydia is truer to the event with her talk of flaming passion. The ambiguity of 'nec quisquam potior' is paralleled with 'non alia magis'; again, this could mean 'so long as there was nobody else you were passionate about rather than me', but it is equally likely to mean 'so long as there was nobody else you were more passionate about than me'. The latter interpretation is confirmed by the second half of line 6, where the lover is accused of running two girl-friends simultaneously. Lydia has repeated her own name twice now (6 and 7) to allow its foreign, dancing-girl sound, full of Eastern promise, to sink in fully. There is much irony therefore in her description of herself as 'multi . . . nominis', as if she were a Metella or a Livia. There is even greater irony in her vaunting herself as more famous than the mother of Romulus. In order to appreciate the significance of this, we have to look back to the lover's claim to be 'more fortunate than the Persian king'. Just as the two statements as a whole are brought into comparison by matching structure ('donec'/'donec'; 'nec'/'neque'), so these two punch-lines both start with a nationality, contain the same central assertion ('vigui') and conclude with a comparison. The lover, a Roman, compares himself with the Persian king. Lydia, whose name associates her with Asia Minor — one of the traditional areas of Persian rule — compares herself, in lieu of a Roman queen, with Ilia. The lover is thus trumped. But we should pursue further the implications of 'Romana . . . Ilia', not least because Ilia is brought firmly into prominence by the reversal of order from 'rege beatior' (4) to 'clarior Ilia' (8). Her epithet 'Romana' seems otiose until one remembers that the versions of Rome's foundation which refer to Ilia rather than Rhea Silvia tend to have Ilia as daughter of Aeneas (so Ennius: cf. Servius on Virgil, *Aeneid* VI.777) and named after Aeneas' home of Ilium/Troy: Lydia may be using 'Romana' ironically to imply that even the mother of Romulus had strong connexions with Asia Minor.

With the lover's reply in line 9, the focus of the poem shifts abruptly to the present. He asserts, somewhat bluntly: 'Thracian Chloe now queens it over me.' All is not what it was in line 4 when the lover saw himself as superior to the Persian king. Now he is the subject, and his ruler comes from an area which Romans would have regarded as uncivilised — in the light of which, line 10 looks like over-compensation. The lover declares himself ready to die for Chloe 'if fortune will spare my darling to survive me'. The lover will die so that Chloe may continue living.

Lydia's reply is once again structurally similar. Initial 'me' in line 9 is picked up by 'me' in line 13; the present tense is again followed by a future declaration; the name and details of the loved one reappear; 'pro qua' in line 11 is met by 'pro quo' in line 15; the final word of both line 11 and 15 is 'mori'; and lines 12 and 16 are identical apart from the substitution of 'puero' for 'animae'. Again the lover is convincingly up-staged. He is ruled by Chloe, but Lydia enjoys a fierce passion (fiery 'torret' in line 13 outroasting 'arsisti' in line 6) which is reciprocal ('mutua') in a way that 'regit' (9) seems to deny. The credentials of her new lover Calais are far more impressive than those of the musical Chloe: Calais is the Greek word for a precious stone; he is respectable enough to be identified by reference to his father; he lives in Italian Thurii, closely associated with the wealth and luxury of ancient Sybaris; he is young ('puero', 16); and he is 'sidere pulchrior' (21). Not even Mrs Bennet could have found more points in his favour. With 'bis' (15), Lydia doubles the stakes — without much regard for logic — and simultaneously improves on the negative 'non metuam' (11) with a more committed 'patiar' (15). 'puero' in line 16 is the only alteration from line 12: could there perhaps be an implication here that the poet is no longer so young? On Williams' dating (1972), Horace would have been between thirty-five and forty-two when he wrote *Odes* I—III, though he is not necessarily writing in character (see below). Chloe's supposed age may be indicated by her name, which is the Greek for young grass or corn.

The lover in lines 17ff. again changes tack. 'What if our former love returns?' The high-flown imagery of line 18, so far unparalleled in this poem, is immediately shattered by the hard worldliness of lines 19 and 20. The nature of their renewed relationship is clearly characterised in line 18: love is not a bed of roses but a metal yoke lovers are compelled to wear (note the sombre 'ō'-alliteration). It is an irony that the most rhetorical line should contain the most hard-nosed sentiments. Such notions leave no place for Chloe, whose real charm turns out to be her blonde hair (another carefully placed sensual detail, like 'candidae' in line 2). Lydia is to be readmitted to the lover's house and affections.

Lydia's reply also oscillates between the extravagant and the harshly realistic. She caps 'flava . . . Chloe' with her Homeric description of Calais as 'sidere pulchrior'. Then the asyndeton in line 22 points up

the contrast between 'ille' and 'tu'. The lover missed his opportunity of
describing Lydia in line 20, but Lydia not only implies that the lover is
substantially less beautiful than a star, but goes on to give a less than
flattering character-analysis. Nonetheless, she does see the lover as a real
person, reminiscent of his own reassessment of the nature of love in
lines 17—18. Calais, like Chloe in line 19, is characterised solely in terms
of physical beauty. Lydia wants more than this, and her final declaration is not the empty rhetoric of lines 11—12 and 15—16, but a simple
and touching revelation of a love which recognises flaws and accepts
them as part of the deal. The repeated 'm'-sound enhances the softness
of the line. Lydia wants a lifelong relationship with this lover, not an
unsustainable scorch. When death has to come, it will not be a solo
gesture but a shared exit, and one that does not so much take courage
('non metuam' 11; 'patiar' 15) as will be faced with cheerfulness ('libens'
24).

The poem moves in a world that is established as Roman by the
references to Ilia and Venus, but which has a distinctly Greek atmosphere to it. Chloe, Lydia and Calais are Greek names, such as were no
doubt common among the *demi-monde* in Rome and in the sometime
Greek colonies of Southern Italy. The renewed relationship between
the lover and Lydia appears to be of a permanent nature, both as viewed
by the lover ('iugo . . . aeneo' 18) and as viewed by Lydia (line 24).
Williams (1968: 210) says that in lines 18 and 24 there are overtones of
the Roman marriage ceremony, but that there is of course no need to
suppose that an actual marriage was ever in question (404—5). The issue
is complicated by what looks like a reference to Horace's own character
(lines 22—3): Williams (1968: 210) points out the similarities with what
Horace says about himself in *Satires* II.3.321—6 and *Epistles* I.20.25. It
may indeed be the case that Horace was hinting at his own character,
but the details of the affair are not therefore to be taken as autobiographical, or indeed as descriptive of any one real-life relationship.
Horace is simply providing his reader with an entertaining and thought-
provoking picture of the way two lovers can come to a deeper understanding of what love involves.

The closest Latin parallel to the structure of this poem, where one
speaker caps another, is Catullus *Poems* 62 — and this may prove a useful comparison-piece. Such an amoebean form necessarily imposes a
strong pattern on the poem. Something of this pattern should have
emerged from the discussion above. Wilkinson (1963: 27) describes the
poem rather colourfully as 'like an antiphony on the virginals', which
Williams caps (1969: 76) with 'a blithe Mozartian duet'!

Questions

1 What is the characteristic pattern of this poem?
2 How does Horace make it clear that the reader should take

lines 1—4 and 5—8 in contrast? Give two clear examples of
Lydia scoring off her lover.

3 What are the points of contrast between lines 9—12 and 13—
16? Consider, e.g., Horace's use of proper names.

4 What sort of picture are we given by Lydia of her lover in lines
22 and 23? Would it be in any way significant if we could
prove Horace himself to have had similar traits of character?

5 Is it fair to quote only the first four lines and say that 'Horace's
sentiment is conventional without being true to life' (R.G.M.
Nisbet in Sullivan, 1962: 185)? Or is it possible to see in the
course of this poem a progression from a dewy-eyed, unrealistic,
conventional conception of love towards a soundly-based,
enduring relationship?

6   amantium irae amoris integratiost
    'lovers' quarrels renew love'
                          Terence, *Andria* 555 (quoted by Page)
Is it unavoidable that the more passionate a love-affair or
friendship the greater the risk of quarrelling? Does a strong
relationship benefit from occasional argument?

7 Consider again the pattern of this poem. The upstaging dialogue
(with Speaker Two always attempting to surpass Speaker One
in virtuosity) is so familiar to us that we are almost bound to
find this pattern satisfactory. What examples can you draw
from our own society: joke-telling at parties; insult-swapping;
the gossip of neighbours; the interplay of jazz soloists?

VII.3 Ovid, Amores *I.11*

Context

On Ovid's *Amores* see note on Context of IV.2. *Amores* I.11 is addressed
to Corinna's maid Nape, and forms a diptych (one of six in *Amores*)
with its neighbour (see VII.4). The reader finds himself eavesdropping
on a meeting between Ovid and Nape. This and the circumstances underlying the meeting are left to be inferred as the poem unwinds. Perhaps
illustrate with *CLC* Unit IV slide 58.

Language and content

1—8 These complex lines are probably best approached by pupils after study
of the main clause (see pupils' text). The boundaries of the various subordinate clauses can then be mapped out by a clear reading, followed
perhaps by group-work drawing on the reconstructions in the pupils'
text.
crines: see note on IV.2.11. On the dangers of being an *ornatrix*, see
Martial *Epigrams* II.66.

2 docta: high praise from a *poeta doctus* (Luck, 1969: 43—4) — cf. VIII.
2.7, Propertius *Elegies* I.7.11 of Cynthia, and Propertius *Elegies* III.23.1

of *his* writing-tablets — but here wittily qualified so that it means 'clever' rather than 'eloquent' or 'soaked in *doctrina*'. The construction with infinitive is imitative of Greek.

Napē: a Greek name.

3 **ministeriis furtivae . . . noctis:** Du Quesnay (in Binns 31) points out the sacral connotations of 'ministeriis', and translates 'at the nocturnal rites of illicit love'.

4 **ingeniosa:** with Form C (dative) of gerundive, unique to Ovid.
notis: ambiguous between either winks and nudges in a secret sign language, or letters (cf. VII.3.14; VII.4.8; Du Quesnay in Binns 30).

5 **Corinnam:** see Barsby 15—16, for a clear statement of the view that 'no such person as Corinna ever existed and that, whatever genuine amatory experience underlies the *Amores*, the Corinna affair is largely the product of a lively imagination and a well-stocked literary memory'.

7 **mane:** position shows it is better taken with 'peraratas'.
peraratas: the metaphor is very infrequent before this passage. The root reference, ploughing a furrow through the wax, is therefore prominent.

9 A commonplace of great antiquity: Barsby cites Homer and Aeschylus, in addition to Tibullus and Ovid.

11 **Cupidinis arcus:** the elegiac poets frequently compared love with warfare. See particularly Ovid *Amores* I.9, and the comments in Barsby 107, 109.

13 **quid agam:** cf. 'quid agis?' = 'How are you?' in VIII.2.4.
noctis: 'a night's lovemaking'.

15 **dum loquor, hora fugit:** modelled on Horace's 'dum loquimur, fugerit invida/aetas: carpe diem, quam minimum credula postero', *Odes* I.11. 7—8 ('While we talk, jealous time has fled: snatch at today, trusting as little as you can in tomorrow'). Ovid does put his trust in tomorrow, and is to be disappointed.

19 **iubeto:** the archaic future imperative.

23 **graphio:** apparently an original coinage, modelled on the Greek.

25 Victorious generals sent letters crowned with laurel to announce their victory to the Senate.

26 Ovid intends to dedicate ('ponere') the tablets in the temple of Venus as a sign of success (cf. crutches at Lourdes). Barsby points out the pun on 'tabellas' (= (i) writing-tablet; (ii) votive tablet), and also gives parallels from Propertius and Horace. The important difference between our passage and the others (Propertius *Elegies* II.14a.23—8 and Horace *Odes* III.26) is that Propertius and Horace are celebrating success, while Ovid has unwisely assumed it.
morer: technically a potential subjunctive, but the present subjunctive fits well at the end of a pentameter and often conveys little more than the sense of the future indicative.

Discussion

The opening passage (1—6) is a sustained *captatio benevolentiae*, an attempt to win Nape's co-operation. Her name is held back to the end of line 2 and the main verb till line 7 in a period designed to excite the reader's curiosity about what Ovid wants of the *ornatrix*. The apparent complexity of this sentence is in fact carefully controlled and it should not present serious difficulty. The first couplet gives us our addressee, an *ornatrix*; the second couplet (3—4) gives Nape's qualifications for employment by a lover; and in the third couplet (5–6) Ovid introduces both his own *persona* and Corinna for the first time, and admits to frequent employment of Nape as a go-between. After 'docta' (2), held over from line 1, it is the penultimate word of all the other lines in this section which provides the fundamental word of reference to Nape on which the other words of description depend: viz. 'habenda', 2; 'cognita', 3; 'ingeniosa', 4; 'hortata', 5; 'reperta', 6. This pattern welds the whole together, and makes the reader's job less strenuous.

Line 1, with its purring 'r's introduces us to the *ornatrix*, taking the reader in imagination into the mistress's boudoir — an appropriate location for elegy. The flattery of her begins in line 2. 'docta' is held over the line-end with great effect, and then immediately trumped by the suggestion that Nape is too good to be thought of as a mere 'ancilla'. The archaic feel of the reversed 'ancillas inter' (2) is striking. Equally so are the use of the infinitive with 'docta'; the quasi-religious connotations of 'ministeriis . . . noctis' (3); the uncommon usage of 'ingeniosa' (4); and the repetition of 'saepe' (5 and 6) in such a strong position. All these combine to give the introduction an unmistakably rhetorical flavour calculated to overawe a mere serving-maid. 'Nape could hardly fail to be flattered and impressed by such a display' (Du Quesnay in Binns 31). The ambiguity of 'notis' in line 4 is a witty touch: at this stage Ovid is merely preparing the ground and his remarks are thus kept general and non-committal. It is in lines 5–6 that Ovid begins to come to the point of his address, and he contrives to introduce 'Corinnam' (5) and 'mihi' (6) in such a way that each word is set in the strong final position, excluded from the balanced 'saepe' + participle clauses of the two lines: 'saepe . . . hortata Corinnam', 5; 'saepe . . . reperta mihi', 6.

With 'accipe' (7) the tension built up in the long introduction is released. A new urgency presents itself as two more imperatives are introduced in line 8, but the rhetorical elegance remains in the structural similarity of lines 7 and 8 ('accipe et . . . -ās'; 'perfer et . . . -ās'); Nape has still to be persuaded. The whole couplet is redolent of effort — on the part both of Nape and of Ovid, for in this venture both are to co-operate. Ovid's first characterisation of himself was as 'laboranti' (6): now we have the three imperatives, the repeated 'per-', the ploughing connotations of 'peraratas' (7), the suggestion implicit in 'mane' that the letter has been written in the early hours after a sleepless night (cf. Ovid *Amores* I.2.3–4; Catullus *Poems* 50.10–16, = *CLC* Unit IV 'odi et amo', poem XI), and the hard application suggested by 'obstantes sedula pelle moras' (8). The intensity of Ovid's passion is now clear.

With the die cast, Ovid spends two more couplets (9–12) confirming his hold over Nape. He appeals to her softness of heart and to her sophisticated view of life, and suggests that she and Ovid are soldiers fighting on the same side. 'The comparative brevity of the phrases and the commonplace metaphors bring a lighter tone: but there is still a certain formality in the repetitions "nec . . . nec . . . nec", the impersonal "credibile est", and the antiquity of the formula in the first hexameter' (Du Quesnay in Binns 31). There is an irony too in the application to Nape of the flint/iron phrase, which is usually found applied to either the lover or his lass. And the climax of the tricolon in lines 9—10 turns out to be wittily double-edged: Ovid's readers would no doubt appreciate, even if Nape's *doctrina* did not extend so far, that lack of 'simplicitas' was not wholly complimentary and that a sneer can be seen as underlying 'ordine maior' (10). In the next couplet too 'et te' (11), though properly taken as 'you as well as Corinna', does admit to misinterpretation as 'even you'. But such poking fun at Nape is no more than incidental. Ovid's primary purpose is to engage her sympathies, and in this final couplet of flattery Ovid adapts the old metaphor of love as a kind of warfare to cover the anticipated co-operation between himself and Nape. A final couple of blandishments are slipped in to tip the balance: Nape is attractive enough to have felt the power of Cupid, and she, a slave-girl, fights as a soldier, alongside a male and a citizen in love's warfare. After such a barrage, Nape is to be considered won over, and it only remains for her to be given her marching orders.

Ovid now (13) invites Nape, and his readers, to make an imaginative leap to the scene where Nape confronts Corinna. This is the nearest we get to an appearance by Corinna in this diptych. The dialogue begins with a conversational platitude, to be answered bluntly by Nape. Again Ovid's urgency obtrudes, and the short, snappy clauses contrast markedly with the grand rhetorical structure of lines 1—8. Ovid has no time for platitudes. The sweet talk is all in the letter. In line 14, Ovid dwells a little on the artistry of his letter; the reader who has experienced Ovid's address to Nape feels he knows the style. But time is pressing on, and 'pelle moras' of line 8 is supplemented by the swiftly dactylic 'dum loquor, hora fugit' (15) in a suggestive allusion to Horace. It is as if he has caught himself gloating over the artistry of his letter. Now the instructions rap out with a profusion of imperatives and hortative subjunctives. 'vacuae' is emphatically placed and its sense underlined by 'bene': Corinna must be alone. 'continuo' (16) keeps up the pressure. The next couplet (17—18) provides us with a prophetic glimpse of the crucial moment when Corinna reads the letter. It is done vividly and in close-up. Ovid will want the full story when Nape returns, not just Corinna's official reply, which Ovid is by now taking for granted as favourable. The pressing 'nec mora' (19) introduces an appropriately compressed hexameter. 'iubeto' (19) is not necessarily as strong as the English 'order!', but Du Quesnay (in Binns 33) is probably right in suggesting that we must suppose an Ovid who enjoins this on a slave-girl to have 'lost contact with reality'. Alternatively, we may suppose that it is merely an extension of his flattery (cf. 'neque ancillas inter habenda',

2): he is treating her like his subordinate in the army (12: the metaphor is still in mind in line 25).

Lines 20—4 bring a noticeable change of style. It is almost as if Nape has now left and Ovid can afford self-indulgent rhapsody on the reply he now confidently anticipates. Line 20 is highly ironical. Ovid does not even consider 'cera vacat' as a possibility, though it turns out that this would be far better than the answer he does get: by VII.4.8—10, he is no longer inclined to refer to the wax as 'splendida'. Barsby remarks on the visual contrast between the 'late splendida cera' (20) which Ovid hopes he won't get, and the close-packed lines of writing ('comprimat ordinibus versus', 21) which he hopes he will. There is also a fleeting reminiscence of Nape's hairdressing from line 1 ('in ordine ponere crines'). The extreme separation of 'oculos' (21) from 'meos' (22) and exaggeration of 'margine in extremo' seem designed to emphasise the length of this imaginary letter. Ovid has so convinced himself now of Corinna's pliability that he can afford the luxury of a little sentimentality (23). 'digitos' is brought forward for emphasis and the stilus is described with a disparaging Greek word: Ovid will not have Corinna's lovely fingers tired by a mere instrument, when they are needed for caresses. The answering pentameter (24) is very firm, with initial 'hoc' prefiguring final 'veni' and supported in mid-line by 'scriptum', and with the balanced 'h'/'h', 't'/'t' alliteration. Between line 20 ('odi, cum late splendida cera vacat') and line 24 ('hoc habeat scriptum tota tabella "veni." ') the lover has performed a complete *volte-face*. His passion is one that will brook no delay, and this effectively rules out the lengthy love letter from Corinna which he would like, but cannot have because it *does* involve 'mora' (cf. 'moretur' in line 21 and the time implications of 'lassare tenendo' in line 23). Passion prevails over the finesse of courtship, and passion not only blinds Ovid to the possibility of a negative reply, but allows him to confuse fantasy (where the lover controls what the loved one writes) with reality (where he has to wait and see).

The poem finishes on a triumphant note, as if 'veni' (24) were the actual reply. At first, in lines 25—6, it seems to the reader as if Ovid is being properly cautious, since it is not until the final word of the pentameter (26) that he allows 'morer' to cancel the negative. The rich imagery of line 25 and the detailed commitments of lines 26—8 show the extent of his confidence, which now verges on hybris. The final phrase ('AT NVPER VILE FVISTIS ACER', 28) suggests the nemesis to follow in VII.4: just as the pretensions of the tablets are debunked, so must be those of the lover, and the final word 'ăcer' perhaps suggests the adjective 'ācer' ('sharp', 'severe'). Why does the lover include such a phrase on his dedication? Presumably because the contrast with the supposed new power of the tablets is rhetorically satisfying. In these two final couplets a number of reminiscences of lines 1—6 give the poem a structural unity: 'redimire' (25) reminds one of the *ornatrix* in lines 1—2; 'fidas' (27) picks up 'fida' (6); 'ministras' (27) picks up 'ministeriis' (3); the status-change of 'NVPER VILE FVISTIS ACER' (28) is comparable with 'neque ancillas inter habenda Nape' (2).

The poem seems to demand a sequel. Ovid began with exceptional realism as he described his manipulation of Nape, but gradually moves his *persona* into a world of fantasy where he can be in control of other people's — in particular Corinna's — reactions. We seem to need a harsh return to reality, and that is what VII.4 provides.

Questions

1 What picture of Nape emerges from lines 1—12? Is there any reason to suspect its accuracy?

2 Are lines 1—6 carefully patterned? If so, why?

3 How are the following words ambiguous? 'dominam' (7); 'mane' (7); 'simplicitas' (10); 'et te' (11).

4 What can we learn about the character of Ovid the lover?

5 Analyse the structure of this poem. At what point does Nape leave?

6 How realistic is Nape's imagined interview with Corinna (13ff.)?

7 Why does Ovid write 'AT NVPER VILE FVISTIS ACER' (28)?

8 To what extent is the reader aware of a separation between Ovid the writer and Ovid the lover?

9 Find out about (a) women's hairstyles (see note on IV.2.11); (b) writing materials in the Roman world (see III.1 question 5; Paoli Ch. 16; Hadas 105; *CLC* Unit I slide 43 and Unit II slide 31).

VII.4 Ovid, Amores *I.12.1—10, 21—30*

Context

See on VII.3.

Language and content

1 **tristes:** predicative — 'with a gloomy answer'.
   rediere: Corinna erases Ovid's note with the top of her stilus, and returns the same set of tablets with her answer.
   tabellae: on their construction and use, see Paoli 181—2. Cf. Propertius *Elegies* III.23.1 — 'ergo tam doctae nobis periere tabellae' — where the tablets have been lost.

4 For stumbling on the threshold being a bad omen, cf. the custom of carrying one's bride over it (Catullus *Poems* 61.159—60, with Fordyce's note). In Plutarch *Tiberius Gracchus* XVII.3, one of many omens which fail to deter Tiberius Gracchus is stumbling on the threshold 'so that the nail of his big toe was split and blood ran out through his shoe'.
   digitos . . . icta: see note on VI.3.24.

9 **putŏ:** ironic — we are not meant to take Ovid too seriously.

cicutae: Pliny the Elder says of hemlock (*Natural History* XXV.95.151–
4) that its seeds, leaves and blossom are poisonous, and it was used by
the Athenians for capital punishment; but that the stem is not poisonous and can be eaten either cooked or as a salad; it can be made into an
effective eye-ointment; breasts stay firm if rubbed with hemlock in
youth or lose their milk if nursing; rubbing the testicles with it in
puberty removes the desire for sex.

10   **sub:** the beeswax honeycomb forms the substructure on which the
honey is deposited.

    Corsica: see Pliny the Elder (*Natural History* XVI.28.71) for the bitter-
ness of Corsican honey, resulting from the prevalence of box.

*11–20   Omitted. Ovid's fulminations continue against (i) the wax of the tablets
(*11–12); (ii) their wooden casing (*13–14); (iii) their maker (*15–
16); and (iv) the tree from which they were made (*17–20). He rises to
an emotional peak in lines *19–20, accusing the tree of harbouring
ominous horned owls and the eggs of vulture and screech owl.

11–16   Propertius writes (*Elegies* III.23.17–20) of a love message on his lost
tablets (see on line 1) from a 'volens non stulta puella garrula', and
then says of the tablets:

> me miserum, his aliquis rationem scribit avarus
>   et ponit diras inter ephemeridas!

'Heaven help me! Some miser is writing up his accounts on them and
filing them among his hateful ledgers.'

12   **mollia:** a favourite word of Propertius, common in Tibullus and in
Ovid's love poetry (see Barsby).

13–14   For Ovid's experience of the law, see Introduction 4.

13   **capiant:** potential subjunctive referring to the future – 'they would
more fitly bear . . . '

    vadimonia: legal undertaking, secured by bail, to appear in court on a
certain day. It was read out by the opposing party's lawyer ('cognitor',
14).

15   **iacerent:** potential subjunctive referring to the present – 'they would
be better lying . . . '

16   **fleret:** seems to be an explanatory generic subjunctive (Woodcock section 156). Ledgers are the sort of books over which a miser weeps. The
tense naturally follows that of 'iacerent' (15).

19   **precer:** deliberative subjunctive.

20   **alba:** the wax is currently red ('rubebas', *11; 'color sanguinulentus',
*12). This rather unusual effect – most wax being black-coloured –
was obtained by dyeing with cinnabar (sulphide of mercury) imported
largely from Spain.

Discussion

VII.3 concludes with the ominous 'VILE FVISTIS ACER'. There is no
reconstruction of the scene between Nape and Corinna which follows.
Ovid is more subtle. Just as he has suggested obliquely the style of his
famous letter by means of honeyed words to Nape, so the imagined
interview of VII.3.13ff. does duty for reality. In VII.4 Ovid focuses on
the lover's reaction to rebuff, establishing a stark contrast with the confident, triumphant tone of the lover in VII.3.

The first couplet, indeed the first word, initiates the atmosphere of

gloom. 'flete', 'tristes', 'infelix' (and 'omina', 3) are all placed first word
in their clauses, and 'negat' concludes the couplet very strongly. Further,
the first line and a half is heavily endowed with long vowels, and the
ellipsis of 'eam' in line 2 relieves Ovid from painful reference to Corinna.
But the whole is undercut by 'hodie' (2): these paroxysms of grief result
from Corinna's inability to entertain the poet on the day of writing.
Ovid must here be laughing at the antics of his *persona*. The explicit
reference to Propertius confirms this self-mockery. Propertius is sad
because he has lost his writing-tablets; Ovid is sad because his have
returned.

Grief now spills over into anger, as Ovid manufactures a reason for
his failure in the supposed inefficiency of Nape. He is still not prepared
to admit that his own lack of realism, and possibly the very urgency of
his passion, was at fault. He prefers to find a scapegoat. 'omina sunt
aliquid' (3) is an in-character remark, not necessarily Ovid's own opinion.
Nape's misdemeanour turns out to be amusingly small-scale, and the
deflationary effect of the pentameter (4) is confirmed by the double
allusion to VII.3: in VII.3.2, Nape is introduced with similar emphasis
at the end of the line, but the tone is very different from this peremp-
tory accusation; in VII.3.23, Ovid showed great concern for Corinna's
'digitos', but there is no answering sympathy for Nape's toes! The lover,
however, in his arrogant blindness, takes the point so seriously that he
compounds the humour by addressing a couplet of advice and rebuke
to Nape. The contrast with the deferential address of VII.3 is extreme:
Ovid now implies that Nape is a careless drunkard. The irony is that it
is Ovid himself who most conspicuously lacks circumspection and
temperance.

The pent-up anger is immediately (line 7) redirected against the
writing-tablets. This whirling around from one object of wrath to
another is psychologically plausible even if three addressees in seven
lines make for a rather disjointed poem. Ovid's sights are now fixed
firmly on the tablets — even less deserving of blame than Nape, since
they merely reflect the thoughts of Corinna and himself. They are personified ('ite', 'difficiles', 7) in order to make them a slightly worthier
target and then immediately depersonalised ('ligna', 7; 'cera', 8) as Ovid
considers their constituent substances. There is strong alliteration, particularly of 'f', 'l' and 't', which runs over into the next couplet (9—10)
and fits well with the insulting remarks Ovid addresses to the tablets.
The dislocation of the word-order in line 7 is possibly intended to
mirror the lover's anger; its boldness is certainly intended to appeal to
the reader (cf. Williams, 1968: 726—8, on this sort of patterning).
'funebria ligna' continues the gloom of the introduction, echoed in this
couplet by final 'tabellae' (7 and 1) and 'negaturis'/'negat' (8 and 2).
The unpoetic 'referta' (8) is ironical: Ovid had specifically asked for a
full reply (VII.3.21—2) and a full reply he has received, but with the

'negaturis . . . notis' (8) that he refused to envisage in VII.3. 'puto' (9)
shows that Ovid is not entirely serious in his attack on the wax, which
merits another hexameter (9) with unusual word-order. 'longae' (9)
seems otiose, except in that it assists the prevalent 'l'-alliteration.
'cicutae', placed strongly at the end of line 9, adds to the deadly connotations in 'funebria' (7).

After our omission (see notes), Ovid pauses to reflect with an
incredulous rhetorical question. The depth of feeling comes over in the
heavy metrical centre of line 11, where 'insanus' is used with a nicely
ironical twist: Ovid was not behaving rationally in VII.3, but his
irrationality did not consist in his choice of writing-tablets. 'mollia' (12)
is carefully chosen both as a common descriptive word for elegiac
poetry and as a strong contrast both with Ovid's own tough words
against the tablets and with the 'duro cognitor ore' who appears in line
14. This line (12) also carries the only specific reference to Corinna in
the poem, if we exclude the ellipsis in line 2. Corinna is still 'domina',
and Ovid will no doubt soon be trying his luck again.

For the moment, he shifts his ground to a consideration of better
uses for the 'tabellae'. The substantial reference to Propertius (see notes
on lines 11—16) makes it quite clear to the observant and literate reader
that Ovid is mocking the vigorous attack launched by his *persona*.

> 'Ovid shows a delightful ingenuity in his adaptation of this
> passage: his vignette of the weeping miser is much more vivid
> and amusing than Propertius'; his introduction of the "cognitor"
> with the implied contrast between him and the gentle lover
> intensifies the contemptuous tone; and it was a brilliant stroke
> to transfer the epithet "garrula" from the "puella" to the
> "vadimonia". Even more important is the fact that Ovid has
> completely reversed the sentiments of Propertius. The latter is
> emotionally attached to his writing tablets and fears that they
> are now being used for some menial task. Ovid, on the contrary,
> wishes that his tablets were used for such work so that they
> could not ruin his happiness' (Du Quesnay in Binns 39).

Lines 17—18 remind the reader of the first couplet: the 'tabellae' are
of ill omen. The word-play on 'duplices' (17) is rather heavily protracted
into the pentameter (18). Such a labouring of the number two may be
intended to remind his readers that Ovid has himself paralleled the
double tablets with his pair of poems. 'auspicii . . . non . . . boni', spread
over the line, is very powerful. Ovid concludes with a curse, which,
sinister though it is, we can hardly take seriously. The curse makes a
neat complement to the dedication in the final couplet of VII.3. 'cariosa
senectus/rodat' (19—20) is particularly vivid, not least because of the
stress placed on 'rodat' by its position and the implication that old age
is like a gnawing animal; perhaps the very extravagance of this expression,

applied let us remember to writing-tablets, is intended to undercut any serious interpretation.

VII.4, like VII.3, is a parody of the distracted lover in elegiac poetry. The reader, if he remains alert for the various clues both within the poem and in the corpus of elegy, will laugh with Ovid at Ovid's portrait of himself behaving as lovers traditionally behave.

Questions

1 How does Ovid build up a picture of unrelieved gloom in lines 1–10? Is it in fact unrelieved?
2 Should we modify our picture of Nape derived from VII.3? If not, why not?
3 Are there any indications in this poem that we are not expected to take it at face value?
4 Contrast lines 11–16 with Propertius *Elegies* III.23.17–20. Why does Ovid choose to draw on the Propertius poem? Why does he make the changes that he does?
5 Read in translation Ovid *Ars Amatoria* I.351–98. To what extent does he follow his own advice in this pair of poems?
6 Explore Roman superstition. (Paoli Ch. 26; Balsdon, 1969: 65–7; Hadas 124–5; *CLC* Unit I *Teacher's Handbook* 84–5; *CLC* Unit III *Stage 22*: 18–19; *CLC* Unit III *Teacher's Handbook* 50–1 and slide 8; Lewis and Reinhold II: 568–71.)

VII.5 Martial, Epigrams IV.71

Language and content

1 **quaero:** 'I have been and am still investigating' (cf. note on VIII.2.15), **Safroni Rufe:** Safronius Rufus is again addressed in Martial *Epigrams* XI.103, with the implication that he is over-fastidious and puritanical about sex.
2 **neget:** subjunctive in indirect question.
3 **tamquam:** on comparative clauses containing the protasis of an 'unreal' conditional sentence with suppressed apodosis, see Woodcock section 254.
6 **dat:** for the idiom, see Martial *Epigrams* II.9, with Friedlaender's note.

Discussion

This light-hearted epigram depends for its effect (i) on the supposed promiscuity of girls in Rome (cf., e.g., Ovid, *Amores* I.8.43ff.); (ii) on the idiomatic uses of 'negare' and 'dare'.

The first line is laboriously phrased, with 'totam' widely separated from 'urbem', and metrically heavy. Martial's inquiry has been exhaustive and exhausting. We expect a serious piece of research. The pentameter destroys that expectation, and the amusingly direct and conclusive second half establishes and exaggerates the moral emergency which

Martial is outraged by in the middle couplet and resolves in the third.
The spondees of the second couplet support Martial's measured indig-
nation. He posits a topsyturvy world where the conventionally moral is
viewed as undesirable and intolerable. The tricolon culminates in 'non
liceat' (4), before the conclusion of the survey is reiterated. The third
couplet probes the generalisation by means of an interrogator. The
answer he gets is surprising: 'sunt castae mille'. How can Martial unravel
the paradox? With applomb. His final remark mirrors the repeated 'nulla
puella negat' of lines 2 and 4, and the last two letters of 'negat' (coupled
with the ubiquitous '-ll-') clatter through line 6. Girls are in fact just as
chaste as ever: it is merely the fashion to give the impression of avail-
ability. Safronius Rufus (see notes) would no doubt have been dismayed
at Martial's initial findings, but at least partially mollified by his conclusion.

The epigram was taken more literally by Samuel Pepys (*The Diary of
Samuel Pepys*, 4 September 1660): 'From thence to Axeyard to my
house; where standing at the door, Mrs Diana comes by, whom I took
into my house upstairs and there did dally with her a great while, and
find that in Latin "nulla puella negat".'

Questions

1 Explain what Martial claims to have discovered, and what he
   has in fact discovered.
2 How important are pattern and repetition to the success of this
   epigram?
3 What is the point of the follow-up to this epigram (Martial
   Epigrams IV.81):

> epigramma nostrum cum Fabulla legisset
> negare nullam quo queror puellarum,
> semel rogata bisque terque neglexit
> preces amantis. iam, Fabulla, promitte:
> negare iussi, pernegare non iussi.

4 Is Max Miller making the same point in the following:

> I like the girls who do,
>   I like the girls who don't,
> I hate the girl who says she will,
>   And then she says she won't.
>
> But the girl I like the best of all,
>   And I think you'll say I'm right,
> Is the girl who says she never does,
>   But she looks as though she — 'Ere!
>   (quoted in *Times Literary Supplement*, 17 October 1975,
>   in review of *The Max Miller Blue Book* by P. Keating)

Section VIII

Section VIII contains a selection of portraits. The characters portrayed are with one exception rather unpleasant or unfortunate individuals — or at least that is the view which our authors intend us to take. The exception is VIII.5, Martial's poem on the young Regulus. This would have greater appeal if it did not give the impression of praising the son to secure favour from the father. Nonetheless, the contrast between the mighty institutions of Rome and the two-year-old boy is wittily managed. Catullus' poem (VIII.1, 'salve, nec minimo puella naso') seems devastatingly hurtful, though intended as praise of Lesbia and a general attack on provincial bad taste as much as an attack on the girl concerned. The sarcasm employed by Catullus is typical of Martial, who is almost equally hard on Laetinus (VIII.4) and Fabulla (VIII.6) — both trying to retain their youth in ways which Martial finds unseemly. Unlike Catullus, Martial keeps the epigram personal. There is nothing to soften his attack. Horace's pest (VIII.2) and Ovid's 'lena' (VIII.3) are more substantial creations, though both take their origin as much from literary type as from real life. The treatment of the two is very different, and is largely determined by the particular genre in which the author concerned was working. Horace gives us a slice-of-life, conversational account of a meeting. Ovid draws much more obviously on the work of his predecessors, addressing what he has to say directly to his reader and sustaining an air of fantasy solely for the pleasure of undercutting it.

VIII.1 Catullus, Poems *43*

Context

The subject of our poem is identified with Ameana (if our text preserves the name reliably) of *Poems* 41, 'puella defututa', since each is described as 'decoctoris amica Formiani'.

Language and content

For hendecasyllabics, see notes on II.1.

    5 **decoctoris . . . Formiani:** i.e., Mamurra, an *eques* from Formiae and a regular target of Catullus; Julius Caesar's chief engineer for, e.g., the Gallic campaigns; efficient at making fortunes and squandering them. See further, Fordyce 160.

    6 **provincia:** Caesar spent the winters with his troops in Cisalpine Gaul, so Mamurra would no doubt have created an impression there.

    8 **infacetum:** a vogue-word of the Catullan set, which prized *facetiae*.

Discussion

The lively 'salve' (1) conjures up a chance meeting in the street. As Catullus moves into apostrophe, we expect to hear a few compliments; and this possibility is still just open at the end of line 1, where we anticipate something like 'nec maximo' to set the balance straight about her nose. Instead, we are swept at full tilt into a withering catalogue of plainness — jarring with the tenderness of the diminutive 'ocellis' (2), itself emphasised by assonant 'pu*ell*a' and '*bell*o'. Such a list is the more damning for being modelled on conventional lists of *good* points (see Fordyce; Quinn, 1973). It is curious that there is no mention of hair, which usually figures in such lists. 'salve' (1) is in any case clearly ironical: Catullus does not wish Ameana well. Quinn (1973) refers to the various phrases as 'a series of hammer-blows dismissing Ameana on count after count'. The negative phrasing (cf. I.5) enables Catullus to suggest the positive at the same time as he denies it. Line 4 seems intended as climactic, whether Catullus is criticising vocabulary, accent or (conceivably) sexual catholicism. A more specific apostrophe follows, allowing tentative identification (see note on Context), and for the first time suggesting that Catullus' subject is a real girl. Two heavily-loaded questions bring him to the point of the poem. What galls Catullus, and has occasioned this vitriolic outburst, is that Ameana should be thought the equal of Lesbia. There must surely be an acidic edge to 'provincia' (6). What could Cisalpine Gaul, for all its attractions, know about chic, urbane terms like *bellus*? What standards *are* there outside Rome? The *coup de grâce* comes in line 8, with another favourite Catullan term in the position of greatest stress, and with the heavy privative prefix reinforced by that of 'insapiens'. We have moved from specific to the most general of remarks. Catullus' real target is not the girl, nor even here Mamurra, but tasteless provincialism.

Questions

1 Use lines 1–4 to produce a positive list of points which Catullus admired in women. On what grounds would you criticise this list? Consider the way criteria of beauty change from age to age (cf., e.g., *CLC* Unit IV slides 4, 5, 8). Can any conclusions be drawn?

2 Who or what is the object of Catullus' attack?

3 Is this poem anything more than just a spiteful outburst written in verse? Contrast *Poems* 86 ('Quintia formosa est multis' = *CLC* Unit IV 'odi et amo', poem II).

4 Some commentators punctuate with a full stop after line 4 and a comma after line 5. Is this preferable? (See Quinn, 1973.)

VIII.2 Horace, Satires *I.9.1–21*

Context

This is the opening scene of what Rudd (1966: 75) describes as 'a minia-ture drama'. Horace writes of himself as buttonholed by an insensitive social climber who refuses to be deflected from sharing the poet's walk.

Pupils may well remark on the similarities with *CLC* Unit II *Stage* 17:
6–8 'ad templum'.

Language and content

1 **ibam forte:** an unpretentious introduction to a story.
via Sacra: 'the setting (is) the Via Sacra between the Velia and tribunal
of the Forum' (Dudley 78). Horace is walking towards the Forum. See
CLC Unit III slide 19, and plan in pupils' text.

2 **meditans:** the active present participle is frequently used to supplement
deponent verbs. 'meditans' may suggest that Horace is actually saying
over to himself the 'nescio quid nugarum'.
nescio quid . . . nugarum: for the shortened 'o' here and in line 10, see
Lejay on *Satires* I.1.104. There is no need to assume that 'nugae' are
necessarily poetic trifles, but the word is often used in this sense (cf.
Catullus *Poems* I.4).

6 **cum:** elision of monosyllables is not uncommon, and not restricted to
Horace.
num quid vis?: 'is that all?' 'nothing else, is there?' A conventional
method of breaking off a conversation.

7 **noris:** possibly a potential subjunctive (Lejay), but see Palmer for the
view that 'ut' is to be supplied following 'num quid vis?'.
docti: i.e. steeped in literary culture (cf. note on VII.3.2).

8 **misere:** colloquial.

9–10 **ire, consistere, dicere:** historic infinitives, not identified as such in
pupils' text.

11–12 **o te . . . felicem!:** exclamatory Form B (accusative).

11 **cerebri:** the meaning 'temper' is colloquial. Cf. IX.2.21.

13 **garriret:** colloquial.
vicos: for buildings that might have caught his eye, see Rudd, 1966:
80–1 and n. 52.

15 **iamdudum video:** 'iamdudum' in this sense regularly takes the present
(cf. French 'depuis'). 'I have seen for a long time and I see now.' Cf.
VII.5.1.

17 **circumagi:** seems to be colloquial.

18 **is:** rarely found in poetry.
Caesaris hortos: bequeathed by Julius Caesar to the people of Rome
(Suetonius, *Julius Caesar* 83), these were on the west side of the Tiber
near the Porta Portuensis. To get there, Horace would have to continue
down the Via Sacra to the Forum, take the Vicus Tuscus, go through
the Forum Boarium and cross the Tiber on the Pons Aemilius, from
where there would still be a substantial walk along the Via Portuensis –
Lejay estimates about an hour's walk in all.

20 **auriculas:** the diminutive was regularly used in colloquial speech.
Horace may also be using it to evoke sympathy: 'poor little . . . '; cf.
'asellus'.

21 **dorso:** may mean either '(too heavy) for his back' (so Kiessling and
Heinze) or '(has taken the weight of) with his back' (Palmer).
subiit: the original long vowel is preserved.

Discussion

The impact of the first half-line is considerable. It appeals because of its
simple, conversational style, and its promise of a first-person account.
'via Sacra' adds a precise location, a street that Horace's audience could

not fail to have walked down. This precision is later seen to contrast amusingly with an artful vagueness about the identity of the man who accosts him.

Horace must now establish the light-hearted tone of his poem. 'sicut meus est mos' (1) is so placed that it appears to be describing the walk down the Via Sacra, a habit so common as to be not worth remarking on. It is only as the sentence progresses into line 2, that one realises that Horace does have a significant and amusing habit — working on his poetry in one of the busiest streets of Rome. The reader is clearly intended to find the self-depreciatory attitude of Horace engaging.

The interruption in line 3 by the pest (adopting Rudd's word, *faute de mieux*) is abrupt. The man's aggressive brusqueness is intensified by the repetition of the prefix 'ad-' in the first syllable of lines 3, 4 and 6. In line 3, the verb is brought forward to shatter the poet's train of thought, and this allows Horace to save for last the stinging 'tantum'. The irony is that the name is one of the few things that Horace does not disclose about his interlocutor in the course of the poem, resolutely and disparagingly referring to him as 'ille' (cf. 6, 12, 13). The situation worsens in line 4. We are, after all, in the status-obsessed world of Rome (line 1), so Horace is justifiably shocked when his hand is grabbed by a virtual stranger and he is treated to an extravagantly familiar form of address ('dulcissime rerum'). There follows a series of colloquial remarks, giving the verse great immediacy. These remarks, of course, are intended to confirm relationships rather than exchange information. The precise innuendo is impossible to determine, not least because tone of delivery counts for much here; the quality of the reading must have been crucial when these lines were recited. What is abundantly clear is that (i) the pest makes himself objectionable; (ii) the poet makes polite but cold attempts to extricate himself from the pest's company; (iii) he is unsuccessful in this, because the pest refuses to take the conventional hints. In line 5, 'ut nunc est' may carry the implication that life is fine as things are, and will not be enhanced by the continued presence of the pest. In case this should not be strong enough, the poet sweeps into a conventional formula of disengagement. Literally, of course, the poet's wishes are the precise opposite of the pest's, and this reaffirms the fundamentally humorous character of this piece. The hint is not taken, since the pest is blind, or feigns blindness, to the social niceties. He boorishly keeps in tow — the clumsiness mirrored by the five-syllable spondaic 'adsectaretur'. With his next remark, the poet actually manages to break in before the pest is able to reply. 'num quid vis?' seems to leave no loop-hole for misinterpretation. But 'at' (6) warns us that the pest has not taken the point. 'noris nos' (7) comes strongly at the beginning of the line, following the first enjambment of the poem. The pest has taken Horace's rhetorical question literally, and says that he *does* want Horace to recognise him as a friend and fellow-*doctus*. What the man has not grasped is that by admitting he is no real acquaintance of Horace he condemns his own effusively familiar behaviour: any truly *doctus vir* would be fully alive to the social conventions which the pest so patently flouts. With his next remark ('pluris hoc . . . mihi eris'), Horace perhaps fastens on just this misapprehension. It is uttered in exasperation: verbal communication is no longer possible with a man who seems to speak a different language. 'I shall value you the more', says Horace, 'when you do show yourself *doctus* (i.e. and remove yourself).' That 'hoc' is intended to carry such a weight is indicated by its initial position in line 8 and perhaps also by the future tense of 'eris'. But yet again, what Horace says is open to misinterpretation by the pest, who could understand the same words as meaning 'I shall value you the more for being *doctus*.' Horace can no longer compete verbally, and resorts to evasive action with a chorus of melancholy 'ē' sounds.

Narrative is now resumed (line 9), and the pace is kept fast by the use of historic infinitives, elision and asyndeton. Metre reflects action with particular clarity in line 9: the first two dactylic feet trip along swiftly, and are followed by the unusual combination of a diaeresis after the second foot and no caesura in the third, while the third and fourth feet add to this deceleration with their spondees and lengthier words. The pace picks up again with the frantic and tantalising whisper to the slave, then slows despairingly with the spondaic 'cum sudor . . . aiebam' (10—12) — all but three of the thirteen vowels of line 11 being naturally long. By the end of line 10, Horace is in a sweat both physically, from all the rushing about, and psychologically, from the stress of conflict and frustration. It is a vivid touch, far removed from the social jockeying of lines 4—8.

We have had narrative and we have had dialogue; now, at this point of total exasperation, we have a muttered aside, as 'tacitus' (12) confirms, for the benefit of the reader. With this exclamation (11—12), Horace (i) gives the reader variety; (ii) underlines, by naming even his choleric type, the failure to name the pest; (iii) credits himself, by contrast, with a refined and delicately sensitive nature. 'felicem' (12) is emphatically positioned, and the tense of 'aiebam' suggests that the aside is repeated more than once. Certainly we are expected to infer that Horace is himself 'infelix'. The pest meanwhile chatters aimlessly ('quidlibet') about the topography. The beginning of line 14 is kept slow and gloomy with its heavy, four-syllable imperfect. At which point the pest, in a return to dialogue and in the lighter half of the line, suddenly reveals that he does appreciate that he is unwelcome — the crucial 'abire' kept back to surprise us after 'inquit' — and then has the gall to admit that he has long realised this ('iamdudum video', 15). Horace's initial objection to the man was that he failed to react to the conventions of social discourse. Now he appears in a much blacker light. 'docti sumus' (7) begins to look an even more ridiculous claim:

how could a *doctus vir* behave like this? The nastiness is even more evident in the pest's remaining words (15—16). Horace's attempts to shake
him off are discounted in advance ('nil agis'); 'usque' and the prefix of
'persequar' indicate an ominous perseverance; 'quo nunc iter est tibi'
closes the net prematurely on the sort of escape-route Horace is about
to attempt. The poet's surface politeness remains unruffled as he tells
the pest that there is no need to come out of his way. Horace is now
engaged on his final, desperate attempt to free himself. Not content
with the strong implications of 'nil opus est te / circumagi' (15—16), he
makes his attack three-pronged with the additional assertions that the
invalid ('cubat', 18) he is going to visit is not known to the pest, and
that he lives a long way away. That the invalid is a fabrication must be
intended by the casual atmosphere of line 2. This makes Horace's plight
the more embarrassing (for him) and amusing (for us) when his gambit
predictably fails. 'non tibi notum' (17) is a clear reminder to the pest
that he is outside the charmed circle of Horace and his acquaintances.
(Line 18 incidentally confirms for Horace's readers that the setting is
contemporary. Julius Caesar had bequeathed his gardens only some
nine years previous to publication.) Horace may be desperate but
decorum prevents him from speaking his mind or using physical force.
His three-pronged attack is bound to fail: (i) the pest has specifically
stated that he will follow Horace wherever he goes (15—16); (ii) a man
who addresses a passing acquaintance (3) as 'dulcissime rerum' (4) is
unlikely to be put off by Horace's second argument; (iii) distance is no
barrier to a man who says 'usque tenebo' (15) and 'persequar' (16). For
the sake of form, the pest delivers his *coup de grâce* in line 19. He is at
a loose end and full of energy, and will keep on following ('usque
sequar', 19, effectively picking up and concentrating 'usque tenebo',
15, and 'persequar', 16). Horace's civilised approach to life provides
him with no further resistance, and he deflates. The image with which
this is described is particularly sharp. On the one hand, Horace is no
longer able to voice his feelings ('demitto auriculas', 20), is resentful
('iniquae mentis', 20), is pitiable (the diminutives in 20), and has taken
on more than he can deal with ('gravius . . . onus', 21). On the other hand,
his behaviour is quintessentially that of sophisticated urban man and in
no way brutish; and he is behaving stupidly ('asellus') only to the extent
that he fails to be a little more bestial towards the pest — who more
than warrants a donkey-like kick.

There is no point in trying to fix a name on the pest. Horace con-
scientiously strove to avoid this (see above), and the character could
equally well be a compound of literary types like Theophrastus'
Chatterer and Talker (Penguin translation 29 and 32—3) and personal
experiences (Rudd, 1966: 74—5 and 284, n. 38). The pest is a caricature, closely related to the types of Roman comedy. For Horace,
what seems increasingly unpleasant about him is (i) his presumption in

making contact with a social superior; (ii) his boorish failure to read the semaphore of social disengagement; (iii) his wilful persistence in keeping contact, despite an appreciation of Horace's reluctance. Horace depicts himself as (by implication) a man of status and refinement, but also a man who proves unable in the last resort to descend to vulgar counter-measures. There is no need to consider the self-portrait as any less of a caricature (his lack of temper, e.g., does not square with the putative self-portrait of VII.2.22—3), but it does perhaps show Horace under cover of humour whitewashing his peasant origins. The whole piece is, of course, highly colloquial in diction (see notes), even in the final simile where one might have expected a heightening of language (cf. IV.1).

A reading of Ben Jonson's version of these lines (*Poetaster*, Act III Scene i) would be entertaining, not least for the period detail grafted on by Jonson.

Questions

1. What sort of picture does Horace give us of himself in lines 1— 2? Is it meant to be flattering? Do we modify our opinion as the poem proceeds?

2. Why do you think Horace studiously avoids telling us the pest's name, when this is the one thing he claims to know about the man (line 3)?

3. How seriously are we meant to take this poem? How early does Horace let us know?

4. Translate into colloquial English the exchanges in lines 4—8. In what sense could 'cupio omnia quae vis' be described as ironical? How does the pest misinterpret 'num quid vis?' (6)? Why is the pest anxious to seem *doctus* (7), and is there any reason for thinking him not so? What precisely is meant by 'pluris hoc mihi eris' (7—8)?

5. What might Horace have whispered to his slave (10)? Why doesn't he tell us?

6. Why does Horace introduce his aside to Bolanus (11—12)? Is he telling us something about himself?

7. How effective is the final simile (20—1)?

8. Discuss Horace's use of metre in lines 9—12 (' . . . felicem!').

9. Write an account of this same episode as seen through the eyes of the pest.

10. Write a continuation of this excerpt, showing how Horace escapes, then compare it with the original in translation.

11. Why does Horace dislike the pest? Does your answer tell us anything about Roman society?

12. Use the plan in the pupils' text to plot Horace's route, assuming that he did in fact proceed to Caesar's Gardens (see note on

line 18). Find out what you can (e.g. from Dudley) about the
various buildings, etc., on the way, remembering that the poem
dates from about 35 B.C. Use this information to reconstruct
what the pest might have been saying about the city.

VIII.3 Ovid, Amores *I.8.1—18*

Context

For Ovid's *Amores*, see note on Context of IV.2. *Amores* I.8 is the
longest poem in the collection. It begins with a lively description of a
lena (go-between, procuress; see Williams, 1968: 542—3), excerpted
here. Ovid then imagines he is eavesdropping on a conversation between
the *lena* and a young and innocent girl, in which the girl is given suit-
ably meretricious advice and warned against wasting her talents on her
poet lover. The *lena* is by Ovid's time a well-established literary type,
an imaginative creation: Barsby (93) cites Roman comedy, Greek mime
and Greek New Comedy, and Propertius and Tibullus as well as Ovid.
Ovid, as usual, writes with awareness of precedent, developed for his
own purposes.

Language and content

1　**volet**: no special force to the future.
2　**Dipsas**: cf. Horace's choice of 'Bibulus' in *Odes* III.28.8. Drunkenness
　　was a regular condition of such disreputable old women: see Barsby for
　　references and Ward-Perkins and Claridge item 34, for illustration.
4　**Memnonis**: Memnon was son of Dawn and the immortal Tithonus. He
　　was black from accompanying his mother driving her chariot and horses
　　across the sky. Eventually he became King of Ethiopia, an appropriately
　　hot locality.
5　**magas**: the adjectival use was apparently coined by Ovid.
7　**rhombo**: one of the various devices used in attractive magic (see Gow
　　on Theocritus *Idyll* 2.17 and 30 and Plate V). The 'rhombus' here is
　　probably (see LSJ and L&S) a disc with a double string ('licia') threaded
　　through holes on either side of the centre. The disc is set in motion by
　　twisting and pulling the strings. Revolving this magic wheel was
　　intended to attract a loved one and hold him captive.
8　**virus amantis equae**: a traditional love-charm, usually called by its Greek
　　name 'hippomanes' and often associated with a pregnant mare rather
　　than a mare on heat.
9, 10　**cum voluit**: strongly reminiscent of Tibullus, *Elegies* I.2.49—50:

> cum libet, haec tristi depellit nubila caelo;
> 　　cum libet, aestivo convocat orbe nives.

'When she pleases, she drives the clouds from the gloomy sky; when she
pleases, she assembles snow in the vault of summer.'

See Discussion. For the perfect indicative used to generalise clauses in
the present, see Woodcock section 217 (2*c*).
13　Cf. ?Lucian *Lucius or the Ass* 12—13 (on which is based Apuleius
　　Golden Ass III.21), for a supposedly eyewitness account of a woman
　　turning into a bird.

15 **pupula duplex**: Pliny the Elder, *Natural History* VII.2.16—17, records a
couple of travellers' tales referring to this peculiarity. Those so endowed
could put on the evil eye(s) so effectively that they killed their victims.

Discussion

The description opens on a note of mystery. 'est quaedam' is given
special prominence, isolated by the early caesura; but then Ovid teases
his audience by interpolating the 'quicumque' clause. The solemnity of
the beginning is soon dispelled by the concluding words of lines 1 and 2
('lenam'; 'Dipsas anus'). Ovid is going to introduce his readers to a *lena*.
(Alternatively, the 'quicumque' clause may be parrying, not without
irony, the anticipated objections that the reader may have to the actual
existence of such a *lena*: cf. Williams, 1968: 546.) The second couplet
merely develops the implications of 'Dipsas' (see pupils' text), but does
so with a memorable contrast of diction. 'ex re nomen habet' (3) is
linked to the first couplet by the repeated 'nomine'/'nomen', and like
this first couplet is written in the speech of every day. The clause which
follows ('nigri . . . equis', 3—4) is expressed in elevated, poetic language
arranged in a rhetorically complex pattern. The contrast is even repeated
within the clause through the collocation of 'roseis' and 'sobria'. The
effect is surely one of humour: we are invited to smile with Ovid at his
seedy creation.

The rest of the description (from line 5) relates to the old woman's
magical powers. Witchcraft had been a traditional weapon in the
armoury of the *lena*, at least from the time of Tibullus (*Elegies* I.5.59)
if not from the Hellenistic poets. Ovid's list of his woman's accomplish-
ments may be summarised as follows:

1 spells (5)
2 reversing flow of rivers (6)
3 use of herbs (7)
4 use of *rhombus* (7—8)
5 use of mare-discharge (8)
6 control of clouds (9—10)
7 power over stars and moon (11—12)
8 ability to fly (13)
9 ability to change form (13—14)
10 eyes with double pupil (15—16)
11 power to split earth and call up ghosts (17—18)

Ovid must have had in mind a similar genre poem by Propertius (*Elegies*
IV.5) — always assuming, with Williams (1968: 545), that this precedes
Amores I.8 — and Tibullus' description (*Elegies* I.2.43—54) of the witch
who has promised help to himself and Delia. Propertius' *lena* shares with
Ovid's *lena* powers 5, 7 and 9, and has about five other powers not
mentioned by Ovid. Tibullus' witch overlaps with 1, 2, 3, 6, 7, 11, and
has no clearly defined additional powers. It is already apparent that Ovid

is at pains to produce novelty within the traditional framework. He does
this partly by adding powers 4, 8 and 10; but also, and more subtly, by
varying order, emphasis and details of expression.

The linguistic novelty of 'magas artes', line 5 (see notes), is paralleled
by novelty of content and treatment. Ovid's *lena* knows the spells of
Circe, where Tibullus (*Elegies* I.2.51) gave his witch control over
Medea's herbs. The distinction is inconsequential, a stock variation. In
the next line too (6), Ovid seems to go out of his way to avoid repeating
Tibullus' description of rivers reversed: only the repetition 'artes'/'arte'
(4—5) reminds one of the Tibullus version — in which repetition is particularly marked, reflecting 'among other things, the heightened intensity of ritual' (Putnam, 1973). 'aquas' (6) is held back till after its verb
for effect and perhaps to highlight the paradoxical notion of bending
water ('recurvat aquas'). Ovid's next couplet is devoted to potions and
charms of various kinds, arranged in tricolon; the repeated 'quid' may
be an intentional parody of the witch's formal incantation, and the
effect of the whole is certainly enlivened by the extravagantly precise
description of the whirring *rhombus* (cf. Propertius *Elegies* II.28.35:
'magico torti sub carmine rhombi'), and the uncharacteristic translation
of the technical term *hippomanes* (often retained in magical contexts,
e.g. Propertius *Elegies* IV.5.18). Ovid is enjoying this recital of witches'
powers, without expecting his readers to take the account literally: he
is playing wittily with the conventional descriptions, and he will soon
make this detachment even clearer.

Lines 9—10 are much closer to Tibullus. The striking repetition is
there (see note) and Ovid has borrowed 'nubila caelo' for the end of his
hexameter and 'orbe' for the pentameter. But at the same time, Ovid has
reversed the sense of the two lines, so that Ovid collects clouds while
Tibullus is dispersing them, and has sunshine while Tibullus conjures up
snow-clouds. As the witch's feats become still more outrageous in lines
11 and 12, Ovid gives his readers an explicit warning that we are not to
take this too seriously: 'si qua fides' (11) strongly suggests doubt on the
part of the reader. There is no such hint in either the Tibullus poem
(where the author says categorically 'hanc ego de caelo ducentem sidera
vidi': *Elegies* I.2.43), or in Propertius *Elegies* IV.5. Ovid is again undercutting the seriousness of his description, itself inflated by the 's'-
alliteration and the morbid prominence of 'sanguine' in line 11 (repeated
in line 12). By contrast with such melodrama, Tibullus merely has the
stars drawn down, and Propertius lamely has his *lena* impose 'leges' on
the moon (*Elegies* IV.5.13). Line 13 opens with another echo of Tibullan
phrasing ('hanc ego . . . ': *Elegies* I.2.43), but again Ovid is more extravagant. His *lena* has the power of flight and can change her shape, not
into a mere wolf (as in Propertius *Elegies* IV.5.14), but into the less
common bird — probably an owl, whom Propertius' *lena* actually had
to consult (*Elegies* IV.5.17). The hexameter (13) creates atmosphere

and suspense which is punctured by the pentameter (14). 'suspicor'
(14) shows far less certainty than the qualified 'vidi' of line 11, let alone
the unqualified 'vidi' of Tibullus (*Elegies* I.2.43). Even the poet's
persona is proving short on 'fides'. The undercutting is confirmed by
the amusing precision of 'pluma corpus anile tegi' (14). The process of
withdrawal from commitment to the truth of these tales continues in
line 15. 'suspicor' is picked up and 'et fama est' is added as if in con-
firmation! Ovid's picture ultimately relies on no more than rumour. He
adds one further invention of his own in the rest of lines 15 and 16,
resonant with 'l' and 'u'. The notion of a double pupil was considered
just within the bounds of possibility, but again Ovid uses the pentameter
to mock the idea. 'fulminat', placed strongly, and 'lumen', starting the
second half of the line, create a ludicrously exaggerated picture of
thunder and lightning emerging from the witch's eyes. The description
finishes on another note of homage to Tibullus, whose description of
the summoning of the dead is the longest (two couplets) and the most
memorable section in his passage. This is why Ovid puts it emphatically
last. He wants to be quite sure that his readers will pick up the references to contemporary poetry. This particular reference is confirmed
by verbal echoes: Tibullus has 'cantu finditque solum' (*Elegies* I.2.45)
as against 'carmine findit humum' (18); ends a line with 'sepulcris' (cf.
17); and uses the word 'devocat' (cf. 'evocat', 17). Tibullus is chillingly
serious; Ovid again establishes an equally serious atmosphere in the hexameter (the incantatory 'proavos atavos' helps, and they are physically en-
cased in 'antiquis . . . sepulcris'). Readers who have come to expect a
deflationary pentameter will see how the two prosaic adjectives ('solidam
longo', 18) which Ovid foists on Tibullus create just such an effect. Her
chant is long-winded and the ground is rock-solid. Furthermore, as in lines
9—10, Ovid's *lena* gets the process the opposite way round from Tibullus
— who has the ground split before the dead are summoned. In lines 9—
10, the order was not important: in lines 17—18, there seems to be a hint
that the order is distinctly wrong. There is little point in asking the dead
to walk forth if they then have to wait for the conclusion of a long spell
('longo carmine', 18) before they can get through the earth!

Ovid, of course, draws more widely for his portrait of a witch than
on just Propertius and Tibullus. Nonetheless, the evidence of both
detailed borrowings and the overall propensity to repetition, shared
with Tibullus, makes it clear that Ovid relied heavily on his readers'
knowledge of Tibullus *Elegies* I.2, and probably Propertius *Elegies* IV.5,
for a full appreciation of the author's progressive dissociation within
this passage from the credibility and seriousness of what he relates.

Questions

1 What is the effect of repeated 'est quaedam' and interposed
'quicumque' clause in lines 1—2?

2 Collect examples of repeated words. Is the incidence unusually
   high? What is the effect?
3 To what extent is Ovid committed to the truth of what he
   describes in lines 5—18?
4 Compare this passage with Tibullus *Elegies* I.2.43—54. Is there
   enough evidence for us to assert that Ovid had these lines in
   mind when he wrote VIII.3? How does he differ from Tibullus?
   Try to account for these differences.
5 Find out what you can about magic in the ancient world. (See
   VII.4 question 6.) Make a magic wheel (see note on line 7).

VIII.4 Martial, Epigrams *III.43*

Language and content

1 **tinctis ... capillis:** Pliny the Elder (*Natural History* XXVIII.51.191)
   refers to a dye for reddening the hair made from beechwood ash and
   goat suet. See also note on III.7.2; Barsby 147, n. 1; Martial, *Epigrams*
   VI.57.
   Laetine: referred to again in Martial, *Epigrams* XII.17, where he is
   pictured as a rich epicure.
3 **Proserpina:** see *CLC* Unit V slide 26.
4 **personam:** see *CLC* Unit I slides 47—8. An actor's mask was designed to
   cover the whole of the head and the hair attached to the mask was
   coloured to match the part portrayed.
   capiti: Form C (dative) is regularly used with verbs of taking away.

Discussion

Two hexameters, carrying the burden of what Martial has to say, are
developed by answering pentameters, each strongly metaphorical.
'mentiris iuvenem' (1) is brutally direct, and the idea of deception is
picked up in 'fallis' (3) and 'personam' (4). The choice of images in line
2 is conventional, for ravens are regularly found as a type of blackness
and swans as a type of whiteness. The change effected by the dye is
exaggerated to grotesque proportions by the use of such colour-
opposites. 'subito' (2), with its supporting 'modo', helps to establish the
comical nature of the change by reminding us that it took place overnight. (For the violence of some such preparations, see Ovid *Amores*
I.14.) Line 3 is mock-solemn — witness the reference to the Underworld
and the superfluity of spondees spilling over into the pentameter. The
change of tone is surprising, for the reader expects Martial to cap 'non
omnes fallis' (3) with '*I* know your secret'. The metaphor becomes
theatrical in line 4, as Proserpina quickly (dactyls resuming in second
foot) lifts off Laetinus' mask to expose his white hair. Even if Laetinus
should succeed in deceiving everyone else (and line 2 suggests that he
will not), there is no way in which he can deceive Proserpina and defer
his entry to the Underworld.

Questions

1 How well chosen are Martial's metaphors in this epigram?
2 Why is Proserpina introduced in line 3?
3 Why has Laetinus dyed his hair? Why does Martial criticise
  him? Why are jokes about, e.g., hairpieces always good for a
  laugh?

VIII.5 Martial, Epigrams *VI.38*

Language and content

2 **Regulus:** son of the lawyer Marcus Aquilius Regulus (see *CLC* Unit IV
  Teacher's Handbook 129—31 on Regulus and *captatio*), who was
  described by Pliny with uncharacteristic acerbity as 'omnium bipedum
  nequissimus', 'the biggest crook on two feet' (*Letters* I.5.14). He had
  been deeply involved in the treason trials during Nero's reign. His son
  was born in A.D. 87 or 88, and is described by Pliny as 'acris ingenii
  sed ambigui, qui tamen posset recta sectari, si patrem non referret'
  (*Letters* IV.2.1: 'quick-witted but untrustworthy; yet he could have
  made an honest living had he not taken after his father').
5 **centum . . . viri:** a court consisting of up to 180 jurors, under the
  Empire, and dealing with important disputes about wills and inheritances. 'As it was the only court of private or civil law with a jury, it
  attracted the outstanding advocates of the day, such as Pliny and
  Regulus, who liked the popular audience' (Sherwin-White, 1966, on
  Pliny, *Letters* V.9).
6 **Iulia tecta:** during the early Empire, the Centumviral Court sat in the
  Basilica Iulia (see *CLC* Unit IV slides 29—30), which had been finally
  completed and dedicated by Augustus in A.D. 12. The building was
  101 metres × 49 metres, sited on the south side of the forum, with a
  wooden roof and an outside originally of white marble (Platner and
  Ashby).
7 **acris:** may be taken with either 'equi' or 'suboles'.
9 **servate:** Regulus' son died young (in A.D. 102 or 103) and the father
  was disconsolate. Pliny tells how he had the boy's ponies, dogs, nightingales, parrots and blackbirds killed round the funeral pyre (*Letters*
  IV.2.3), commissioned a multitude of statues and portraits of the boy
  (*Letters* IV.7.1) and arranged for an encomium to be declaimed publicly
  throughout Italy (*Letters* IV.7.2).

Discussion

That Regulus' son was to die when only fifteen was an irony not of
Martial's making. This epigram is light and hopeful, and provides by
implication a much more generous assessment of the father and his
abilities than we have from Pliny. Two couplets of rhetorical question
are followed by two couplets of statement and a concluding prayer in
a single couplet.

'aspicis' (1) involves the reader (second person) and suggests that this
is a real scene which Martial will allow the reader to share. The diminutive size and age of the boy are stressed in line 1 at some length (with a

Graecism that seems a little ponderous for a two-year-old) in order to
provide a foil for Regulus junior's precocity — he can hear *and* appreciate his father's rhetoric (2) — and to set him off against the importance
of his father. Martial is writing about a contemporary orator, so there is
no need to do more than allude to Regulus senior's fame with 'auditum'
(2) and 'laudet et ipse' (2), implying that everybody else as well as
young Regulus is congratulating his father. The second couplet adds a
hint of bravery, for 'maternos sinus' (3) reminds us that young Regulus
is not yet three — but no sooner does he see his 'genitor' (the grandiose,
poetic word) than he makes straight for him like any true Roman. In
line 4, 'patrias laudes' again suggests the merits of Regulus senior, for
whose eyes, no doubt, the poem was intended; and 's'-alliteration gives
the line some prominence. The next couplet (5—6) evokes vividly, as
the alliteration changes to 'c'/'q', the noisy, crowded atmosphere of the
Centumviral Court. 'densum', 'corona' and 'vulgus' (5) all separately
contain the idea of a mass of people, and 'corona' (strongly placed)
again points to support for Regulus the father. All these things might
be thought frightening for a two-year-old, but young Regulus finds
them positively attractive. 'infanti' is held back partly to allow the
evocation of the court-scene to collect impetus, and partly to provide a
witty contrast with 'Iulia tecta' (6) across the caesura: one of the finest
buildings of imperial Rome is subjected to the scrutiny and evaluation
of a toddler. (There is also the paradox of a talk-shop appealing to an
'infans', 'non-speaker'.) The secret, of course, is in the breeding, and
exploration of this in lines 7—8 allows Martial (i) to drop incidentally
yet another compliment for Regulus the father; (ii) to widen the area
of discourse, providing a distinct change of scene for the reader. The
animal similes are balanced, and yet by no means tediously symmetrical.
Both have a young animal as grammatical subject, 'sic' to indicate the
simile, and the same broad pattern of subject + Form E (ablatival)
adjective + intervening word + Form E (ablative) noun + verb in third
person singular of present tense. On the other hand, Martial varies the
position of 'sic', varies the means of describing the youthfulness of the
beast, and varies the function of the Form E (ablative). 'magno' in line
7 is used both literally ('deep') and metaphorically ('famous', 'important'), and 'pulvere' alludes to any scene of action, but perhaps particularly racing. Line 8 introduces, or reintroduces from lines 1 and 3, a
note of vulnerability with 'molli' and the soft 'l'-alliteration. This leads
easily into the prayer of the final couplet, which builds up to the
wittily elliptical final line. This is a conscious development of line 2,
but now 'Regulus' refers to the father rather than the son. The prayer
is as much a prayer for long life for father (and mother) as for survival
for the son.

Questions

1 To what extent does Martial recreate the scene in visual terms?

2 Can we conclude anything about Martial's relationship with Regulus the father? Investigate Pliny's picture of Regulus (note on line 2): does this affect our view of the Martial poem?
3 Why does Martial lay so much stress on Regulus junior's youth?
4 Could lines 7–8 be omitted without loss?
5 What can we learn from this poem about the rôles of women and children in Roman society? Supplement this picture from, e.g., Lewis and Reinhold I: 484–7, 489–90, 507–9; II: 47–52, 252–4, 287–94, 380–3, 403–5, 407–8, 543–6; Balsdon, 1962; Paoli, Chs. 9, 15, 21; Carcopino; Balsdon, 1969; Liversidge 73–6; and Hadas, s.v. 'women' and 'children'.

VIII.6 Martial, Epigrams *VIII.79*

Language and content

For the hendecasyllabic metre, see notes on II.1.
1 **vetulas**: predicative — 'all the friends you have are . . . '
4 **porticus**: see note on I.2.8.
5 **Fabulla**: elsewhere presented by Martial as 'cretata' ('powdered') and hence frightened of rain (*Epigrams* II.41.11); purchasing false hair (*Epigrams* VI.12); inclined to boast about her supposed youth and riches (*Epigrams* I.64); and reacting too seriously (*Epigrams* IV.81) to Martial's strictures on Roman women (quoted in VII.5 question 3).

Discussion

The humour lies (i) in the perversity of Fabulla's behaviour; (ii) in the withholding of the addressee till the end, thus persuading the reader to suppose a masculine subject. The sordid picture of line 1, with the exaggeration ('omnes') essential to Martial's point, gives place (2) to an even more sordid picture in which the three adjectives reinforce one another. The 's'-alliteration runs over from these two sneering lines into the third, which suggests pressure ('trahis') put on the women by the subject. This may raise doubts in a perceptive reader's mind, for if a gigolo is the subject it is more likely that he will be dragged around by his ageing mistresses than *vice versa*. The stark list in asyndeton of the places where one has to be seen (line 4) indicates a rather empty-headed perseverance, and in structural terms balances the adjectival list in line 2. Martial now reveals all with his cutting last line, held together with the alliteration and assonance of 'formosa Fabulla puella' (5). Like so many of Martial's poems, this is a hard attack on a credible human weakness, and the exaggeration of 'omnes' (1) does not make Fabulla any the less plausible. There is no sympathy here; only a barely muted impatience with the vanity of the lady concerned.

Questions

1 What is the effect of withholding 'Fabulla' till line 5?
2 Is Fabulla credible?

3 Is Martial's tone one of serious criticism, light-hearted reproach
   or gentle sympathy? or none of these?
4 Are there any noticeable sound-effects in this epigram?

Section IX

Section IX is about travel. Catullus' 'phaselus' poem (IX.1) is the only
passage which concentrates entirely on travel by water. It is different in
other ways too. It has an elaborate but not stifling symmetry, with
which the ring-composition of IX.3, Martial's farewell to Domitius, can
scarcely be compared. With its talking boat and back-reference to
dedication-verse, it is more imaginatively conceived than the others. It
is metrically more adventurous and ultimately more intriguing. With
IX.3 it does have in common the use of collected proper names for
almost incantatory effect. Martial's epigram might have revolved simply
round the colour-changes of Domitius. Instead, he introduces a second
strand, the social comment on Rome's unhealthiness, and this gives the
poem a particular interest in addition to the wittiness of word-play and
paradox. His other poem (IX.4) is much more slight: here the wit lies
in the apology that is stood on its head to become criticism. Horace, in
our excerpt from the Journey to Brundisium (IX.2), also confounds
expectation by opting for the mundane in preference to the cosmic.
The particular appeal of this piece for a modern reader is that it captures, perhaps better than anything else in Roman literature, the feel of
ancient travel. The Roman reader would no doubt have appreciated the
concealed art with which this is achieved, but would have been perhaps
more aware of the great irony of the political hiatus.

IX.1 Catullus, Poems *4*

Context

For the view that this poem cannot be fully understood without reference to *Poems* 46 ('iam ver egelidos refert tepores') and 31 ('paene
insularum, Sirmio, insularumque'), see Putnam, 1962.

Language and content

The metre, pure iambic trimeters, is rare. Quinn (1973) talks of it 'giving the
poem a buoyant vitality'. The scheme is:

phăsēlŭs īllĕ quĕm vĭdētīs, hōspītēs

The final syllable is *anceps.*

1 **phaselus:** literally a kind of bean, so presumably *phaseli* were slim and
   low like a bean-pod. See further, Casson, 1971: 167–8.
   hospites: guests, strangers, passers-by (Williams, 1968: 193). The singular
   is the equivalent of Greek 'ō xeine', so frequent in sepulchral epigrams.
2 **ait fuisse navium celerrimus:** the Form A (nominative) + infinitive is a
   Greek construction rare in Latin (see Fordyce).

3   **impetum trabis**: epicism.
6   **minacis**: storms blew up (and still do) very quickly in the Adriatic.
7–9   **-ve, -que**: used interchangeably.
8   **Rhodum . . . nobilem**: 'Rhodes . . . has such exceptional harbours, streets, walls and other fixtures that I am unable to cite any other place as even approaching it, let alone superior to this town . . . It is adorned with many votive offerings . . . of which the best is the Colossus of the Sun . . . but this has been knocked down by an earthquake and now lies broken off at the knees' (Strabo *Geography* XIV.2.5: Strabo was born 64/63 B.C.).
9   **Propontidā**: this anomalous lengthening of a naturally short vowel probably reflects Greek practice (see Fordyce).
11   **iugo**: the hills inland from Cytorus. 'The whole of the south coast of the Pontus was forested and provided wood for the local industries of shipbuilding . . . and smelting' (Fordyce).
13   **buxifer**: epicism. Boxwood from Cytorus was so famous that a Greek equivalent of 'carrying coals to Newcastle' was 'taking boxwood to Cytorus'.
14   **tibi**: the neighbouring ports of Amastris and Cytorus are henceforth treated as a single area.
18   **impotentiā**: see note on 'Propontidā' (9).
19   **erum**: the slave's term for his master.
    laeva sive dextera. 'Ancient square-riggers, with their broad mainsail as principal driver, were designed first and foremost for traveling with the wind astern or on the quarters. But, when pressed, the ancient mariner could also sail a close-hauled course with the wind abeam or forward of the beam . . . although, with his relatively inefficient rig he could probably point no closer to the wind than seven points . . . When his destination lay well to windward he resorted, as ships willy-nilly did until the age of steam, to tacking, i.e., he pursued a zigzag course with the ship taking the wind first on one bow and then being swung about to take it on the other' (Casson, 1971: 273–4).
20–1   **utrumque . . . in pedem**: with the wind astern, both sheets are under equal tension.
22   **vota**: vows to dedicate, e.g., a votive tablet should the ship escape imminent danger (see Ogilvie, 1969: 37–9).
23   **sibi**: glossed as 'a se', the Form C (dative) of agent emphasising the boat's personality. But the alternative meaning 'on its behalf' lurks in the background to remind us that this is in fact a boat and not a person.
    esse facta: best taken as 'had been made' (so Williams, 1968: 191).
24   **novissimo**: see, e.g., Fordyce and Quinn (1973) for the problems associated with this word.
26   **senet**: archaism.

Discussion

I take the view (following Copley) that this poem stands on its own merits as a piece of literature and does not necessarily benefit from analysis in the light of either Catullus' career or of other poems in his corpus (see note on Context).

Catullus is pointing out a *phaselus* to a group of unidentified passersby. Unless we have read the poem before (in particular, lines 26–7), we do not at this stage recognise it as belonging or related to the specific type of dedication-poem in which someone retiring from a profession dedicates his equipment to a god (see *Palatine Anthology*, Book VI; cf. Williams, 1969, on Horace *Odes* III.26). Indeed, we are more likely to reject this possibility, in the absence of early mention of the god, and to follow the lead given by 'hospites' (see note on 1) towards interpreting the poem as a sepulchral epigram. In the manner of many such epigrams, we proceed to achievements and career, related by the dead person — except that in our poem (i) the subject speaks not directly but through the poet as interpreter; (ii) the boat is not in fact a person, though strongly personalised throughout (e.g., 'ait', 2; 'palmulis', 4; 'comata', 11; 'loquente', 12; 'dicit', 16; 'erum', 19; 'vota ... sibi ... facta', 22–3).

That the *phaselus* is somehow at rest is confirmed (Kenney in Greig 14) by the perfect tenses of 'fuisse' (2) and 'nequisse' (4). Her sailing days are now finished. But in her prime, the boat continues, she was the fastest thing on water. Speed is given great emphasis (note 'volare', 5) in a complex tripartite boast which culminates at the end of line 9 with her back at the Black Sea where she was constructed. The tone is light, for there is something endearing about the boat's swelling rodomontade expressed in the sort of syntax that foreigners from the east might very well use (2) and with an amusingly heavyweight epic phrase in line 3 reminiscent of the great boat-races of epic poetry and effectively depriving the opponent ('natantis ... trabis') of the sort of claim to personality made by our own heroic *phaselus*. The metre, itself something of an exoticism, keeps the poem bowling along.

With the third leg of the boast (6–9), we find ourselves journeying from Italy to the Black Sea, and we end our travels at Cytorus (10–12) where the *phaselus* grew as timber. We travel all this way in the time it takes to read a few lines: the boat's claim to speed is fully vindicated. Furthermore, the grandiose implications of 'impetum trabis' (3) are sustained by the epic conglomeration of place-names, most with their attached epithet. We are left with high estimations of a boat which seems to be on speaking terms with 'noble Rhodes' (8), and which is sufficiently tough to have survived '*minacis* Hadriatici' (6), '*horridam* ... Propontida' (8–9) and '*trucem* Ponticum sinum' (9). The contrast with its peaceful birthplace (11–12) is marked, and is to be re-echoed in lines 25–7 by the peace of its retirement. Quinn (1973) draws attention to 'the highly tensioned, artificial verbal structure' of line 12, presumably intended to fix our attention on it as we rest at the poem's turning-point.

The return journey begins in line 13, with the apostrophe of the boat's home towns. Again, the effect of the grand epithets, particularly 'buxifer' (13) and the very notion of invoking such insignificant places, is mock-solemn, if not downright amusing. They are appealed to as witnesses, much as a local boy made good would expect his home town

to know all about his subsequent career. (Quinn's objection that 'intimate knowledge . . . of what happened after the yacht left home waters
is not easily ascribed to Amastris—Cytorus' seems pettifogging.) The
whispering voice of the *phaselus*, perhaps suggested in 'saepe sibilum'
in line 12, is sustained by the marked 's'-alliteration of:

> tibi haec fuisse et esse cognitissima
> ait phaselus: (lines 14—15)

and the perfect infinitives of lines 16, 17 and 19 may be felt to carry on
this effect.

   Just as the first section began (1—2) with 'phaselus . . . ait fuisse', so
this second part is initiated by 'fuisse . . . ait phaselus' (14—15), and
'the journey back is not this time conveyed by place-names; the correspondence (in reverse) of lines 18—24 to lines 6—12 is signalled by the
reference in both passages to the sailing qualities of the boat (3—5 =
19—21)' — Kenney in Greig 15. We start with first beginnings, lines 15—
17 roughly paralleling lines 10—12. 'inde' in line 18 (both spatial and
temporal as Quinn, 1973, states) carries the reader to the next section,
where 'impotentia freta' (18) are strongly reminiscent of the rough seas
of lines 6—9 (see above). At the same time, there is more than a hint of
the 'powerless' meaning of 'impotens' (see III.3 Discussion 65): the
winds and waves have no power over our *phaselus* — a point developed
in lines 22—3. In line 19, the boat for the first time introduces its
owner, in terms ('erum') that suggest a servile relationship. There is
nothing to suggest that the boat's master is the poet, except our knowledge from the other poems of Catullus' journey to Bithynia, and (more
persuasive) the close relationship implied in lines 1—2. Catullus' readers
would no doubt have made the equation; but it is surely wrong to tie
the poem down too strictly to a particularity which Catullus could have
made much more explicit had he wished (cf. Quinn, 1972: 106—7). The
focus is kept continually on the boat, and not allowed to shift with any
precision to its master. What Catullus does clearly intend is that the
'hunc' of line 24 should bring us back from faraway places into eyeshot
of the *phaselus* (cf. 'videtis' in 1). There are also two contrasts suggested
by these final lines (Kenney in Greig 15—16): that between the rough
seas of earlier times and the 'limpidum lacum' (24) in which the boat
now rests; and that between the boat's second boast (for the first, see
above on lines 2ff.) about its independence of the gods of the shore,
and its self-dedication (in the final two lines) to the Dioscuri. Kenney
comments that 'the two contrasts convey the same mood of retirement
and peace after stress and adventure'. The boat has relinquished the
excitement of singlehanded battle against the elements in favour of a
secure retirement covered by the insurance of divine protection. Notions
of peace and quiet are exceptionally prevalent in lines 24—6 ('limpidum',
'recondita', 'quiete', even the archaising 'senet'); and the gentle 'l'-

alliteration of the final line is reminiscent of line 1, neatly rounding off
the poem. (Observe also how the assonance of line 1 — '-elus'/'ille',
'-etis'/'-ites' — is echoed by repeated 'gemelle Castor' in line 27.)

The last lines mark this piece as inspired by epigrams of dedication
rather than of burial (see above). It is amusing to have our expectations
thwarted and our boat's boasting (22—3) overturned, and amusement is
in order in a light-hearted poem which has a ship precisely characterised
(a proud old slave) and whispering its story into the ears of the poet.
Under what circumstances did Catullus imagine such a dedication? What
picture would occur to the minds of Catullus' readers? The most persuasive modern treatment of these questions is in Williams, 1968: 192—
3 — though certainty is impossible. Williams argues that an ancient
reader would identify the poem with the special kind of dedicatory
inscription appended to wall-frescoes, and that Catullus therefore wanted
his readers 'to visualize a painting of the ship in the setting of a placid
lake' (193). This interpretation has at least two advantages: (i) 'hospites',
not found in the plural in sepulchral epigrams nor at all in true dedicatory epigrams, now has a clear reference to a group of visitors admir-
ing the painting; (ii) there is no longer any need to explain either the
circumstances or the omission from the narrative of the boat's extraordinary journey from the sea to an inland lake, this being a lake of the
imagination (perhaps see *CLC* Unit IV slide 17).

The qualities of this poem are manifold. It is a metrical *tour de force*,
with the inherent monotony of the iambic beat well disguised by such
devices as enjambment and diverting the reader's attention with extravagant diction. There is an amusing contrast between the artifice of the
mannered style (epic words, repetition, apostrophe, etc.: Fordyce 97)
and the portrait of the narrator as an old boat. The structure is exceptionally neat, but with symmetries adumbrated rather than hammered
out. The development of Greek epigram is achieved with wit and
panache. The whole provides not only a clever encapsulation of ancient
travel (with oblique reference to Catullus' own journey to Bithynia),
but also a suggestive treatment of the universal themes of hazard and
achievement balanced by retirement and security.

For an ancient parody, see Quinn, 1973: 102.

Questions

1 Who is the narrator?
2 Does the *phaselus* acquire any special character from lines 2—
   9 and 18—23? What evidence is there in the poem that Catullus
   wants us to view the *phaselus* in personal terms?
3 Are the place-names of lines 6—11 in any particular order?
   Find them on the map in the pupils' text.
4 In what sense could the centre of the poem be said to fall
   between line 12 and line 13? What evidence can you find?

5 How does Catullus characterise the sea in this poem? What
   does he contrast it with? Would this view of the sea be a common Roman view? (See, e.g., Balsdon, 1969: 226—7; Casson,
   1971 and 1974; *CLC* Unit IV *Bithynia* I (a); Copley 12; Greig
   17.)

6 Is it more likely that this poem was written about a real
   phaselus in which Catullus sailed from Bithynia to Italy and
   which he had transported inland to Lake Garda; or that he
   wrote the poem as a dedication for a model or a painting of a
   phaselus? (See Williams, 1968: 192—3.) Is it important to
   know?

7 Do we need to look outside the material given if we are to
   understand this poem? Is your conclusion universally true
   about poetry?

8 Write a parody, closely modelled on this poem, about, e.g., a
   motor car. Bring out its close involvement with its master/
   mistress and its success in outlasting the dangers of the highway.

IX.2 Horace, Satires I.5.1—33

Context

In *Satires* I.5, Horace gives us a first-hand account of a journey from
Rome to Brundisium down the Via Appia (see map in pupils' text 1).
This excerpt covers the first 100 km or so from Rome to Tarracina
(= Anxur). That there is something special about this journey does not
become plain until we are told of the eminent fellow-travellers in lines
27—9 and 31—3. Horace apparently accompanied a diplomatic mission
intended to reconcile Octavian and Antony. The date and precise circumstances are disputed (see, e.g., Rudd, 1966: 280, n. 1) but there is
a general consensus in favour of 38 or 37 B.C. when 'the predominance
of Antonius was secured and reinforced' (Syme 224). Octavian in 38
B.C. insisted on attacking the fleet of Sextus Pompey, against the
express warnings of Antony, was soundly defeated, and thus driven to
seek help from Antony in a series of diplomatic encounters. A rather
ramshackle agreement was put together at Tarentum in 37, and this
may well provide the background for our excerpt (so, e.g., Syme 225;
Earl 40). But politics intrude very little. Instead, Horace gives us a series
of vivid snapshots recreating with exemplary freshness and precision the
circumstances of ancient travel.

Language and content

1 **egressum:** Rome would be left by the Via Appia (see the plan in pupils'
   text 3).
2 **rhetor:** see *CLC* Unit I *Stage 10*: 15, and references in *CLC* Unit I
   Teacher's Handbook 101.

Heliodorus: see Rudd, 1973: 153, n. 2, for the view suggested in the pupils' text. Apollo = sun = *helios* (Gk). Cf. *O.C.D.* s.v. 'Apollodorus (5)'.

3 **longe**: used with superlative by Horace only twice.

Forum Appi: in the malarial (cf. 'culices', 14) Pomptine Marshes. A 28 km ship-canal ran from here to Feronia's temple near Tarracina. The boats were pulled by mules. Travellers preferred to travel on the water-way, which ran parallel to the Via Appia, since (i) the journey could (usually) be done overnight; (ii) it saved the expense and danger of a 'taberna'; (iii) the concentration of numbers would provide a little more security against the bandits who inhabited this sort of country. The canal explains the presence of sailors in Forum Appi, which was not on the coast.

5–6 It is possible that Horace and his party went on foot as far as Forum Appi. From the point of view of distance, this is quite feasible. Horace was under thirty at the time and about 65 km in two days would have been a very straightforward undertaking in an age where 'the ordinary man walked and might hope to average up to twenty-five miles (40 km) a day' (Balsdon, 1969: 226). On the other hand, it is much more likely that a man of Horace's status on a mission of such importance would have travelled in a litter or a *raeda* (as in *86): 'anybody who wished to travel comfortably . . . went in a carriage' (Paoli 229). See *CLC* Unit IV slide 43. Balsdon reckons that it would be difficult to average more than 75 km per day even in a carriage, and there may have been attendants on foot and ox-wagons keeping the pace much slower. (See also Liversidge 164–6; Casson, 1974: Ch. 11 with illustration 13.)

6 **Appia**: the Appian Way was Rome's principal road to the south. It was initiated in 312 B.C. by Appius Claudius Caecus, and when complete ran for 374 km from Rome to the port of Brundisium via Beneventum, Venusia and Tarentum. It was only wide enough between the pave-ments for two vehicles to pass each other, and this would have made swift travel difficult if the road were crowded (Lejay).

7 **aquam**: bad water is referred to four times in the poem.

9–10 **terris, caelo**: probably Form C (dative) after compound verbs – see Woodcock section 62.

11 **nautis**: suggests the embarkation point for the canal (see on line 3).

12 **ingerere**: historic infinitive.

trecentos: regularly used of an indefinitely large number – 'hundreds'.

13 **dum aes**: see note on VIII.2.6 'cum'.

14 Cicero refers to the noise of the frogs in this area in a letter written in April; cf. Rudd, 1966: 280–1, n.1.

15 **absentem . . . amicam**: cf. graffito in Inn of Sittius at Pompeii, telling us that Vibius Restitutus slept there alone, and longed for his Urbana.

16 **vappa**: see note in II.2.3.

18 **pastum**: glossed in pupils' text, but see further Woodcock section 152.

20 **cum**: inverted, hence 'sentimus' is indicative. Cf. I.1.24 with notes.

23 **quarta . . . hora**: about 9.00 to 10.00 a.m. See note on I.4.1. The season is probably springtime.

24 **lavimus**: as much a ritual gesture in honour of the goddess as a welcome chance to refresh themselves.

Feronia: she had a temple in the Campus Martius, and her cult was widely spread in central Italy (see *OCD*).

lympha: a poetic word.

25 **milia . . . tria**: about 4.5 km.

26 **Anxur**: Volscian name for the town of Tarracina, which stood high above the marshes. The massive supporting arches of the first-century

B.C. Temple of Jupiter still stand on the heights overlooking modern Terracina. 'Tărrăcĭnă' will not fit into a hexameter. For an Italian hill-town, see *CLC* Unit III slide 33.

28 **Cocceius:** Lucius Cocceius Nerva had been with Antony in Syria in 41 B.C., and had helped Maecenas (for Octavian) and Pollio (for Antony) to negotiate the Pact of Brundisium in 40 — 'a friend of Antonius but acceptable to the other party' (Syme 217).

magnis de rebus: the imminent summit conference.

28–9 **missi . . . uterque legati:** it is easy to see how 'uterque' (= both of them) can have plural words in agreement.

29 **aversos soliti componere amicos:** the reference must be to the Pact of Brundisium, which healed an alarming breach between Octavian and Antony.

30 **collyria:** illustrate with *CLC* Unit II slide 22. A similar stamp found at Cirencester (and in the Corinium Museum) belonged to the oculist Atticus and one of its four inscriptions reads as follows:

ATTICI LENE AD OMNES DOLO-
RES POST IMPETVM LIPPITV(DINIS)
'Atticus' mild (salve) for all pains: after the onset of eye-inflammation.'

The ointments would be ground to a powder in a mortar, and then mixed with egg or another liquid.

31 **illinere:** historic infinitive.

32 **Capito:** 'About C. Fonteius Capito (cos. suff. 33) precious little is known. One of the negotiators at Tarentum in 37 B.C. . . . , he was sent on a mission to Egypt by Antonius in the following winter' (Syme 267, n. 6).

32–3 **ad unguem factus homo:** 'the metaphor is from workers in marble or wood, who test the smoothness of the material by passing their nail over it' (Palmer). The phrase apparently lacks the opprobrious over-tones of English 'smooth'.

Discussion

Whether or not Horace is describing a real journey is immaterial. What matters is that the conception rings true and the artistry pleases. (But see Rudd, 1966: 54–6, for the view that the poem as a whole is to be taken 'as a piece of authentic narrative'.) Horace clearly wants to keep the political dimension in reserve so that in line 27 he can spring Maecenas on his reader. There are no earlier clues, unless 'Heliodorus' carried more significance than we realise (see note). The reader thus takes the beginning of the poem as an account of the commonplace journey which well-to-do Romans would regularly tackle on their way, e.g., to the delights of Baiae.

Rudd (1966: 57) stresses the compression of Horace's writing. He cites the first eight words, where 'the departure is contained in "egressum", the arrival in "accepit", and Aricia, as well as being con-trasted with mighty Rome, is defined by the type and quality of its accommodation'. Compression is, of course, greatly helped by the avail-ability of the deponent participle (cf. line 25). That 'Aricia' should be placed next to 'Roma' effectively enhances the contrast between them,

and a chiastic pattern is created with 'magna . . . Aricia Roma / . . .
modico'. This artful beginning and the swiftness of pace takes the
reader's attention and sweeps him along into the body of the poem.
The process is further assisted by making the very first word a word of
departure, and by the introduction of 'me' in promise of a lively eyewitness account. There is also a strong suggestion that the tone will be
light: the placing of Aricia in parallel with, and next door to, Rome
cannot be fully serious, and the reference to the quality of the inn
('hospitio modico', 2) prefigures the kind of practical, everyday observation which is to be Horace's chosen subject matter for this poem.

The inn may have been sordid, but the company was elevated. Even
if Horace's audience were able to identify Heliodorus, they would not
necessarily associate the trip with a summit conference — especially
after such an unpretentious beginning, designed to put them off the
scent. Horace is seen to be travelling with a Greek intellectual, and the
super-superlative ('longe doctissimus', 3) contrasts well with 'modico'
(2) and the low-life of line 4 — introduced by the down-to-earth
'differtum' and with 'atque' placed so as to throw emphasis on
'malignis'. There may also be a further contrast between the learned
Greek and the local riffraff that follow. Logically, Heliodorus should
have been mentioned before the party left Rome, and one might well
have expected a few more details about the entourage. The catching of
the reader's interest justifies the compression of line 1, while the
deferred mention of Heliodorus (i) fills the time-gap between Aricia and
Forum Appi; (ii) hints at the sort of scholarly conversation Horace must
have enjoyed on this leg. Horace is both compressing his material and
selecting the occasional choice detail to create atmosphere.

After arrival at the harshly-characterised Forum Appi, Horace at last
slackens the pace and allows himself the luxury of a reflection (5—6).
The stress here is on the easy-going nature of this first stage of the
journey: 'ignavi' (5) and 'tardis' (6) are specific, while 'altius ac nos/
praecinctis' (5—6) indicates that Horace and Heliodorus took the
journey very easily. We acquire the impression that there is no pressure,
that the travellers' first concern is for comfort ('minus . . . gravis', 6). I
can only think that Horace is again trying to conceal the purpose of the
journey, in order to give the début of Maecenas in line 27 greater
impact, while for those who have heard the poem before and know the
circumstances, the lack of urgency must be an amusing sidelight on this
diplomatic journey.

Throughout the poem, Horace is at pains to avoid providing a tedious
list of places, each with its appropriate word-picture. It is interesting to
observe how he manages the transition from Forum Appi, described in
line 4, to the arrival at Anxur in line 26. Two lines (5—6) are spent in
reflection, set in contrast with a piece of detailed personal reminiscence,
spreading out (in line 8) to include the rest of the party. At the caesura

in line 9, there is a marked change of mood as the diction becomes
extravagantly epic and the scene moves (for one-and-a-half lines) away
from the travellers to the night and the heavens. Time has been subtly
advanced ('cenantes', 8; 'nox', 9), and almost before we realise it
'nautis' (11) takes us to the night-ferry in an amusing reversion to the
world of the everyday, soon to be spiced with direct-speech colloquial-
isms (12–13). What follows is the nearest Horace gets to a sustained
description (13–23), though even here he is picking out amusing or
significant details in a way which he could easily have applied to the
Rome-to-Aricia leg had he wanted. There is no description of such
things as getting on board, the sleeping arrangements, or of fellow
passengers in any detail. The selectivity is that of the cine camera, even
to the jump-cut after line 19. The party disembarks in line 23. The
shrine of Feronia is not described, but the address to the goddess and
the use of the word 'lympha' elevates the writing in such a way as to
suggest the precinct. Straight narrative takes us to Anxur (26), strikingly
described in terms which uniquely (Rudd, 1966: 59–60) bear no
relation to the comfort and entertainment of the travellers. Such
variety of technique continues in line 27, as Horace casually drops his
bombshell.

There are at least three other ways (cf. Rudd, 1966: 58–9) in which
Horace avoids the travelogue stereotype: (i) by choosing colourful
travel-words ('accepit', 1; 'repimus', 25) and sometimes omitting their
prosaic equivalents ('inde Forum Appi', 3); (ii) by ringing the changes
on specifications of time (meal, 8 and 25; night and day, 9 and 20;
hour, 14; time of day, 23); (iii) by enjambing many new entries, so that
the narrative has a continuous flow (3; 9; 23).

The *detail* of lines 7–26 is equally skilful. In line 7, 'ventri' is put
under pressure by its position at the end of the line and by the conversational interjection of 'quod erat deterrima'. The enjambment lays
stress on the mock-heroic 'indico bellum', bounded by the caesura in a
hexameter of appropriate heaviness, and placed in the vivid present for
even greater effect. The figure of speech, once one becomes aware of
the circumstances of Horace's journey, is breathtakingly bold: civil war
is in the offing, but the only war Horace can make is on his bowels.
There may be a similarly glancing reference to affairs of state in 'haud
animo aequo' (8): in retrospect this clearly belongs with 'exspectans'
(9), but for the listener or reader aware of the political overtones the
word-order and run of the hexameter seem for a moment to attach the
phrase to 'cenantes' (8), for it is clear that their meal may well have
been disturbed by thoughts of political turbulence. The grandiose diction of 'iam nox . . . parabat' (9–10) follows, but this extravagant roll
of drums yields only a humorously bathetic scene of dockside banter
(11). The line is nonetheless artfully patterned in chiasmus so as to
suggest the interaction between slaves and sailors, and acts as a general-

ised introduction to the lively dialogue which follows. Horace prefers to compress and keep the poem moving, rather than specify precisely who says what. In fact 'huc appelle!' (12) has to be the shout of the slave on the canal-bank trying to get preferential treatment for his masters, while the cautious reply must be from the skipper of the barge. There follows the collection of fares and the harnessing of the mule (13), and again the stress is on the unhurried non-urgent nature of the journey — in line 19 the sailor is to be 'piger', just as Horace and company have been 'ignavi' in line 5. As we realise that it is time to go to sleep, the metre slows from the dactyls of line 14 to the heavily spondaic lines 15—17. The singing sailor is introduced by a singular verb ('cantat', 15), and 'atque viator' (16) is an amusingly unexpected addition, immediately trumped (after a pregnant pause at the line-end) by 'certatim' (17) — not even a co-operative effort. The proliferation of long 'ā's is positively operatic. Both in line 17 ('fessus') and in line 18 ('missae') the participle is heavily worked to get the maximum amount of information into the minimum space: for lines 17—19 even the excellent Penguin translation (Rudd, 1973) has thirty-six words to Horace's eighteen. The first scene of this comic episode ends magnificently. The repetition of 'viator' at the end of line 17 appears to establish a contrast between the 'viator' and the 'nauta' with whom he has been coupled. The 'viator' goes to sleep and we expect the sailor, who seems to be the only one awake, to attend to his duties and get the boat moving. Instead he proves to have only sufficient energy to unharness the mule ('religat', 19, clearly echoing 'ligatur' in 13, where the process took a lot of time and effort) and tie it up for the night before succumbing to sleep in a memorable phrase ('stertitque supinus', 19). The opening of line 20 is sharp and direct, again with an epic feel to it (e.g., inverted 'cum'-clause) and a world away from the comic slackness of the preceding lines. 'nil' (20) is brought forward out of its clause to start the second half of the hexameter with emphasis. 'sentimus' (21) suggests that Horace and his party have just woken up and gradually become aware of the lack of motion. At this point the metre lightens as the 'cerebrosus' man leaps to his feet in a line which resounds with 's'-alliteration and the rhyming '-brōs-', 'prōs-'. There follows a thrashing — its results marked by '-ae', '-ae-', '-ōs', 'ō', the first three corresponding with the verse ictus. Willows may well have grown along the canal banks and it adds to the liveliness of this scene if one imagines the 'cerebrosus' man tearing off a branch before setting to.

The move from the barge to the shrine is covered by the curious slide from 'hōrā' (23) to 'ōra' (24). Still in the vivid present, which Horace uses from line 8 almost without exception, we are now taken quickly through the morning meal and up the steep gradient to Anxur. The goal is left till last, while the remainder of line 26 memorably recreates the view of the little hill-town which must have been before the eyes of the climbers.

Horace in line 27 admits the significance of this journey. Maecenas'
name comes first, as we would expect, and the importance of the
mission is shown by the spondaic nature of lines 27—9. The rather arch
references to 'magnis de rebus' (28) and the 'aversos . . . amicos' (29)
warn the reader not to expect at this late stage a swing to politics.
'amicos' is used advisedly. The poem seems to have been written soon
after the event, at a time when *amicitia* was the official doctrine —
which Horace could hardly afford to ignore. But *amicitia* was often a
political rather than a personal friendship, and 'amicos' seems to be
reserved for the end of line 29 because it is intended to surprise — one
does not usually reconcile friends but enemies. (Are we possibly meant
to take the word proleptically?) The allusive, unspecific nature of these
words, produces a sense of secret deals being worked out behind the
scenes. Something of the power and influence rubs off on Horace, who
chooses this moment (30) to remind us of his continuing presence,
sandwiching himself between Maecenas about to come and Maecenas
arriving. Of all the circumstances he could have mentioned (e.g.,
Maecenas' greeting to him on arrival) he chooses to write about putting
ointment on his eyes. The contrast is great, and intentional. Horace
seems to be saying (i) diplomats are human and are equally liable to
suffer from the human condition; (ii) there is an amusing contrast
between the sort of things Maecenas achieves and what Horace does on
such a journey; (iii) this poem is intended to be an inside-out view of
political activity, so it is necessary to bring the level of discourse down
to earth when politics obtrudes. With the arrival of Maecenas, Cocceius
and Fonteius Capito (32), our excerpt finishes.

Questions

1 Follow Horace's journey to Tarracina on the map in the
   pupils' text. Why do you think Horace does not take a more
   direct route to Brundisium?
2 What is meant by describing the first eight words as highly
   compressed? Can you translate them in eight words?
3 Analyse Horace's use of contrast in the first four lines.
4 What does Horace imply about himself and Heliodorus in lines
   5—6? Why?
5 When do you think Horace's reader would understand the
   significance of this journey?
6 How does Horace try to make the barge episode (11—23)
   comic?
7 Why do you think Horace included 'hic oculis . . . illinere'
   (30—1)?
8 List the words Horace uses to describe travelling and the places
   where a travel-word is understood (e.g 'inde Forum Appi', 3).
   How successfully does he avoid repetition?
9 'The poem is interesting, but on the whole disappointing: con-

sidering the company he was travelling in, it is wonderful how
little Horace has told us worth remembering' (Palmer). 'The
maxim that every thing in great men is interesting applies only
to their minds and ought not to be extended to their bodies'
(Gibbon, quoted by Rudd, 1966: 57). Are these fair comments
on this excerpt?

10 Contrast this excerpt with another poem about a journey,
Philip Larkin's 'Whitsun Weddings'. This also looks at something important from an unusual, everyday angle. Cf. also
W.H. Auden, 'Le Musée des Beaux Arts' (with *CLC* Unit IV
slide 2).

IX.3 Martial, Epigrams X.12

Language and content

1 **Aemiliae**: the Via Aemilia, one of the most important routes north-west
across the Italian peninsula, was built by Marcus Aemilius Lepidus in
the early second century B.C. It carried traffic for about 300 km from
the north-east coast of Italy (Ariminum) to the northern provinces (see
map in pupils' text 1). If Domitius set out from Rome, it would be a
dog's leg to travel north-east up the Via Flaminia and north-west up this
road in order to get to Vercellae. Martial may have envisaged him travelling along part of it only, or else perhaps had in mind the Via Aemilia
Scauri, built in the late second century B.C. and running up the west
coast of northern Italy from Vada Volaterrana (south of Pisae), through
Genua to Vada Sabatia and (curling round north-east) to Dertona on a
tributary of the Padus (= the Po). On modes of travel, see IX.4 question
4.

2 **Phaethontei . . . Padi**: Phaethon, son of the Sun, drove his father's
chariot for a day, scorched the earth and was killed by a thunderbolt
from Jupiter. He fell into the River Eridanus, commonly identified with
the Po. For the story, see Ovid *Metamorphoses* I.750—II.408. The Po is
Italy's longest river, and the neighbouring land is very fertile (Pliny the
Elder *Natural History* III.16.117).

3 **ne vivam, nisi . . .** : 'may I perish if I don't . . . ' — a strong declaration
of intent. Cf. VII.1.2.
Domiti: tentatively identified by Friedlaender with Domitius Apolli-
naris, consul designate in ?97, friend of Pliny, literary patron and valued
critic of Martial (see, e.g., *Epigrams* IV.86).

8 **dum . . . eris**: when 'complete coextension is indicated, the temporal
clause normally has the same tense as the main clause' (Woodcock section 219). Here the verb of the main clause ('eris') is in ellipsis.

9 **amicis**: Form C (dative) of agent after gerundive (Woodcock section
202).

Discussion

Martial has apparently written a straightforward little poem of the type
known to literary critics as *propemptikon* (a farewell to a departing
traveller). A prescription for poems of this type survives from the Greek
rhetor Menander, probably written in the third century A.D., but con-

taining much earlier material (Russell and Winterbottom 580–3).
Menander writes that, of the various varieties of *propemptika*, 'a second
type allows the expression of a loving and passionate attitude to the
departing person without the addition of advice; this is when the reputation and position of the two parties are equal, e.g. when a friend sends
off a friend'. This may give us some clue to the relationship between
Martial and Domitius. Of the various topics which Menander recommends
for a *propemptikon*, Martial includes only three: the description of
Domitius' journey (1–2) and the country through which he travels; the
expression of dismay (4) at Domitius' departure; the beauty (8) of
Domitius. Martial is merely using the form of the *propemptikon* as the
basis for an epigram, and he therefore fixes on Domitius' suntan in the
second half of the poem and develops the colour-contrast between
Domitius and his fellow-Romans — far too frivolous a topic for
Menander's handbook.

The first couplet introduces the faintly adventurous theme of travel
in the very north of Italy. The proper nouns help to establish this, provide some lively alliteration ('l' in 1; 'p' in 2) and are no doubt also calculated to impress Domitius with Martial's geographical and mythical
expertise. The fifth-foot spondee in line 1 is also remarkable. After this
exotic start, the emphatic 'ne vivam' of line 3 leads the reader to expect
a protestation of the poet's intention to stop Domitius leaving (after the
manner of Menander), but Martial lightly overturns expectation with
'dimitto libenter', underlining the humour with his 'Domiti, dimitto'
jingle. 'libenter' (3) is extraordinary, and is rightly given prominence at
the end of the line. The traditional expression of regret in the pentameter (4) only complicates the issue further; not least since 'grata' is
brought forward from its clause to chime paradoxically with 'libenter'
(3). The next couplet (5–6) provides the necessary resolution: the
benefits to Domitius outweigh the 'desiderium' (5) felt by Martial,
though the grudging 'vel una' (5) suggests that the balance is fine.
'messe' (5) is our first indication of the time of year, an important
element, and it is immediately buttressed by the heat-implications of
'perusta' (6). The mention of harvest prepares the way for the splendidly
apt comparison of urban man to the bullocks with necks rubbed sore by
pulling heavy carts. As usual, Martial keeps the surprising word for last:
city life is like a galling yoke on Domitius.

The second half of the epigram begins sharply with the monosyllabic
imperative, cushioned by parenthetic 'precor' (7). Martial has now
ceased analysing his own reaction to Domitius' departure, and turns his
attention to the pleasant effect of the sun on Domitius' appearance.
The sun, inflated by 'totos' (7) and the poetic plural, is now viewed as a
sort of cordial to be downed as therapy for urban deprivation. 'avida'
clearly suggests such deprivation. 'combibere' is regularly found in metaphorical uses, but is not used of sunbathing before Martial; drinking the

thirst-inducing sun is a witty, if incidental, word-play. For the pentameter (8), Martial jump-cuts to the fulfilment of the hexameter's imperatives. Domitius is lionised in the heavy 'ō quăm fōrmōsŭs' (8); and the answering 'dum peregrinus eris', naturally descriptive at first reading, acquires an edge to it in the light of the poem's conclusion, *viz.* you are *only* tanned while out of Rome. Lines 9—10 see Domitius, in Martial's imagination, returning to Rome: 'et venies' (9). Domitius will be so brown and healthy that even his friends won't know him. But Martial is now concentrating on the whey-faced Romans: 'albis' (9) and 'pallida' (10) are supplemented by the unhealthy colour-connotations of 'livebit' (10), and all share 'l'-alliteration. By contrast, there has been no explicit colour description of Domitius' cheeks. The final couplet is strongly reminiscent of the first, with its reference to 'via' (11) and its proper names. Even 'Apollineas' and 'Phaethontei' (1 and 2) are now activated in retrospect, and we remember the scorching drive of Phaethon son of Phoebus (Ovid *Metamorphoses* I.750ff.), the Sun, and how he brought 'nigrum colorem' to the Ethiopians (Ovid, *Metamorphoses* II.236). (There may also be a play on Domitius' cognomen —see note on line 3.) 'dederit' and 'rapiet', with their fussy consonantal sound, are set next to each other across the caesura of line 11: no sooner does Domitius get his tan than Rome grabs it away (another striking metaphor). And the couplet finishes with some marked assonance of 'ō' and 'ōr', and with Domitius' colour at last described — but grossly exaggerated for maximum effect in its strong final position. The real point of the epigram now emerges: Rome is so unhealthy that it can turn even a black man white.

Questions

1 What is the effect of the proper names in lines 1—2?
2 What is there to surprise the reader in the second couplet (3—4)?
3 Discuss Martial's use of metaphor in this poem.
4 Is Martial really trying to squeeze two topics into one epigram? If so, is the poem the worse for this?
5 Is it possible to determine from this poem what sort of relationship Martial had with Domitius?
6 Draw a map of the Roman road-network in Italy. (Use, e.g., Grant, 1971 (2), map 49; Forbes II: 140—56; *OCD* s.v. 'via'; *CLC* Unit IV slide 45.) To what extent does this reflect (a) the relief geography of Italy; (b) the modern system of major roads?

IX.4 Martial, Epigrams *XI.79*

Language and content

1 **primum . . . lapidem:** Martial is on his way from Rome to Paetus' suburban estate. On milestones, see Liversidge 162—3, with illustration.

decima . . . hora: see I.4.6 and note on I.4.1 for the ninth hour being the regular time for *cena*.

4 **Paete**: Martial refers to a Paetus on four occasions, characterising him as a hard businessman.

Discussion

Martial, supposing himself an hour late for dinner, makes play with the two numbers in line 1. He then imagines himself on a criminal charge for 'pigritia' ('sloth'), a surprise ending to line 2 which doubles the force of 'lentae'. The second couplet is the speech for the defence, delivered with passion (repeated 'non est' in line 3) and attempting a daring reversal with 'sed tua culpa est' (3). In the final line, spoken with deliberation (spondaic first half and 'm'-alliteration), Martial humorously claims that his host was at fault for sending Martial inefficient transport. Martial contrives to portray a kindness ('tuas', 4) as blameworthy without being truly critical of anything but the mules. Paetus, if a real occurrence is being described, could hardly have been much offended at such a cheeky excuse.

Questions

1 How important to the epigram is the legal imagery of line 2?
2 Why is 'tuas' isolated at the end of the poem?
3 How did Martial expect Paetus to react? Would he be justified in reacting differently?
4 Investigate methods of travel in the ancient world. (See, e.g., Casson, 1974: Ch. 11; Tingay and Badcock, Ch. 7; Lewis and Reinhold II: s.v. 'transportation'; Balsdon, 1969; Hadas, s.v. 'travel'; Paoli, Ch. 20; Liversidge Ch. 7.)

Section X

This section indicates something of the range of Roman religious and philosophical belief. Horace's proclaimed rejection of Epicureanism (X.1, 'parcus deorum cultor') turns out to vary in tone from the flippant to the committed and to extend from the abstract philosophies of its first stanza to the clearly visualised conceptions of the divine in its last few lines. Its attitude to Jupiter and all his thunderous panoply seems gently sceptical, though there is a healthy respect for the power of chance. The other Horace poem (X.2, 'Faune, Nympharum fugientum amator') is far less devious. Despite its surface glitter, it reflects a warm, unsophisticated commitment to the gods behind natural forces. It shares this sincerity with X.3 (Ovid's lines on Terminus), where we have a highly sympathetic picture of the traditional Roman religion as practised in the small, peasant communities throughout Italy. The communal nature of the ritual is prominent again in the other excerpt from Ovid (X.4, on Anna Perenna). These are joyful verses expressing frank pleasure in simple things and not drawing too hard a line between the religious and the secular. Such an attitude clashes sharply with the cynicism with which Martial credits Segius (X.5) and with the apparently rather patronising treatment of Apollo in X.6, where the god's name and the ceremonial of the prayer are made to serve Martial's wit and to boost the status of Domitian.

X.1 Horace, Odes I.34

Context

The first three books of the *Odes* seem to have been published in *c.* 23 B.C., but there is no reason to suppose that this poem was not in circulation, at least among a limited public, some years before. In view of line 15, it is interesting that the next poem in Book I ('o divä, gratum quae regis Antium') is addressed to the goddess Fortune, who is urged to protect Augustus. In our poem, there are no overt politics.

Language and content

The metre is alcaic, and the form is as follows:

pārcŭs dĕōrŭm / cūltŏr ĕt īnfrĕquēns
īnsānĭēntīs / dŭm săpĭēntĭaē
cōnsūltŭs ērrō, nūnc rĕtrōrsŭm
vēlă dăr(e) ātqu(e) ĭtĕrārĕ cūrsŭs

The first two lines are identical. The final syllable of all four lines is *anceps*.

1 **parcus**: sacrifice and paying of vows could be expensive.
   cultor: at this period a rare, high-flown word.
2 **insanientis . . . sapientiae**: i.e. Epicureanism. Cf. I.1 Discussion 19—20 and, for a clear and full statement of Horace's Epicurean doctrine, see De Witt.
3 **erro**: Lucretius (*De Rerum Natura*, II.10) uses the word of non-Epicureans, watched with some smugness by Lucretius and his fellow-thinkers from their 'bene munita templa' built up by 'doctrina sapientum'.
4—5 **iterare cursus . . . relictos**: cf. Nisbet and Hubbard on the problems of 'relictos'. 'iterare' must mean 'to go over something again'. One way out of the problem is to steer closer to the literal sense of the metaphor. Nisbet and Hubbard wish to see 'cursus' as 'the path between piety and doubt'. If instead we think of 'cursus' as merely the course of Horace's ship, then 'iterare cursus relictos' means 'to retrace a course which had been left (far) behind'. The skipper, realising that he is off course, back-tracks ('iterare . . . cursus') until he reaches the point of deviation. Horace, similarly, will write off his Epicureanism (though a substantial feature of his past life) and take up orthodoxy from where he left off.
5 **Diespiter**: archaic and grandiose.
7 **plerumque** has a scientific flavour (Nisbet and Hubbard).
   tonantes: thunder was popularly supposed to be the rumbling of Jupiter's chariot over Olympus.
10 **Taenari**: the Greek promontory of Taenarum (modern Cape Matapan) was at the southern extremity of Laconia, and was supposed to contain a cave giving entrance to the Underworld.

11 **Atlanteusque finis**: a grandiloquent term for the western portion of the
modern Atlas Mountains.

12–13 **ima summis/mutare**: reminiscent of the terminology of radical political
change and revolution (Nisbet and Hubbard).

14 **obscura**: the generalising neuter plural is commonplace in gnomic utterances (Nisbet and Hubbard).

apicem: the conical hat with an olivewood peak worn by Roman priests
('flamines'), but applied also to kings' crowns.

15 **fortuna**: closely associated with 'Diespiter' (see Discussion 174), for Fate
and Zeus had been identified by the Stoics. Fortune was commonly
seen as the bringer of revolution, and the notion of Fortune's wheel (cf.
e.g. Horace, *Odes* III.10.10–11) was powerful both in classical times
and in medieval and later writing. See *CLC* Unit III slide 50.

Discussion

The confessional seriousness of the first line, with grandiloquent 'cultor'
and the two words of reproach enclosing the line, is soon undercut. The
double paradox of 'insane wisdom' (2) and 'erring expert' (3), the
amusing irony of 'erro' (3), together with the revelation — held back till
the final syllable of the clause — that the defaulter is Horace himself, all
combine to amuse the reader and deflate the tone. (There may even be
a further suggestion of paradox in 'parcus . . . cultor', 1, since a penny-
wise worshipper would not be dignified by such a grand word.) Appreciation of this low-key beginning is vital, since Nisbet and Hubbard (377)
are surely right in seeing it as evidence that we must not take seriously
(*pace*, e.g., Ogilvie, 1969: 18) Horace's recantation of Epicureanism.
They quote Dr Johnson's remark about this poem: 'Sir, he was not in
earnest: this was merely poetical.'

'nunc' (3) brings us back to the present, and Horace embarks on an
expansive metaphor, in contrast with the economical expression of what
precedes it. The enjambed 'cogor' (5) is strongly placed and is a clear
indication of the new creed, for the gods of Epicurus were remote and
did not exercise such control. The agent of 'cogor' is 'Diespiter',
balancing it at the end of the line, and implied by 'namque'. By using
the name 'Diespiter', rather than the more regular 'Iuppiter', Horace has
consciously opted for an archaic grandeur. This high style is sustained
by the stirring imagery of Jupiter splitting the clouds with his lightning
(onomatopoeically 'corusco') and galloping across the heavens in his
chariot. It is only later that we realise the significance of 'nubila'.
'plerumque' (7) prepares the way in a line which is expressive with 'p'
and '-rum' sounds. The exactitude of 'plerumque' (see notes) in its
exposed position pulls the reader up short and focuses his attention on
'per purum' (7) and, retrospectively, 'nubila' (6). The stanza finishes
(8) with the delayed complement of 'Diespiter', the chariot and horses
of popular fancy (alliteration of gutturals and final '-urrum' adding to
the sound-effects). It seems likely that these pyrotechnics were meant
not to support, but to demonstrate the insincerity of Horace's palinode:

a serious rejection of the somewhat cerebral Epicureanism might lead to a revived faith in Jupiter, but hardly to a literalist belief in Jupiter's chariot.

The relative 'quo' (9) links the two central stanzas, and the loftiness of diction and content also carries over. Here we have detailed for us the effects of Jupiter's thunder. The verb 'concutitur' (12) is saved up for the end of the stanza, and in its strong position, placed in an 'epic and grand' historic present (Nisbet and Hubbard), it acquires very great emphasis. In the rest of the stanza there is some neat patterning and balancing. 'bruta' (9) is complemented by 'vaga' (9) and paralleled by 'sedes' (11). 'tellus' (land) and 'flumina' (rivers), balanced in line 9, are set in chiasmus against the river Styx and the promontory of Taenarum in line 10. The world above, 'Atlanteus . . . finis' (11) is set against the Underworld (10); and we remember that the Styx and Taenarum are traditionally located in nearby Greece, while Mount Atlas (like the Pillars of Hercules) marks the end of the world. Atlas too 'suggests fixity (like the Rock of Gibraltar)' (Nisbet and Hubbard), making 'concutitur' the more powerful. The whole stanza acquires an air of morbidity and ill omen from the inclusion of the Underworld in line 10 with its effectively juxtaposed 'invisi horrida' (the elision of the long 'i' across the caesura is unique in Horace's alcaics: Nisbet and Hubbard xli).

After such a powerful demonstration, there is no prize for guessing the subject of 'valet' (12), itself brought forward to give extra support to 'concutitur'. The present tenses are now gnomic, and the political overtones of 'ima summis' (12) facilitate the transition from the physical world to mankind. Change is the key concept of the final stanza — indeed of the whole poem, for the first stanza's transfer of loyalty is explained by the two following. 'mutare' is emphatic in line 13, and 'insignem attenuat' once again shows change being imposed on a human object. The subject of 'valet' finally appears and 'deus' (13) following its second verb is very forceful. The word is non-specific (so, Fraenkel 253) and selected in order to provide a neutral link between 'Diespiter' and the goddess 'fortuna' (15) — who are fundamentally inseparable, merely two aspects of the same deity. Certainly the actions of the deity in lines 12–14 ('valet . . . promens') are precisely the actions of Fortune. And Fortune is introduced as a character in the vivid concluding image. By now there is no hint of levity. Fortune is a monstrously sinister, harpy-like creature introduced by the resonant 'hinc apicem rapax' (14) and screeching into action (15) — note the four long vowels of 'strīdōr(e) acūtō' — in a phrase which chills rather than amuses, not least when one discovers her smiling in the final word of the poem. The speed of her movement is indicated by the instantaneous perfects 'sustulit' and 'posuisse' (Nisbet and Hubbard): 'Fortune's action is so quick that it is over before one can describe it.' That the object of her swoop should be a priest's hat is interesting. Of course, the word has wider connotations, but are Nisbet and Hubbard justified in concluding: 'We should perhaps think of convulsions in the Parthian kingdom'? Is it not more reasonable to take 'apicem', at least primarily, in the light of stanza one? Horace has decided to return to the traditional religion, and presumably expects some protection against the rigours of Fortune. But if even a *flamen* is likely to lose his hat, what chance has Horace?

Poetry of this sort is not biography, and discussion of whether or not Horace in fact relinquished Epicureanism or heard thunder from a clear sky is largely off the point. That many Romans 'who should have known better' accepted the occurrence of thunder in such conditions is well attested (Nisbet and Hubbard 376). It is also clear that thoroughgoing Epicureans could not accept it (Lucretius, *De Rerum Natura* VI.400—1). Horace, who was by no means doctrinaire in his Epicureanism, either hears thunder when the sky is clear, or for the sake of a poem light-heartedly imagines that he has. His reaction is entertainingly exaggerated: Epicureanism must go, and the great panoply of the traditional worship moves in to replace it. As the poem becomes more and more serious, Jupiter is revealed as Chance, against whom even the traditional priest-hoods provide no defence. It is the fortune-dominated world of the final stanza which merits the term 'insanientis' (2), not Epicureanism. The implicit response must be a return to the orderly explanations of Epicureanism, where chance is kept in her place (Nisbet and Hubbard 378). At the same time, Horace retains a sincere respect for the power of Fortune, and thus dedicates to her the next poem in the collection.

Questions

1 What has Horace decided to do (1—5)? Is this a reasonable response to lines 5—8?

2 How are we invited to picture Jupiter in lines 5—8 and Fortune in lines 14—16? Which is the frightening picture?

3 What is the significance of the proper names in the third stanza? Would other places have done as well?

4 Is there anything to show that the first stanza is less serious than the others?

5 Are we to take this poem literally, as an account of a sudden conversion? If not, why not? Does any single strong belief of Horace emerge from the poem?

6 Do the lines which describe sound show evidence of verbal sound-effects?

7 To what extent do Horace's sentiments about Fortune corre-spond with those expressed in these verses from a thirteenth-century poem (in Carl Orff's selection of the *Carmina Burana*):

Fortunae plango vulnera
stillantibus ocellis,
quod sua mihi munera
subtrahit rebellis.

in Fortunae solio
sederam elatus,
prosperitatis vario
flore coronatus;

quidquid enim florui
felix et beatus,
nunc a summo corrui
gloria privatus.

Fortunae rota volvitur:
descendo minoratus;
alter in altum tollitur
nimis exaltatus.

rex sedet in vertice:
caveat ruinam!
nam sub axe legimus
Hecubam reginam.

X.2 Horace, Odes III.18

Context

See on III.3.

Language and content

The metre is sapphic:

Faŭně, Nȳmphârŭm // fŭgĭēnt(um) ămātŏr,
pĕr mĕōs fīnēs // ĕt ăprĭcă rūră
lēnĭs īncēdās // ăbĕāsquĕ pârvīs
aĕquŭs ălŭmnĭs.

The final syllable of all four lines is *anceps*.

1 **Faune**: a mythical early king much concerned with agriculture and
cattle but also a huntsman. He was later deified as god of fields and
shepherds, and his festival, the Faunalia, was held on 5 December (10).
Faunus was also credited with a tendency to frighten mortals. Dionysius
of Halicarnassus (V.16.3) says: 'To this deity the Romans ascribe panic,
and any frightening apparitions ... or supernatural voices ... they
credit to the activity of this god.'
fugientum: *sc.* 'te'. Faunus is assimilated to the Greek rural deity Pan
(cf. 'panic', note on 1), who was susceptible to nymphs and who would
take in good part such a teasing epithet. For an amusing story of
Faunus' lechery, see Ovid *Fasti* II.303–58.
5 **si**: no doubt is implied as to the fulfilment of this precondition. Williams

In the first couplet, perhaps intended to recall the pious language of Tibullus, *Elegies* I.1.11f., Ovid establishes his own boundaries. He is concerned with Terminus as a god of private field-markers, and not with Terminus in his temporal sense or as god of the public boundaries. 'stipes' is forcefully placed to give bite to 'tu quoque', and 'ab antiquis' (2) is prominent before the caesura and at the beginning of its clause: Terminus is unlovely and very old. Furthermore, Terminus actually *is* the stone and the stump, which Ovid credits with the possession of 'numen' (2). The ritual begins in the following couplet (3–4), and the liturgical significance of the crowning is assisted by the strong alliteration and the repeated 'binaque' balancing the pentameter. The worship of Terminus is essentially a shared activity, so we are not surprised to find Ovid emphasising duality ('duo', 'diversa', 3; 'binaque', 'binaque', 4) in close connexion with 'te' and 'tibi' (= Terminus).

The simplicity of 'ara fit' (5) is extreme, and Ovid offsets it with a few details of human interest. No doubt he intended a contrast with the polished worship of Rome. His urban audience would not be used to the crucial flame arriving in a chipped cooking-pot: 'rustica' (5), with its non-urbane connotations, completes the picture. But this is no sneer. In the pentameter (6), we discover that the 'rustica' is not a slave but the farmer's wife ('colona' being held back to create this surprise) who has herself picked out the warm coals. 'focis', the last word of line 6 and juxtaposed with 'colona', is important. In this simple ceremony the principal actors are nonetheless in immediate touch with the hearth, the centre of family worship and the embodiment of the physical welfare of the family.

Every member of the family plays his part. The old man chops his wood (with suggestive repetition of 'con-', 7), and we get from 'solida' and 'pugnat' (8) a lively and humorous picture of his perseverance. In order to break the symmetry of one subject per couplet, Ovid lets his activity spill over into the following hexameter. Line 9 is a clear example of metre adapted to sense. The old man's laborious coaxing of the fire is well caught in this spondaic line, and 'flammas' is appropriately held back to the end. With 'stat puer' (10), Ovid returns to his starkly economical description, now reminiscent of the formulaic sacrifice-descriptions of Homer. As the staples of life are thrown on the flames, the spare, paratactic clauses of lines 12–18 — almost every line starting with a new main verb — underline the rustic simplicity of the event. The focus is on the detail of the ceremony. Ovid makes us aware of the participants and onlookers, but only as vaguely differentiated shapes defined in terms of their participation in the sacrifice. Towards the end of the piece, Terminus himself returns to prominence, at first in the third person, but soon (18) to be apostrophised again, in preparation for the hymn which follows. Terminus is now (15) characterised as 'communis', a god of sharing and co-operation, precisely the virtues which have been evident in the ritual just performed. With 'nec queritur' (16), Ovid is possibly allowing himself an entertaining understatement. But it is more likely, taking into account the serious tone of the context, that he is correcting the tradition that Numa founded the worship of Terminus and laid down that the god of friendship and peace should not be worshipped with blood sacrifice; and this may also explain the reference of 'et' in line 15. The final couplet of our excerpt, again with insistent alliteration, takes us on to the feasting and hymn-singing which followed the sacrifice, and it ends with a powerful reference to the name and holiness of Terminus.

Questions

1 Tabulate the events of the ceremonial as described by Ovid. Write your own version of the occasion as seen through the eyes of the 'puer' or 'filia parva'.

2 How does Ovid indicate that this is not a sophisticated ceremony?

3 Is it possible to discover Ovid's attitude to this occasion?

4 How could the worship of Terminus be said to exert a positive force on Roman society?

5 Discover what you can about (a) methods of sacrifice; (b) the lesser-known gods of the Roman world. See, e.g., *CLC* Unit III slides 51—4; Ogilvie, 1969: Chs. 1 and 3; Carcopino 227ff.; Hadas 121—2, 74—5 (illustration); Grant, 1971: 96—7 (illustration); Tingay and Badcock, Ch. 17; Lewis and Reinhold I and II: s.v. 'religion'; Liversidge, Ch. 8.

6 If repetition and alliteration are a feature of Roman prayers (Cato *De Agri Cultura* CXLI.2—3), we might expect Ovid to use them in this sort of piece to establish the sanctity of the occasion. How marked is Ovid's use of repetition and alliteration?

7 Read in translation Tibullus' account of a rustic feast (*Elegies* II.1; especially lines 1—30 and 81—90).

X.4 Ovid, Fasti III.523—40

Context

On Ovid's *Fasti*, see note on Context of II.4. The lively festival of Anna Perenna was held on 15 March (*Idibus Martiis*). Ovid concludes his account of this day, after some aetiological tales about Anna Perenna, with an explicit reference to Caesar's assassination and praise for the *pietas* of Augustus who had revenged his father's murderers at Philippi (*Fasti* III.697—710).

Language and content

See Wilkinson, 1955: 273 for a translation of the bulk of this passage.

half-line. It is as if they had been touched and blessed by the deity. To us, the festival seems entirely non-religious. For the Romans, it may have been enough to attend the festival and to enjoy the drinking and hilarity. We must beware of being too dogmatic about what precisely does and does not constitute religious activity, particularly with reference to a deity about whom so little is known; and we must bear in mind too that Ovid's account is necessarily selective, concentrating perhaps on the peripheral and assuming that he could take for granted in his audience an awareness of the central ritual and worship.

Questions

1 'Anna Perenna cannot be said to have had any religious meaning at all' (Ogilvie, 1969: 80). Does our passage provide any reason for disbelieving this? Is it likely that Ovid provides the whole picture? Contrast X.3.

2 Why might Ovid in line 2 address the Tiber by his Greek name and call him 'advena'?

3 Does Ovid's attitude to the goings-on emerge at any point? What picture of the *plebs* is given by these lines?

4 Why would it be wrong to interpret this passage as an attack on the abuse of alcohol?

5 Find out what you can about the Roman theatre. (See Carcopino 243ff.; Beare; Bieber; Balsdon, 1969: 270—88; Paoli, Ch. 24; Liversidge 92—5; *CLC* Unit I *Stage 5*: 11—15 and slides 47—9 with *Teacher's Handbook* 73—5, Unit II slide 29 and *Teacher's Handbook* 114—16.)

X.5 *Martial*, Epigrams *IV.21*

Language and content

For the hendecasyllabic metre, see note on II.1.
2 **Segius**: mentioned only here.

Discussion

The epigram is neatly balanced, with central Segius flanked by 'affirmat' and 'probat', and his severe declaration in line 1 matching the proof in line 3. The somewhat contorted order of line 3 results in his conclusive piece of evidence — that he has had a lucky break — emerging with great vigour in final position.

Questions

1 Write a rejoinder (in English verse) to Segius' discovery.

2 How persuasive is Segius' argument (a) generally; (b) in the context of Roman religious beliefs? (See, e.g., Ogilvie, 1969: Introduction and Chapters 1—2; X.3 question 5.)

X.6 Martial, Epigrams *IX.42*

Language and content

For the hendecasyllabic metre, see note on II.1.

1 **dives:** either 'sis' is to be understood, in which case 'dives' is predicative and controls 'campis . . . Myrinis'; or 'fruare' is to be supplied from line 2 (as in pupils' text), in which case 'dives' is merely descriptive of Apollo. See Discussion.

    sic: introduces the various inducements to Apollo conditional on fulfilment of lines 6–7.

    Myrinis: there was a famous oracle and temple of Apollo at Gryneum in the territory of Myrina in Asia Minor (Strabo *Geography* XIII.3.5).

2 **senibus . . . cycnis:** swans were popularly supposed to sing only at the moment of death (hence 'senibus'), and Apollo was strongly associated with music.

5 **Palatia:** see *CLC* Unit IV slide 28.

6 **bis senos . . . fasces:** these bundles of rods, bound by red thongs and originally containing axes, were carried by *lictores* before all Roman officials with an active power of command (*imperium*). The number of *fasces* varied with the rank of the magistrate: consuls were entitled to twelve. See *OCD* s.v. 'fasces'. For illustration, see *CLC* Unit IV slide 27.

7 **Stellae:** Lucius Arruntius Stella put on games to celebrate Domitian's victory over the Sarmatae in 93, and he wrote love poems to Violentilla, later to be his wife. He became suffect consul in A.D. 101.

9 **rusticas:** presumably on Martial's suburban estate.

10 **aureis:** victims' horns were regularly gilded.

Discussion

Martial's epigram purports to be a prayer to Apollo. It falls into four parts. In lines 1–5, Martial makes a number of propitious wishes on Apollo's behalf, all conditional ('sic'). In lines 6–7, Martial outlines what he wishes Apollo to bring about. In lines 8–10, the sacrificial inducement is detailed. The last line marks a distinct change of tone, as Martial attempts to put pressure on the god for a speedy outcome.

    The first line reads like a real prayer, with name and whereabouts of the deity both detailed. As we read on and appreciate the conditional force of 'sic' and the susceptibility of 'campis' to construction with 'fruare', it becomes clear that Apollo is not being addressed as 'rich in plains of Myrina', but rather Martial is saying: 'May you continue to be rich and take pleasure in the plains of Myrina, so long as you . . . ' We move from prayer to a mild sort of blackmail. This is much more high-handed than the normal contractual arrangement between man and god, in which an offering is humbly promised if the god fulfils a request (Ogilvie, 1969: 37). A contract *is* proposed later in the poem, but again with an arrogance (11) which would not have been a feature of a real prayer.

    The liturgical character of most of this poem is underlined by the formality of structure, with each of lines 1–5 containing a single new wish for Apollo's welfare. It is difficult to avoid seeing a snatch of

— *Cities of Vesuvius* (Weidenfeld and Nicolson, 1971) (1)

— *Ancient history atlas* (Weidenfeld and Nicolson, 1971) (2)

Graves, R. *The Greek myths* (Penguin, 1955)

Hadas, M. *et al. Imperial Rome*, rev. ed. (Time—Life International, 1971)

Hodges, H. *Technology in the ancient world* (Allen Lane, 1970)

Lewis, N. and Reinhold, M. *Roman civilisation: sourcebooks I and II*, Harper Torchbooks (Harper and Row, 1966)

Liversidge, J. *Everyday life in the Roman Empire* (Batsford, 1976)

Meiggs, R. *Roman Ostia*, 2nd ed. (Oxford U.P., 1973)

Ogilvie, R.M. *The Romans and their gods in the age of Augustus*, Ancient culture and society (Chatto and Windus, 1969)

Paoli, U.E. (trans. Macnaghten) *Rome: its people, life and customs* (Longmans, 1963)

Seager, R. (ed.) *The crisis of the Roman Republic* (W. Heffer, 1969)

Singer, C. *et al.* (ed.) *A history of technology* (5 vols., Oxford U.P., 1954—8)

Syme, R. *The Roman revolution* (Oxford U.P., 1939)

Tingay, G.I.F. and Badcock, J. *These were the Romans* (Hulton Educational Publications, 1972)

Toynbee, J.M.C. *Death and burial in the Roman World* (Thames and Hudson, 1971)

— *Animals in Roman life and art* (Thames and Hudson, 1973)

Ward-Perkins, J. and Claridge, A. *Pompeii AD 79* (Imperial Tobacco Ltd., 1976)

Witt, R.E. *Isis in the Graeco-Roman world* (Thames and Hudson, 1971)

Yavetz, Z. 'The living conditions of the urban plebs', *Latomus* XVII (1958), 500—17 (also in Seager, 162ff.)

c. Art and architecture

Ashby, T. *The aqueducts of ancient Rome* (Oxford U.P., 1935)

Boardman, J. *Greek art*, rev. ed. (Thames and Hudson, 1973)

Brilliant, R. *Roman art* (Phaidon Press, 1974)

Dudley, D.R. *Urbs Roma* (Phaidon Press, 1967)

Grant, M. *The Roman Forum* (Weidenfeld and Nicolson, 1970)

Platner, S.B. and Ashby, T. *A topographical dictionary of ancient Rome* (Oxford U.P., 1929)

Richter, G.M.A. *A handbook of Greek art*, 6th ed. (Phaidon Press, 1969)

SELECT GLOSSARY OF
TECHNICAL TERMS

aetiological: concerned with assigning origin or causes

amoebaean: responding alternately

anceps: syllable which may be metrically either light or heavy

apodosis: the clause in a conditional statement which gives the consequence attending the condition

apostrophe: a breaking off from the narrative to address a person or thing

assonance: similarity of vowel sounds

asyndeton: omission of conjunction(s)

bathos: anticlimax — descent from the elevated to the trivial

bucolic diaeresis: diaeresis following a dactylic fourth foot in a hexameter

caesura: the division of a metrical foot between two words

chiasmus: rhetorical arrangement whereby the order of words in one phrase is reversed in the next

colon: distinct constituent part of a sentence

diaeresis: division between words in a metrical line, the end of a foot coinciding with the end of a word

diptych: a pair of poems intended as companion-pieces

disjunctive: necessitating a choice between two or more things

ellipsis: omission of words that can be supplied from the sense

enjambment: the flowing-over of sense over the line-end into the next line before a pause is reached

epistolary imperfect: convention whereby letter-writer uses imperfect to describe current events

formulaic adjective: adjective regularly applied to specific noun in epic poetry

gnomic: concerning what is generally true, e.g. maxims, proverbs

golden line: a verse consisting of two adjectives, a verb and two nouns, in the order a b C A B

heavy syllable: 'long' syllable

ictus: the beat of the verse-rhythm, e.g. on first syllable of each hexameter foot

irony: saying one thing and meaning another; ('dramatic') situation where audience has a deeper awareness of the significance of words and actions than characters in the drama

jump-cut: abrupt change of subject matter, often marking passage of time

light syllable: 'short' syllable

litotes: understatement, esp. where positive statement is made by negating the contrary

metron: the basic unit in a verse-rhythm, e.g. ˇ - ˘ - in iambics

molossus: the metrical foot - - -

morphology: the grammar of inflexion and word-formation

neologism: a newly-coined word or phrase

onomatopoeia: correspondence between sound and sense

192

oxymoron: association in one phrase of normally contradictory words
palinode: recantation
paradox: an apparent self-contradiction
para-rhyme: assonance approaching but not quite achieving rhyme
parataxis: arrangement of clauses without connectives so that they are in parallel rather than dependent
pathos: style intended to arouse emotion, especially pity or sadness
patronymic: name derived from name of father or ancestor
periodic sentence: = period, a well-formed sentence of elaborate construction
periphrasis: roundabout expression, circumlocution
prolepsis: stating as current fact something which will not be the case till later
protasis: the clause in a conditional statement which expresses the condition, the 'if' clause
synecdoche: part used for whole, or whole for part
tmesis: separation of a word into two parts by intervening word(s)
topos: element of a literary genre
tribrach: the metrical foot ˅ ˅ ˅
tricolon: group of three cola, often with increasing members ('ascending', 'crescendo')

INDEX

Intro. = *Introduction*   *Note* = *Introductory note to each Section*

Achilles IV.5
Adonis VI.3
Adriatic IX.1
Aeneas V.3; VI.2; VII.2; X.4
Aeschylus VII.3
Aesop I.1; III.1
Afer II Note; II.7
Africa V.3
Agrippa, Marcus Vipsanius I.2; I.6;
    IV.2; IV.5; VI.4
Alcaeus III.3
Amastris IX.1
Ameana VIII.1
amicitia IX.2
amoebaean verse VI.3; VII.2
an III.2
Anchises V.3
Ancus Marcius VI.2
angustus clavus V.2
Anna Perenna X Note; X.4
Antony, Mark (Marcus Antonius) IX.2
Anxur IX.2
aorist, generalising VI.4
apex X.1
Apollo III.3; III.8; VI.2; VI.3; IX.2;
    IX.3; X Note; X.4; X.6
Appian Way *see* Via Appia
Apuleius, Lucius Intro. 2*a*; VIII.3
Apulia Intro. 2*a*; III.3
aqueducts *see under* Rome
arbiter III.6
Arbuscula III.2
Arellius I.1
Arellius Fuscus V.2
Aricia IX.2
Ariminum IX.3
Asia Minor Intro. 2*a*; VII.2; X.6
Athena III.8
Athens Intro. 2*a*
Atlas Mountains X.1
Attalus III.5
Auden, W.H. IX.2

Aufidus, River III.3
Augustus Intro. 2*a*; I.2; I.6; II.4; III.3;
    V Note; V.2; V.3; V.5; VI.4; VIII.5;
    X.1; X.4; *see also* Octavian
aulaea IV.1
aulos III.8
Ausonia V.3

Baiae IX.2
Balatro, Servilius IV.1
barber *see tonsor*
bargemen III.4; IX.2
bar mitzvah V.2
baths IV.5
Beneventum IX.2
Berger, John I.1
Betjeman, Sir John X.2
Bibulus VIII.3
Bilbilis Intro. 2*a*
biography Intro. 2*a*
Birmingham I.6
Bithynia Intro. 2*a*; IX.1
Black Sea Intro. 2*a*; IX.1
boats III.4; IX.1; IX.2
Bononia IV.4
books and writing implements I.4;
    III.1; III.2; *see also* papyrus rolls;
    stilus; writing-tablets
box VII.4
Brundisium IX Note; IX.2
Brutus, Marcus Junius Intro. 2*a*
bucolic diaeresis *see under* metre
burial *see* funeral

Caecilianus III.6
Caecus, Appius Claudius IX.2
Caelius Rufus, Marcus I.3
Caesar, Gaius Julius Intro. 2*a*; VIII.1;
    X.4
Calais VII.2
Callimachus, influence of Intro. 2*b*;
    III.1

Calvus Macer, Gaius Licinius Intro. 2*b*; VI.1
Campania II.2; IV.1
canals IX.2; *see also* Rome, *euripus*
Candidus II.6
Capito, Gaius Fonteius IX.2
caprimulgus III.1
captatio II.3; VI.2; VIII.5
captatio benevolentiae VII.3
Capua V.4
Carmina Burana X.1
Carthage V.4
Cato, Marcus Porcius V.4
cats I.1
Catullus, Gaius Valerius *passim*; life Intro. 2*a*
caupo I.5; IV.4
Celsus, Cornelius II.2
censor perpetuus I.4
Centumviral Court Intro. 2*a*; VIII.5
Cervius I.1
Chance *see* Fortune
Charidemus V.4
chariot-racing IV.2
chiasmus I.1; I.5; II.4; II.6; III.1; III.4; III.5; IV.1; IV.2; IV.5; VI.5; IX.2
children VIII.5
Chloe VII.2
Cicero, Marcus Tullius Intro. 2*a*; I.3; II.2; III.2; III.8
Cincinnatus, Lucius Quintius II.4
cinnabar VII.4
Circe VIII.3
Cirencester IX.2
Cisalpine Gaul Intro. 2*a*; VIII.1
clepsydra III.6
clientela Intro. 2*a*; I.4; II Note; II.6; V.1
Clodia Intro. 2*a*
Clodius, Publius I.3
cobblers IV.4
collyria IX.2
Colossus of Rhodes IX.1
Columella, Lucius Iunius Moderatus III.4
comissatio I.4
Corbulo, Gnaeus Domitius V.3
Corfu VI.3
Corinna IV.2; VII Note; VII.3; VII.4
Cornelius, Fidus V.3
Corsica VII.4
cosmetics III.7
courts and law I.4; VII.4; IX.4; *see also* Centumviral Court
cradle V.4

Crassus, Marcus Licinius I.3
cratera X.2; X.4
Creusa V.3
cum, inverted I.1; I.4; V.2; IX.2
Cupid VI.3; VII.3
curse VII.4
cursus honorum V.2
cyathus X.4
Cyclopes V.3
Cynthia V.3
Cyrenaica V.3
Cytorus IX.1

Dama II.3
dance X.2; X.4
Daunus, King III.3
Dawn VIII.3
decemvir stlitibus iudicandis Intro. 2*a*
declamation II.4
dedication IX.1
defeat of expectation Intro. 2*b*
Delia VI.3; VIII.3
Delphi III.3
depositio barbae V.4
Dertona IX.3
dice-box IV.6
Dickens, Charles IV.1
Diespiter X.1
Dionysius of Halicarnassus II.4; X.2
Dioscuri IX.1
Dipsas VIII.3
doctor II.2
doctus VII.3; VIII.2
Domitian Intro. 1, 2*a*; I Note; I.4; I.5; V Note; V.5; X Note; X.6
Domitius IX Note; IX.3
doors I.1
Dryden, John III.2
dum III.3
dye VIII.4

eating *see* food and drink
Eliot, T.S. V.3; X.4
ellipsis VII.4; VIII.5; IX.3
Elysian Fields VI.3
enim IV.2
epic and mock-epic I.1; I.4; IV.1; V.3; VI.2; VII.2; IX.1; IX.2; X.1; X.3
epicedion VI.3
Epicureanism *see* philosophy
Epicurus X.1
epigram Intro. 2*b*; VI.5; IX.1
equites Intro. 2*a*; III.2; III.4; V.2; VI.3; VIII.1
Eridanus, River IX.3

Erotion Intro. 2*a*; VI Note; VI.5
Eryx, Mount VI.3
Ethiopia VIII.3; IX.3
Etruria X.4
Euphemus I.4
Eutrapelus III.7
evil eye VIII.3
exile Intro. 2*a*; I.2; III.4; V.2; V.3
eye-ointment IX.2

Fabulla VII.5; VIII Note; VIII.6
facetiae VIII.1
fasces X.6
Fate X.1
Faunus X.2
Feronia IX.2
fires I.3
fish IV.3
Fishbourne I.2
Flaccilla Intro. 2*a*; VI.5
Flaminian Way *see* Via Flaminia
flattery Intro. 2*a*; I.4; I.5; II.3; IV.5;
    VII.3
food and drink I.1; I.4; II.2; IV.1;
    IV.5; IX.4
food-taster I.1
Formiae VIII.1
Fortune II.4; IV.1; VI.4; X Note; X.1
Forum Appi IX.2
fossor III.4
Fowles, John III.2
freedmen Intro. 2*a*; II.3; II.6
frogs IX.2
Frontinus, Sextus Iulius Intro. 2*a*; I.2;
    I.6
Fronto Intro. 2*a*; VI.5
fulling IV.4
fultura II.2
Fundanius, Gaius IV.1
funeral V.3; VI.3; VI.5; VIII.5
Furius II.1
future perfect indicative, second singular VI.2

Gallus, Gaius Cornelius IV.2
gambling IV.2; IV.6
games IV.5; IV.6
Garda, Lake Intro. 2*a*
Gaul VIII.1
Geminus, Quintus Varius V.2
Genua IX.3
Germans I.5; I.6
gladiatorial shows IV.4
glass III.6
goats X.2

gods VI.3; IX.1; IX.2; X.1; X.2; X.3;
    X.5; *see also names of individual
    gods*
Golden Age Intro. 2*b*; II.4
golden line I.1; II.4
Gracchus, Tiberius Sempronius VII.4
Graces VI.2
graffito IX.2
Graves, Robert III.2
Greece X.1
Greek IX.2
Greek influence Intro. 2*a*, 2*b*; II.3;
    II.4; II.6; III.3; IV.5; VII.2; VII.3;
    VIII.2; VIII.3; IX.1; IX.3; X.2; X.4
Gryneum X.6

hair III.8; IV.2; IV.5; VII.3; VIII.1;
    VIII.4; VIII.6
Hardy, Thomas III.2
Hector V.3
heir II.2; II.3; VI.2
Heliodorus IX.2
hemlock VII.4
Hercules, Pillars of X.1
Herodotus III.8
hippomanes VIII.3
Homer II.3; V.2; VI.3; VII.2; VII.3;
    X.3
homosexuality III.7
honey VII.4
Horace (Quintus Horatius Flaccus)
    passim; *Carmen Saeculare* Intro.
    2*a*; III.3; VI.2; life Intro. 2*a*; V.1;
    VII.2; VIII.2; *Odes* I–III III.3;
    Odes IV III.3; VI.2; *Satires* Intro.
    2*a*
hospites IX.1
hours I.4; IX.2; IX.4
house prices and rents *see under* Rome
Housman, A.E. VI.2
humour Intro. 2*b*; II.2; III.5; IV Note;
    IV.1; IV.2; IV.3; IV.5; V.4; VIII.2;
    VIII.3; VIII.6; IX.1; IX.2; IX.4;
    X.1; X.2; X.4; X.6
hunting IV.3; X.2
hymn X.2

Ilia VII.2
Iliad VI.3
Ilium VII.2
imperfect, epistolary III.4
Indians II.2
infinitive, historic I.1; V.1; VIII.2;
    IX.2
inscriptions I.1; III.3; III.4; VI.5

Isaiah X.2
Isis VI.3
Italy V.3; VII.2; IX.1; IX.2; IX.3; X
    Note; X.2
Iulus V.3
ius trium liberorum Intro. 2a; V Note;
    V.5

Jackman, Brian IV.3
Janus II.4
Jerome, Eusebius Hieronymus Intro.
    2a
Johnson, Samuel X.1
Jonson, Ben VIII.2
Jupiter II.4; III.3; V.3; IX.2; IX.3; X
    Note; X.1; X.3
Juvenal (Decimus Iunius Iuvenalis)
    Intro. 2a; I.3; I.4; III.7; IV.1

Laconia X.1
Laertes VI.3
Laetinus VIII Note; VIII.4
Larkin, Philip IX.2
Latium II.4
latus clavus V.2
law and lawyers *see* courts and law
leather III.8
legacy-hunting *see captatio*
lena VIII.3
Lepidus, Marcus Aemilius IX.3
Lesbia Intro. 2a; VII Note; VII.1;
    VIII Note; VIII.1
lethargus II.2
Libitina III.3
Libya V.3
lightened syllables Intro. 2b
litter IX.2
Livy (Titus Livius) II.4
Lucian VIII.3
Lucilius, Gaius Intro. 2b; I.1; III.2;
    V.1
Lucretius Carus, Titus III.3; X.1
Lupercus III.7
Lydia VII Note; VII.2
Lysippus I.2

Macrobius, Ambrosius Theodosius II.4
madness II.2
Maecenas, Gaius Intro. 2a; IV.1; V.1;
    IX.2
magic *see* witchcraft
make-up *see* cosmetics
malaria IX.2
Mamurra Intro. 2a; VIII.1
mantica III.1

Mantua V.3
mappa IV.1
Marcella Intro. 2a
Marcia V.3; *see also* Rome, Aqua
    Marcia
marriage VII Note; VII.2
Mars II.4
Marsyas III.8
Martial (Marcus Valerius Martialis)
    passim; life Intro. 2a; V.4; V.5
mask VIII.4
Matapan, Cape X.1
Maximus, Paullus Fabius V.3
Medea VIII.3
Melpomene *see* Muses
Memmius, Gaius Intro. 2a
Memnon VIII.3
Menander of Laodicea IX.3
Menogenes IV Note; IV.5
Messalla Corvinus, Marcus Valerius
    Intro. 2a; VI.3
Metellus Celer, Quintus Caecilius Intro.
    2a
metre *passim*; alcaic X.1; asclepiad
    III.3; VII.2; bucolic diaeresis I.1; II.3;
    III.2; hendecasyllabic II.1; iambic
    trimeters IX.1; iambic trimeters
    and dimeters II.5; sapphic X.2;
    scazon, limping iambic trimeter
    III.1; III.8; teaching methods Intro.
    3c(ii); *see also* lightened syllables
'middle' voice VI.3; VII.4
milestones IX.4
Miller, Max VII.5
miser II.2; VII.4
mixing-bowl *see cratera*
mock-epic *see* epic and mock-epic
Molossian I.1
monasteries IV.3
money II.2; II.4; II.5; *see also* poets'
    poverty; Rome, house prices and
    rents
mules III.4; IX.2
Mulvian Bridge II.5
munus see gladiatorial shows
Muses I.4; III.3; V.2; VI.3
Mutina IV.4
Myrina X.6

nail, used to test smoothness IX.2
names, Horace's choice of I.1
Nape VII.3; VII.4
Nasidienus Rufus Intro. 2b; IV Note;
    IV.1
-ne IV.1

negative enumeration I.5; V.3; VIII.1
Nemesis VI.3
neque III.2
Nero I.6; III.7; IV.5; VIII.5
Nerva, Lucius Cocceius IX.2
Nestor X.4
Nomentanus IV.1
Nomentum Intro. 2*a*
nugae VIII.2
Numa Pompilius X.3
Nymphs VI.2; X.2

Octavian IX.2; *see also* Augustus
Odysseus *see* Ulysses
Odyssey VI.3
Olympus, Mount I.4
omens VII.4
Opimius II.2
Orwell, George I.1
otium V.2
Ovid (Publius Ovidius Naso) *passim*;
    Amores IV.2; *Epistulae ex Ponto*
    I.2; *Fasti* II.4; life Intro. 2*a*; V.2;
    V.3; *see also* I.2, for Ovid's third
    wife; *Remedia Amoris* IV.3; *Tristia*
    III.4; V.2

Padus, River (modern Po) II.2; IX.3
paedagogus III.8; V.4
Paeligni Intro. 2*a*; V.2
Paetus IX.4
Palace, Imperial I.4; X.6
Palatine Anthology IX.1
palimpsest III.1
Pan X.2
papyrus rolls III.1; *see also* books and
    writing implements
paradox II.2; II.4; III.2; III.3; III.5;
    VI.1; VI.2; VI.4; VII Note; VII.1;
    VII.5; VIII.3; IX Note; IX.3; X.1;
    X.4
parataxis II.6
parody Intro. 2*b*; VII.4; IX.1
Parthians X.1
participles I.1; IV.3; V.1; VIII.2; IX.2
patronage *see clientela*
Penelope VI.3
Pepys, Samuel VII.5
perfect tense, instantaneous X.1; X.2
Persian king VII.2
Persius Flaccus, Aulus II.2
Petronius Arbiter II.3; IV.1; X.4
Phaeacia VI.3
Phaedrus III.1
Phaethon IX.3

phaselus IX.1
Phidias I.2
Philippi Intro. 2*a*; V.1; X.4
philosophy Intro. 2*a*; I.1; II.2; IV.1;
    X Note; X.1
Phoenicia V.4
Pindar III.3
plebs X.4
Pliny the Elder I.6; II.2; II.4; III.1;
    III.4; III.7; VII.4; VIII.3; VIII.4;
    IX.3
Pliny the Younger Intro. 2*a*; I.4; II.2;
    III.4; III.6; IV.3; V.3; VIII.5;
    IX.3
pluperfect forms, for perfect I.3; V.4
Plutarch VII.4
Po, River *see* Padus, River
poetae novi Intro. 2*a*; III.1
poets' poverty II.1; III.1
Polla VI.4
Pollio, Gaius Asinius IX.2
Pompeii I.5; IV.1; IV.4; IV.5; IX.2
Pompey (Gnaeus Pompeius Magnus)
    III.6
Pomptine Marshes IX.2
Pontifex Maximus III.3
Pontus *see* Black Sea
Pope, Alexander I.1; III.2; V.2
popina I.5
Porcius IV.1
Porcius Latro V.2
porticus I.2; VIII.6
Praxiteles I.2
prayer-language Intro. 2*b*; III.3; VI.5;
    X.2; X.3; X.6
prices *see* money
prolepsis I.4; III.3
Prometheus III.1
propemptikon IX.3
Propertius, Sextus Intro. 2*a*, 2*b*; I.2;
    IV.2; V.2; V.3; VI.2; VI.3; VII.3;
    VII.4; VIII.3; X.4
Propontis IX.1
Proserpina VIII.4
pupil (of the eye), double VIII.3
purple V.4
Pythia X.6

Quintilia VI.1
Quintilian (Marcus Fabius Quintilianus)
    I.2
Quirinus *see* Romulus

raeda IX.2
ravens VIII.4

Regulus, Marcus Aquilius II.2; II.3;
VIII Note; VIII.5
relegatio Intro. 2*a*; *see also* exile
Restitutus, Vibius IX.2
Rhea Silvia II.4; VII.2
rhetoric Intro. 2*a*; II.4; IV.2; V.2; VI.4;
VII.2; VII.3; VIII.3; IX.2; IX.3
Rhine, River I.6
Rhodes IX.1
rhombus VIII.3
rhyme V.3
rice II.2
ring-composition I.3; IX Note
roads IX.3; *see also* Via
Rome *passim*
Aqua Marcia I Note; I.6
Aqua Virgo I.2; VI.4
aqueducts I.6
Argiletum II.4
Basilica Iulia VIII.5
Campus Agrippae VI.4
Campus Martius I.2; VI.4; IX.2
Capitol I.6; II.4; III.3; VI.3
Circus Maximus IV Note; IV 2
Colosseum Intro. 2*a*; IV.5
Esquiline Hill Intro. 2*a*; IV.5
euripus I.2
Forum Augusti I.2
Forum Boarium VIII.2
Forum Iulium I.2
Forum Romanum I.2; II.4; VIII.2
Horti Agrippae I.2
Horti Caesaris VIII.2
house prices and rents I.3; II.1
Hut of Romulus II.4
Janiculum Hill X.4
Mons Pincius I.2
Palatine Hill II.4
Pantheon IV.5
Pons Aemilius VIII.2
Porta Portuensis VIII.2
Porticus of Livia I.2
Porticus of Octavia I.2
Porticus of Pompey I.2
Porticus Vipsania VI.4
shops I.5
Stagnum Agrippae I.2
Temple of Iuppiter Capitolinus
II.4; X.3
Temple of Iuppiter Feretrius II.4
Temple of Mars Ultor I.2
Temple of Venus Erycina VI.3
Theatre of Balbus I.2
Theatre of Marcellus I.2
Theatre of Pompey I.2

Thermae Agrippae I.2; IV.5
Thermae Neronianae IV.5
Thermae Titi IV.5
Thermae Traianae IV.5
tribunal VIII.2
Velia VIII.2
Via Portuensis VIII.2
Via Sacra VIII.2
Vicus Tuscus VIII.2
Romulus II.4; VII.2
Rufinus, Publius Cornelius II.4
Rugby School III.8

Sabine Hills Intro. 2*a*
sacrifice X.1; X.2; X.3; X.6
Safronius Rufus VII Note; VII.5
salutatio I.4
Sappho III.3
Sarmatae X.6
satire Intro. 2*b*
Saturn II.4
schools III Note; III.2; III.8; V.2; IX.2
Scopas I.2
scriba quaestorius Intro. 2*a*
scutica III.8
Scythia III.8
sea IX.1
seal III.3
Segius X Note; X.5
Senate Intro. 2*a*; VII.3
Seneca the Elder II.4; V.2
Seneca the Younger Intro. 2*a*; I.2; V.3
Severus, Cornelius I.2
sextarius V.4
Sextus Pompey (Sextus Pompeius
Magnus Pius) IX.2
sheep X.2
shepherd III.4
ships *see* boats
shoes IV.1; IV.5
shops I.5
shorthand III.8
Sibyl X.4
Sicily Intro. 2*a*; IV.3; VI.3
sistrum VI.3
slaves I.6; III.4; IV.1; V.4; VI.5; IX.1;
IX.2
Spain Intro. 2*a*; II.5; VII.4
spinning III.4
sportula II.5
Statius, Publius Papinius I.4
statues II.4
Stella, Lucius Arruntius X.6
stilus III.2; VII.3; VII.4; *see also* books
and writing implements

Stoicism *see* philosophy
Strabo I.2; IV.1; IX.1; X.6
Styx, River I.2; X.1
subjunctive, uses of I.1; II.4; III.1;
    III.2; III.3; III.4; III.5; IV.1; IV.3;
    V.3; V.4; VI.3; VI.5; VII.2; VII.3;
    VII.4; VII.5; VIII.2; X.4
Suetonius Tranquillus, Gaius Intro. 2*a*;
    I.2; I.3; I.4
Suffenus Intro. 2*b*; III.1
Sulmo V.2
Sun-god IX.3
superstition VII.4; X.1; *see also* omens
supine IX.2
swans VIII.4; X.6
Swift, Jonathan II.3
Sybaris VII.2
Syria IX.2

Tacitus, Cornelius I.6
Taenarum X.1
tamquam VII.5
Tarentum V.1; IX.2
Tarquinius Priscus II.4
Tarracina IX.2
Tartarus VI.3
teacher *see* schools
temples I.2
Terminus X Note; X.3
Terracina *see* Tarracina
theatre I.2; III.2; VIII.4; X.4
Theophrastus VIII.2
Thrace VII.2
thunder X.1
Thurii VII.2
Tiber, River I.2; II.5; VIII.2; X.4
Tibullus, Albius Intro. 2*a*, 2*b*, 3*d*; I.1;
    II.4; III.7; IV.2; VI Note; VI.3;
    VII.4; VIII.3; X.3
time III.6; *see also* hours
Tiresias II.3
Tithonus VIII.3
Titus Intro. 2*a*; IV.5; V.5
tmesis I.1
toga II.3; II.6; IV.2; V.2; X.4
Tomis (modern Constanta) Intro. 2*a*;
    I Note; I.2; II.4; V Note; V.3
Tongilianus I Note; I.3
tonsor I.5; III.7; V.4
Torquatus VI Note; VI.2
Trajan IV.5
Transpadane Gaul III.4
tresviri V.2
triens V.4
trigon IV.5

Trimalchio II.3; IV.1; V.4
tripudium X.2
triumph III.3
Troy V.3; VII.2
trulla II.2
Tuccius Intro. 2*a*; II Note; II.5
Tullus Hostilius VI.2
Tunisia IV.3
Tyre V.4

Ulysses II.3; VI.3
Umbria X.4
Underworld X.1
unguenta V.4
Urbana IX.2
ut I.1
Utica V.4

Vada Sabatia IX.3
Vada Volaterrana IX.3
vappa II.2; IX.2
Varius Rufus IV.1; V.1
Varro, Marcus Terentius II.1; III.4;
    V.2
Varus III.1
vates VI.3
Venus IV.2; VI.3; VII.2; VII.3; X.2
Venusia Intro. 2*a*; IX.2
Vercellae IX.3
Verona Intro. 2*a*
Vestal Virgin III.3
Via Aemilia IX.3
Via Aemilia Scauri IX.3
Via Appia IX.2
Via Flaminia II.5; IX.3; X.4
Vibidius IV.1
villa, siting of II.1
Violentilla X.6
Virgil (Publius Vergilius Maro) Intro.
    2*a*; I.5; III.3; V Note; V.1; V.2;
    V.3
Virro IV.1
Viscus IV.1
Vitruvius I.2; II.4; III.6
Vulca of Veii II.4

waiters I.1; IV.1
walking IX.2
water-clock *see clepsydra*
water transport *see* boats
wills II.3
wine *see* food and drink
wine-ladle *see cyathus*
witchcraft VIII.3
women VIII.5

writing-tablets VII.3; VII.4; *see also*
  books and writing implements

Zeus X.1
zodiac III.8